WHO OWNS SCHOOL?

Authority, Students, and Online Discourse

NEW DIMENSIONS IN COMPUTERS AND COMPOSITION

Gail E. Hawisher and *Cynthia L. Selfe*, editors

WHO OWNS SCHOOL?

Authority, Students, and Online Discourse

Kelly Ritter

University of North Carolina—Greensboro

HAMPTON PRESS, INC.
CRESSKILL, NEW JERSEY

Library of Congress Cataloging-in-Publication Data

Ritter, Kelly.
  Who owns school? : authority, students, and online discourse / Kelly Ritter.
      p. cm. -- (New dimensions in computers and composition)
  Includes bibliographical references and index.
  ISBN 978-1-57273-952-9 (hardbound) -- ISBN 978-1-57273-953-6 (paperbound)
  1. Computers and literacy--Moral and ethical aspects. 2. Authorship--Moral and ethical aspects. 3. Plagiarism. 4. College teaching. I. Title.
  LC149.5.R58 2010
  808'.0420285--dc22
                                     2010000629

Hampton Press, Inc.
23 Broadway
Cresskill, NJ 07626

CONTENTS

ACKNOWLEDGMENTS

I would like to thank a number of individuals who helped me to bring this book to its final form. For their review of, and feedback on, Chapter 1, I thank Jesse Blackburn of the University of Arkansas and Will Duffy of the University of North Carolina-Greensboro (UNCG). For his tireless reading (and re-reading) of the earlier/article version of Chapter 4, I thank Scott Ellis of Southern Connecticut State University. For their assistance in submitting surveys to first-year composition students in fall 2001, as outlined in Chapter 3, I thank the participating faculty in the English Department at Southern Connecticut State University: Andrea Beaudin, Alex Boateng, Donna Carbone, Christopher Dean, the late Sharleen Dickinson, Rick Farrell, Patti Hanlon, Nicole Henderson, Liz Keefe, Debbie Malewicki, Sharon Nolan, Pamela Roberts, and Cindy Stretch. At the University of North Carolina-Greensboro, I thank my fall 2008 English 747 class (Jacob Babb, Dan Burns, Mercer Bufter, Jason Cooke, Joe George, Erin Houlihan, Zach Laminack, Andrew Pisano, Brian Ray, Christine Tobin, Amelie Welden, and Anna Whiteside) for doing the same survey with their own first-year composition students. I also thank my department chair at UNCG, Anne Wallace, for her support of my work and her ongoing confidence in me. I thank my research assistant in 2008–2009, Jeff Martin, and the five doctoral students at UNCG who served as my assistant composition program directors or English 747 course interns while this book was in progress, and who thus enabled me to have more time to write: Brandy Grabow, Mary Beth Pennington, Will Dodson, Will Duffy, and Alan Benson. Finally, I thank Gail Hawisher and Cindy Selfe and Hampton Press for their faith in this project.

I especially thank my husband, Josh Rosenberg, and my daughter, Sarah Rosenberg, for their continued patience, support, and love.

Earlier versions of the following chapters have been previously published: chapter 3: *College Composition and Communication* 56.4 (June 2005): 601–631 and chapter 4: *Rhetoric Review* 27.3 (July/August 2008): 259–280.

ABOUT THE AUTHOR

Kelly Ritter is Associate Professor of English and Director of Composition at the University of North Carolina–Greensboro. She is the author of *Before Shaughnessy: Basic Writing at Yale and Harvard, 1920-1960* (Southern Illinois UP, 2009), and co-editor, with Stephanie Vanderslice, of *Can It Really Be Taught? Resisting Lore in Creative Writing Pedagogy* (Boynton Cook, 2007). Her articles and essays on writing pedagogy, history, and theory have appeared in *College English, College Composition and Communication, Composition Studies, Pedagogy,* and *Rhetoric Review,* among others. Her current project is on women's literacy education, specifically the institutional intersection of composition and creative writing pedagogies in the postwar public women's college.

INTRODUCTION

School For Sale

Making the critical decision to say "no" to authority is a supposed rite of passage for every child coming of age, at least in the mainstream, youth-centered culture of the United States. We like to pride ourselves on the idea that we are a nation of rebels, of nonconformists, and independent thinkers, particularly among our youth. That conception may be true to an extent; certainly it is evident in key historical and political events that have taken place in the twentieth century. The promise of rebellion guides much of our thinking about the ways in which we live, work, and communicate (or fail to communicate) with one another as social beings within the public sphere, which includes, for those of us who are teachers, the spaces of the classroom.

But as teachers know, when it comes to the public secondary and post-secondary educational system that functions as a subset, and sometimes symbol, of American culture, there is rebellion, and then there is rebellion. How far-flung a challenge to authority can actually be is limited by the extent to which standardized labels such as "student," "teacher," and "text" can be successfully reified in the already deeply entrenched system of schooling, and in the accepted learning processes by which authorial, textual, and intellectual ownership are acquired. Ask an average college student, especially one going through the often lamented motions of general education courses at the freshman and sophomore level—including courses such as first-year writing—what she thinks about the level of control she has over her own education. After likely expressing surprise at being asked the question in the first place—having had little to no role in the crafting of the requirements she must fulfill—she might very well

1

invoke in her response, as a commonplace analogy, the long-standing mantra of the District of Columbia: *taxation without representation*.

As someone who belongs to the just-previous generation, my own response as a teenager to this question would have been to have no response at all, reflecting the method by which I was taught to engage with counter-statements. In my years of high school, through the completion of my undergraduate degree, I was about as far from a rebel as you could get. If ever there was the perfect embodiment of the bow-to-authority teenager (and young adult), someone who believed mightily in the power of social and educational hierarchies, who never talked back to a teacher or thought ill of a rival student, who never dared question a policy, that was me. Pollyanna-esque though this description may be, I assure you that it is true. I was the meek and acquiescent product of parents who, true to their own generation and upbringing, ascribed mightily to such cut-and-dry value systems. So, of course, I was secretly fascinated—above all other things—by those among my classmates who, conversely, took every available opportunity to *challenge* authority, either in large or small doses. I carefully studied, like an anthropologist of teen behavior who herself can never be part of the tribe, those students who acted without apparent particular fear of retribution, or loss of their fragile institutional reputations. I silently scrutinized those who never outwardly wondered, "How *will* this transgression affect my [fabled] permanent record?"

Particularly fascinating to me were the occasions when my fellow students committed acts of rebellion that made a big, noisy splash, but didn't really *harm* anything or anyone. Even better were the counter-authority moves that made an interesting point about the day-to-day structures of school that we all took for granted—because we had never *been* presented with a viable alternative to our educational trajectory. The exception was the "alternative" high school, and to get into that you needed only do one or the following: (a) become strongly associated with one or more recreational drugs; (b) commit some sort of embarrassing public act that shamed your family, which commonly, but not necessarily, meant (for girls, anyway) to (c) get pregnant. So "alternative" wasn't a particularly positive or empowering word in the old high school lexicon. Rebellion had to be carefully contained—or had to masquerade as a short burst of exuberant freedom, less against the system than cheerfully beside it, performed as a charity skit for the elders who would respond with polite, if slightly nervous, applause.

Such was the case with the "senior prank" pulled each year at my high school, near the end of the spring semester. Our school sat atop a hill, overlooking several acres of rolling green lawn peppered with varied foliage (to illustrate the breadth of this scene, let me say that our varsity golf team used the front lawn as a nine-hole practice range). Local lore claimed that shortly after the school was built in the late 1960s, an expectant father drove his laboring wife to its front door, thinking it a maternity hospital. Other popular fiction claimed that the school was *actually* built as a sanitarium, but then a population explosion caused need for a new high school instead, and so the original plans for mental health patients were scrubbed. Either way, we are talking about a stately and foreboding amount of institutional green.

I remember approaching the campus on the school bus one sunny morning in my junior year, about a week before the end of classes. The night before, as was the developing annual tradition, several senior boys had gathered twenty or thirty "For Sale" signs from the yards of unsuspecting homeowners all over town. They then transplanted these signs all across the front lawn of the high school. The signs were densely packed without rhyme or reason, like candidate advertisements just outside the legal boundaries of a polling place on election day. The boys then set up webbed lounge chairs to lie in with welcoming smiles and (I assume) non-alcoholic umbrella drinks, doing a good imitation of real estate agents hosting an especially grand open house on the beach.

This confident—one might even say *smug*—display made it into the yearbook that particular year—1986—and as I look back at that photo, as I have a few times over the years, I think it emblematic of something more than a senior prank. These boys' faces are so assured, so relaxed, even in the space of inevitable suspension, and a stern talking-to from their parents (and probably the homeowners, who were frantically phoning their agents that morning, wondering what had happened). Obviously they are skipping class—or about to—in order to hold court on the front lawn. Obviously, they have committed some sort of petty theft, however innocuous, and are smiling about it. It is as if these classmates of mine—to none of whom I dared ever speak for fear of fainting dead away from their sheer, awesome hubris—were thinking (if not saying, under their breath), *we own this school. And so, we have the right to do with it whatever we wish.*

I'm sure the principal of our school, Mr. A., who was already a generally irritating and condescending man from what I recall, did not agree with this juvenile assessment of ownership. But the cheers emanating all around me from the lines of the full and rollicking school buses that morning told a different story. The "For Sale" signs ultimately stayed up all of that day, left unattended by the students and unfettered by the faculty and administration. Who was supposed to take them down? And when and if they came down, where did they *go?* Such an unusual dislocation of ownership—houses from real estate signs, owners from their products, agents from their advertisements—was not served by an easy clean-up. Such retrenchment of a complex market system takes time. So the signs remained, well into the afternoon, and were visible as we leaned out the windows of our classrooms to get a second look, from high up on the hill.

***

I tell this story not just to wax nostalgic—even though some seemingly benign images are powerful, and they stay with us, inexplicably, for the whole of our lives. I tell this story instead to make a point about the subject of this book—student ownership of and control over their own learning, and the concomitant processes by which students are *supposed* to learn, including the shifting role of the student against/with/beside the teacher, or teacher-figure, in this learning process. The Internet, as I argue in the chapters to follow, has caused an up ending of the expected relationships between students and the educational system and its spokespeople, much like the up-ended relationship between properties and owners during that prank at my high school, in three distinct ways.

First, the Internet has changed the relationship between students and texts, altering how they read, how they value the act of reading, and how this affects or is affected by the texts themselves. As students increasingly read both assigned and nonassigned, supportive, or ancillary texts online, and within online dialogic environments, the importance of the teacher is invariably lessened and held less valuable than the global accessibility of one's reading peers—both in terms of assistance with interpretation and explication and in terms of simple discussion or debate opportunities. Second, the Internet has changed how students view writing, and how they define "writing" versus "authorship," which are no longer viewed as inextricably linked; it would be more accurate, in fact, to say that these terms are seriously at odds in our first-year composition classrooms, due to the economy of scale that dictates the relationship between intellectual effort (and sometimes failure) and ready-made texts acquired with purchasing power.

Third, the Internet has changed the relationship between students and teachers—specifically the methods by which students value and evaluate teaching, and how that information might now be disseminated publicly to other students, so as to make public what most educators prefer to think of as a private, local act of intellectual rather than commodified, free-market exchange. With open online evaluation systems that cross geographical, social, and temporal boundaries, students are no longer content to trust that their individual, on-the-ground assessments of teaching will (or can) make a difference in their local context. Instead, students seek to open up that assessment to the network of like students who consume such assessments, both literally and figuratively. In doing so, the students become the "teachers" of other students—as well as the voices who gain greater authority in the evaluative process, insofar as evaluation becomes a marker of quality expressed by a population more than willing to judge others (teachers) as they are routinely being judged themselves.

Each of these altered states—of reading, writing, and teacher performance, validity, and evaluation—goes to challenging the core of how students learn and even *why* they learn, at least using the traditional methodologies currently in place. For those of us who grew up in the United States, regardless of the specific community where one was schooled, it is very likely that the structures of our educational experiences were strikingly similar. There is a classroom (and more often than not, it is populated with more students than it reasonably should be). Students do assigned work individually, or occasionally in small- and in large-group settings, depending on the subject of the course and the nature of the immediate task. Classes are divided by subject areas of the curriculum, with little overlap from one course to another, or between potentially conversant subjects. Students play a limited role in the scope or direction of the course, and fulfill a series of required assignments and sequences of courses in order to meet state and local mandates. Teachers are in charge of students. Administrators are in charge of teachers.

Texts, however—chiefly print in nature, and frequently canonical or at least "traditional" in scope and content—are the elements that truly rule the day. Work on these texts and *for* these texts, in the case of system-authored texts that dictate the teaching methodologies of the *other* texts, is submitted by the students to the teachers; teachers evaluate the work and return it to the students. At the end of the semester, teachers are evaluated by students (at the college level; no such luck at the secondary level), and via other measurements, by school administrators—in order to determine how well the students have read, memorized, and regurgitated the words in those texts, in order to move to the next educational phase. Nothing changes into the next year, at least nothing visible and significant. Change takes years, even decades, and as such is barely audible over the low din of progress.

This system, situated so deeply that it does not even *seem* like a definable system at all, is certainly ripe for a rebellion. But until the advent of technology, which could bring students together *en masse* outside of the classroom, there was no realistic way to enact change, even if the change was entertained by the institutional structures and systems themselves. Certainly, the various community actions and reactions, within larger cultural movements, of the 1960s and 1970s were one powerful way to illustrate disapproval with the educational system. But even then, the collection of bodies was still often a local one, unable to capitalize on cross-country dialogues or cross-population complaints. Furthermore, the memory of those sit-ins, rebellions, and strikes today—viewed through clouded, historical lenses that make such events seem part of a distant, disconnected past—seem to bear little on students' views of their own disagreements with authority. Instead of mobilizing a physical gathering to descend on a campus building, students "get connected" online and put that gathering into play in a virtual space.[1]

This online communal presence is a seismic shift from even the youth behaviors and motivations of twenty years ago. When I was a teenager in the relatively conservative and (student-wise) orderly 1980s, for example, students could gather in groups to complain, talk on the phone and complain, or cut class—the ultimate complaint, next to dropping out altogether at the age of consent (or getting sent to that spooky alternative high school, never to be seen again). But none of these rebellious-like actions ever changed, ultimately, what we were *supposed* to do. Even the occasional public rebellion that caught the attention of authorities—that senior prank with the real estate signs, or others like it—didn't *change* they way we learned, or the way we were taught, or the ultimate role we played in that process. No one stopped to question, why *this* student group would use *this* method to express themselves. Those senior boys could lounge on the lawn, changing places and faces but not roles, year after year, selling our school and sipping their drinks, feigning adulthood and the trappings of suburbanite community status. But their proposed ownership, however *real* in terms of the daily human capital and intellectual labor that students put into the educational system, never ultimately gave them any real rights to the proceeds of the sale.

The Internet has changed these critical agencies, bringing that implicit student ownership of schooling to the surface, blatantly hoisting it in our faces, at all hours of the day and night and during all days of the year; one cannot simply leave campus, or boldly cross a picket line, to avoid the building online rhetoric of protest. Social networking technologies provide venues for students to propose and confront their personal grievances to a set of peers completely out of any teacher-figure's view. This confrontational and often commercial new omnipresent system—one that relies on a tacit rejection of previously indisputable terms like *authority, teacher,* and *text*—is the subject of this book. In particular, this book focuses on the acquisition of literacy as it occurs without or, perhaps more accurately, despite the direct oversight of teachers or teacher-figures—that which offers students a coherent framework within which they are able to read and interpret texts; respond critically to arguments (both well-reasoned and poorly or falsely constructed); and, chief among all activities, write correctly, persuasively, and eloquently, for these remain the most three popular adjectives attached to "good" writing at the college level, particularly writing done in the first year.

To situate this student response to literacy practices in higher education, I must first posit a definition of literacy that I believe students are both rebelling against and seeking to make more operational in their daily schooling lives. I find this definition in the work of James Paul Gee, whose work I return to in Chapter 2. Gee summarizes that from

> a "discourse-based, situated, and sociocultural view of literacy, we must see reading (and writing and speaking) as not one thing, but many: many different socioculturally situated reading (writing, speaking) practices. It demands that we see meaning in the world and in

texts as situated in learners' experiences—experiences that, if they are to be useful, must give rise to mid-level situated meanings through which learners can recognize and act on the world in specific ways. At the same time, these experiences must be normed and scaffolded by masters and more advanced peers within a Discourse, and such norming and scaffolding must lead apprentices to build the "right" sorts of situated meanings based on shared experiences and shared cultural models. Minus the presence of masters of the Discourse, such norming and scaffolding is impossible. Such "sharing" is always, of course, ripe with ideological and power effects, and it leads us always to ask of any school-based Discourse, "In what sense is this Discourse 'authentic'— that is, how and where does it relate to Discourses outside school (e.g., science, work, communities)?" In the end, "to read" is to be able to actively assemble situated meanings in one or more specific "literate" Discourses. There is no reading in general—at least none that leads to thought and action in the world. (www.readingonline.org/articles/hand-book/gee)

As Gee notes, literacy, in social terms, requires "norming and scaffold-ing" in order to be meaningful in a given sociocultural context. I argue that such norming and scaffolding are exactly what students are selecting to do themselves, without the "masters of the discourse," in this case, classroom teachers. As students assemble "situated meanings," these meanings increasingly take space within peer student communities and in the con-text of Internet discourse, which includes that discourse about higher edu-cation in general, which serves as a dialogic frame for the larger conversa-tion. These students would likely agree with Gee that there is "no reading in general"—that it is all situation and culturally specific, despite the fact that our current system of higher education works to make reading seem exactly that—a "general" process to be mastered with the aid of teachers-as-interpreters of texts, both those under study/previous published and those created by the students themselves. Students who seek to gain their literacy acquisition online would also likely agree with Gee that the dis-course of school needs to also be "authentic outside school," but is rarely framed that way with higher education's standard practices. Even the most liberal and liberated writing classrooms, as I examine in Chapter 1, fail to ring true for many students as enactments of "real" moments of literacy in action, especially when directed so closely in tone and subject matter/approach by the teacher-figure.

I have chosen to focus this book on this process of acquiring one's lit-eracy online without teachers, to borrow from Peter Elbow, within the sys-tem of higher education for two reasons. First, I am a scholar of composi-tion studies, and literacy is therefore the area of higher education about which I can speak the most coherently and authoritatively. I am frankly not equipped to analyze or critique the educational arenas of mathematics, science, social science, or the fine arts (although my background in creative writing does give me some insight into the intersections of so-called "creative" expression and argumentative discourse), nor do I aim to know or understand the equally complex relationships that are in play, and that surely have also changed with the introduction of the Internet and online student discourse, between students, teachers, and texts in these disciplines.

I am also investigating literacy acquisition here, however, because its enterprise is far more *public* an endeavor, I would argue, than these other processes of becoming a mathematician, scientist, social scientist, or artist in twenty-first century American culture. Although such areas of study are often publicly *funded*, through government grants, fellowships, and community programs, and are thus financially scrutinized to the extent that taxpayer monies underwrite certain scientific, mathematical, historical, or artistic projects and pursuits, these areas of scholarship and inquiry are far less frequently perceived as publicly *owned*. Simply put, through the late twentieth- and early twenty-first-century phenomenon of economic disincentives attached to the teaching of "fundamentals" in secondary and postsecondary education, including but not limited to No Child Left Behind (as a mandate) and the Spellings Report (as an ominous directive), the general public has come to see itself as the collective "owner" of reading, writing, and (the more vaguely defined) critical thinking in our institutions of learning. Perhaps this is because one cannot, literally, "get by" in the global economy, or even in our individual home communities, without having some degree of facility in these facets of literacy. Those who study the plight of second-language immigrants and other functionally illiterate adults in the United States (see, e.g., the often read works of Jonathan Kozol and Theodore Sizer on these issues, each of whom appears regularly in first-year composition anthologies) have clearly shown how the distinctive commodification of our culture falsely persuades these individuals to engage in obviously unhealthy/unsafe/uninformed practices detrimental to their own livelihoods, and the livelihoods of their families.

This same embrace of commodification in our culture results in the belief that education, as a system in which participants must *pay* to take part (even if through a sponsored financial transaction, such as a student loan, scholarship, or fellowship, each of which has its stipulations and payback rules), is a commodity unto itself, paid for by the culture and made possible by capitalist economic exchange, at the root of which stand the equations Education = Employment and College Degree = Social/Communal/Financial Respect. Students who, after four years of college, emerge from this economic exchange and its equations having not received, or received fully, the goods (literacy) for which they have paid, in a variety of ways, typically feel cheated. And at the root of this feeling is anger, anger at having unwillingly bought into a system that cannot deliver all that it so seductively promises.

This consumerist attitude very likely occurs in other disciplines and subjects as well; I myself still question why and how, for example, I was allowed to not *really* understand chemistry as a high school student, instead having been encouraged to drop the course so as to not endanger my otherwise solid grade point average via a true grappling with this subject. As a young woman who excelled in English, I surely was marked by counselors and teachers as having a particular future ahead of me (which I did, in fact, fulfill—even if my role as "teacher" became more multivocal in its enactment than these early sponsors of mine may have imagined). Given my memory of this slightly "cheated" feeling I experienced later in life—for example, when I did a public presentation on writing in a chemistry lecture hall, and lamented openly that foreignness of the periodic table on the wall—I certainly do not dispute that in order to push our students through the process of attaining an education—*any* education—we cheat them out of an ideal, rich experience in a variety of ways.

But our popular culture's *focus* on the perceived lack of momentum gained in the "fundamentals" of reading and writing—and the associated "lost" costs thrown toward pursuits of literacy—at the secondary and then postsecondary levels continues to rage on, especially in presidential election years, such as the one in which I am writing (2009). One need not be old enough to remember the infamous *Time* magazine cover in 1975 asking "Why Can't Johnny Read?" to be familiar with the current lament echoing that same query. We rarely (if ever), in comparison, see parents or students who angrily challenge their lack of facility in basic physics or geometry, or even history, in the context of discussions over the cost and value of higher education. We regularly and always see employers, parents, and community members complaining about youth literacy—and craning their necks so as to speak directly to the English teacher in the room.

Barring the availability of a refund, these students' and parents' complaints and, more accurately, fears of their collective economic future, become part of the general public discourse against the ineffective machinery that dictates how literacy is taught, and thus *acquired*, as a tangible commodity, in postsecondary American institutions. If college graduates cannot read, write, or communicate effectively—each of which is learned, I maintain, despite my clearly biased viewpoint, through a process far more subjective than the pedagogies present in mathematics or sciences, wherein there are "right" and "wrong" answers, or even in the social sciences, wherein historical evidence provides a pathway to answering key questions obtainable by all—then the system, surely, is to blame. Given the way in which a college degree is chiefly configured in the twenty-first century, as a certificate entitling the holder to a "good" job that will ensure a "better" place in the difficult American economy, the consequence of poorly taught (or poorly acquired) reading and writing skills is perceived to be potentially lifelong in economic terms. I do not necessarily *agree* with this version of economic theory that has been foisted on writing teachers, but it has been the overarching impulse guiding curriculum, budgets, and even hiring practices in my aggregate educational experiences.

Yet, in order to be able to address this public outcry, which never seems to abate and, depending on other passing cultural phenomena, can rise comparatively, and suddenly, at alarming rates, we first have to be able to clearly define what literacy is and how one can *successfully* acquire it. Although composition studies scholars spend a good deal of their time working with exactly those puzzling parameters in explicit as well as implicit ways, very little of that scholarship likely makes its way to the general public outside academia. Additionally, secondary schools infrequently share the same terms of art and curricular values as do postsecondary institutions and writing scholars, which makes for paradoxical pedagogies, at times. At least this is the case in subjects such as first-year composition, which for the past twenty or so years has commonly been viewed as a course wherein students not only develop and improve on their literacy skills, but also develop and improve on their "critical thinking" skills and, frequently, their sense of intellectual self. Such pedagogy is designed to be empowering in the most basic sense, that is, enter a discourse about reading and writing and discover one's innate social (and political) position in higher education.

But as Sharon Crowley has posited, in the context of first-year composition and its status as a "universal requirement," writing teachers have difficulty *conclusively* defining these larger aspects of literacy when they are viewed as tangible goods to be transferred to students who have been trained to view learning in quantified terms throughout their secondary schooling experiences. Crowley queries:

> What is literacy anyhow? And whose literacy do we teach? Can in fact literacy empower anyone who has achieved it? How does this work? What sort of empowerment are we talking about—political? Ethical? Intellectual? Financial? And if in fact literacy does empower people, for whose purposes does it do so? (234)

Crowley's questions serve to link the two core problems that I explore throughout this book, via an exploration of reading, writing, and teacher–student evaluative practices *sans* the oversight of teachers and other teacher-figures, as represented on the Internet. First, how do students define literacy, inside and outside the classroom, versus how teachers and teacher-figures (such as school administrators) define it? In particular, do students see literacy acquisition as a singular event, or a communal/collaborative one? Do students privilege the mastery of texts, or instead the bland familiarity with ideas and tools toward understanding those ideas, and less so the material staying power of the text itself? Second, in the pursuit of literacy vis-à-vis higher education, what or who is the prevailing discourse of authority? In other words, how and when do we talk about power and authority in the acquisition of literacy, and what role do students truly occupy in that discourse, especially when set "free" from the oversight of teachers?

This book, therefore, illustrates how the extra-institutional discourses surrounding higher education, and literacy acquisition, complicate the traditional answers to these questions—answers that privilege the practices of the educational system while professing to give students critical agencies through student-centered pedagogies, including those that incorporate technology as a minor or major part of the learning process. In addition, this book emphasizes how the increased commodification of learning, which not only allows for but insists on a declaration of ownership—of courses, texts, and intellectual products—works hand in hand with the rise of technological apparatuses that assist students in designing their own economically sanctioned parameters for learning, and for agency-building, outside of the classroom setting.

To introduce the problems inherent in addressing authority issues inside and outside of the classroom, in Chapter 1, I discuss current theories of the benefits and drawbacks of liberatory pedagogy—that popular teaching worldview that attempts to relinquish and relocate authority, control, and ethical representation in the college classroom, specifically the college reading and writing classroom, to "develop citizens who are actively literate, [who are] critical agents of change as social and political activists" (Berlin, "Freirean Pedagogy" 419). In doing so, I query the actual role and value of the teacher or teacher-figure in student learning, specifically whether the teacher has been effectively marginalized such that he or she occupies a liminal rather than centralized place in higher education as we know it. I illustrate the intense push–pull currently in place between well-meaning, and highly self-conscious, teachers and their students, who struggle to find a definition within those classrooms for who and what they are—both individually and as a learning collective set against the larger system—within higher education. To do so, I draw on the work of Richard Miller, arguably one of the most widely known critics of liberatory pedagogy today, in order to apply his theories and criticisms of nineteenth- and twentieth-century schooling to a twenty-first-century virtual educational space.

In Chapters 2 through 4, I transition from this opening theoretical argument regarding teachers, students, and the learning process to a focused spotlight on three separate concepts of educational authority that illustrate this argument via commercial Web sites; I spotlight these sites as core illustrations because they each complicate definitions of and attitudes toward authorship, reading literacies, and teacher evaluation. Chapter 2 analyzes the Web site Pink Monkey, which offers alternatives to traditional reading and textual analysis practices found in secondary and postsecondary class-rooms, and which illustrates the ways in which students read—and value reading—differently when in online collaboration outside the oversight of teachers and institutions. Chapter 3 focuses on the various online "paper mills" and their negative rhetorical appeal as sites of authorship-for-sale, and examines the paradox created when students desire academic success via, among other things, the rewards of authorship, while simultaneously devaluing the process by which one *becomes* an author in favor of embracing consumer-based processes of authorship instead—namely, the purchase of already-"good" writing online. Chapter 4 examines a larger view of literacy and educational practices through the Web site Rate My Professors, and the discourse students engage in on this site related to teacher evaluation and educational reform, a public—and sometimes uncomfortable—discourse which clearly evidences a desire among students for a greater critical voice in their own educations.

When spotlighting these sites, I am cognizant of the argument that the Internet is a transitory space—with content evolving day and night, as we speak, with the result of certain sites, threads, and associated software rising and falling in popularity, accessibility, and therefore use. The three sites profiled in this book, in my view, represent a deep and consistent attention to student extracurricular educational spaces that I believe will remain at the center of online discourse for some years to come, even if the design and/or structure of the sites shift or are amended by future generations of users. Thus, although certain online paper mill sites, for example, may expand or contract, or rapidly proliferate, the core material (papers for sale or trade) will be eternally present now that the technology is readily available, and as long as economic (and educational) demand exists. I offer these representative Web sites/samples, therefore, in order to illustrate larger long-lasting concerns and challenges posed to students and teachers via online communication in twenty-first-century schooling, including those challenges undoubtedly yet to come.

To bring together the core argument of this book, in Chapter 5, I postulate classroom measures and overall pedagogical considerations that balance, but do not completely undermine or cannibalize, these student-led, extra-institutional efforts to reclaim school, in the context of what is possible versus what is desirable where technology and public discourse are concerned. In doing so, I argue that the teacher in the twenty-first century has in fact been reified as object rather than subject, and in the process, the act of teaching has become a highly replicable act, subsequently enacted by students themselves, for one another. As neither this chapter nor this book is a "how-to" lesson in using or addressing online technologies in teaching, Chapter 5 focuses on larger considerations that teachers must openly address both with their students and between themselves as the Internet continues to be a large part of our students' lives outside the institutional space, and as teachers themselves continue to be a comparatively smaller part. In raising these considerations, I sketch a broad future vision of first-year writing pedagogy that takes into account the increasing importance of the text–student relationship and the decreasing importance of the teacher as mediator, or interlocutor in this relationship, as well as the permanent role that economic values and commodified learning practices will continue to play in higher education into the twenty-first century.

Ultimately, the way in which to address the commercialized Internet presence in our students' roads to literacy is not to co-opt these sites (or their methodologies) for classroom use, as a kind of uncomfortable pandering reminiscent of the initial mass adoption of technologies in institutions nationwide, even those for which there existed no rational infrastructure to support—or even simply use—these technologies. Such blind adherence to *any* mass innovation that promises to "connect" the educational and public spheres is at best, financially and institutionally irresponsible and at worst, an even greater sign to students that we, as teachers and teacher-figures, talk a good (money) game, but care little about the rules of (social and intellectual) play. Instead, teachers and administrators must keep the integrity of the external sites of student educational discourse intact, and use the classroom space (whether it be on-the-ground, online, or hybrid in nature) to build stronger relationships between the educator and educated, in order to provide a site of mutual trust and dialogue that adds to, but does not discount, the external commodified practices of reading, writing, and evaluation.

In closing, before I begin my discussion of liberatory pedagogies in Chapter 1, I would like to leave readers with a sound reminder of the inherent paradox that teachers and teacher-figures face in the writing and reading classroom, as posited by Marilyn Cooper some fifteen years ago. I select Cooper as a source here because her concomitant work on writing and technology (specifically online communication) has also been an influence on my work in this book, and because I believe her worldview of "academic" writing and research (both student and faculty) as it intersects with the public sphere is highly applicable to my own understanding of why and how students turn to the most newly available technologies to advance (or, in some cases, laterally move but safely secure) their own schooling beyond the watchful eyes of the educational system.

In discussing the role of the writing center teacher-tutor, specifically "organic" versus "traditional" intellectuals, and the outcomes of this binary in writing center work, Cooper argues that composition studies faculty too frequently "function for the most part as traditional intellectuals of the dominant social group, intellectuals who have lost sight of how their beliefs and practices are dependent on the worldview of the white middle class of America and whose everyday experience is quite separate from and foreign to the life experiences of most students in college writing classes" ("Really Useful Knowledge" 105). Now, my agenda here is not to re- (or de-) intellectualize either writing students or writing faculty; however, Cooper's point—prescient in its applicability to our current digital age—does highlight an important and accepted distinction between what composition studies faculty (as researchers) do in their own work versus how that work truly speaks to—and speaks, if ever, *for*—the students on whom it is frequently based.

Even though in these pages I draw on examples of student writing submitted to other students/peer groups, in public online spaces, I do not claim to speak for students—and highly respect, in fact, scholars such as Amy Robillard, who has vigorously defended students' rights to their own scholarship and intellectual representation in the pages of our field journals and collections.[2] But I do wish to use Cooper's point, which was made in the context of writing center work, to remind readers that this *separation* is real and ongoing—and that consequently to abruptly attempt to "bridge that gap" (an over-used phrase, to be sure) via appropriation of technologies in the classroom is, in my view, a facile solution, fraught with false hope about the ultimate power of the technology itself, divorced from its rightful social context(s). Instead, I hope that the examples I provide in this book will show that we instead must acknowledge and address the teacher–student separation and reconceive of it as occasionally *healthy*, insofar as technological uses (and abuses) of literacy acquisition are concerned. Although our collective physical manifestations of "school" are, I hope, not for sale, our collective definitions of the long-standing terms *student, teacher,* and *literacy* are truly up for some healthy twenty-first-century, Internet-based bidding.

1

WHO NEEDS TEACHERS?

The Generation After Liberatory Pedagogy

My core contention throughout this book is that college and university students do not feel in control of their own education, and consequently resist and reject teacher oversight as they acquire that education, particularly in the highly interpretive and value-laden reading- and writing-centered classroom. To make my case, however, I must first address how and why current pedagogical strategies designed to combat these student perceptions do not necessarily eliminate the problem. Given the popularity of teaching approaches such as liberatory (also known as critical) pedagogy, which aims to privilege student agencies in the classroom—and importantly, attach a measurable cultural and political importance to student literacies—why do students still continue to feel disaffected, and seek other outlets for dialogic learning and literacy acquisition outside the institution?

There exists an immense amount of online student discourse associated with teaching and learning in the twenty-first century; the self-directed nature of this discourse bypasses the teacher-figure in favor of collaborative learning, information sharing, and meta-analysis of the educational system. Such online discourse is, I argue, a response to/outgrowth of student disenfranchisement with the educational system, a symptom of the continued limitations of how empowered our students actually feel in traditional classrooms, even within the positive intentions and progressive frameworks of liberatory pedagogies. I submit that in the context of these growing online student communities, the core goals of liberatory pedagogy have not been as fully realized as its supporters may imagine. These core goals are first, that students become empowered through their education so as

15

to become fully cognizant political citizens, and second, that the teacher in the classroom evolves to be a participant and a facilitator of knowledge-making, rather than a centralized figure in imparting abstract wisdom that continues the cycle of the oppressor (authoritative subject/teacher) in shaping and imprinting the values of the state on the oppressed (educational object/student).

In this chapter, I examine the core tenets of liberatory/critical pedagogy in light of the seemingly disappearing teacher within students' perceptions of and practices toward literacy acquisition. Specifically, I question whether this teacher or teacher-figure, however empowering or politicizing, is any longer of significant use-value when students have (a) access to the technology necessary to create cross-cultural and cross-global communities of learners; (b) access to a variety of viewpoints and counter-viewpoints on the common subjects under study (or debate) in our secondary institutions, and (c) an innate, economically rooted drive to be independent learners and thinkers, as defined on their own terms, rather than those of the institution, in exchange for the college degree—a prize earned through survival of the educational fittest, and not necessarily compatible with theories of a politically enlightened, liberatory-centered education.

In order to ground my argument in current theoretical perspectives, I first examine several scholars' support of both liberatory pedagogy and the more general radicalized teacher-figure inside English studies, specifically first-year composition classrooms. Next, I focus on the contrarian work of Richard Miller, who raises legitimate and pressing questions about liberatory pedagogy and the bureaucracies of higher education that I find parallel, in part, to my own. Overall, I demonstrate broad ways in which the socialized, online practices of students in the twenty-first century eclipse and even conflict with liberatory methodologies in ways that may make teachers—even the most radical among them—uncomfortable with their resulting (lesser) positions in higher education.

I do *not* aim to argue, certainly, in this chapter or in the book as a whole, that *every* student is happy without the influence of *any* teachers. I work with students every day who seemingly appreciate and respond to the presence of a teacher-figure, as well as the expertise that he or she can offer. These students, however, happen to be graduate students, and are themselves part of the teacher-figure construction as they serve a dual role as teaching assistants and/or instructors for their own undergraduate courses. Nonetheless, I am willing to believe that a certain type of undergraduate student also still exists out there—somewhere—as a segment of the first-year or undergraduate population, one who does want the ongoing influence of a teacher in his or her learning life. But that student also is concomitantly influenced by other students who have none of these needs, and who are available 24/7 online, unlike teachers, as part of that student's extra-institutional electronic media community. Given this reality, I disagree in part with scholars such as Susan C. Herring, who has argued in regards to the patronage of the Internet that

> [A]dults create and regulate the media technologies consumed by young people, and profit financially from them. More insidiously, mainstream media commentators interpret new technologies and youth practices in normative, moral terms, a process that reinscribes youth as "other." New media scholars also view the Internet through an adult lens . . . in ways that exoticize technologically mediated communication and its youthful users. While the Internet may seem perfectly ordinary—even banal—to today's youth, it is not a native medium for most adults who write about it. Yet, with the exception of teen bloggers, it is adults who are doing most of the writing. (71–72)

Certainly adults (and here I define this term as individuals outside the educational enterprise, as well as outside the traditional age group for college students, i.e., 18- to 25-year-olds) do gain profit from even student-led Web sites; as a negative example, the online paper mills profit not only from students' purchases of papers, but also from the sponsors who buy advertising space on the sites themselves. But Herring's argument that adults do "most" of the writing on the Internet seems to overlook the type of other sites I profile in this book—those that are created for students, are fueled *by* students, and serve to further the dialogic aims of students regarding their educational agencies. Arguments such as Herring's lead us to believe that students read, write, and dialogue with one another on the Internet simply in the service of "adults" who realize a profit from this discourse. Discounting the actual *content* and *purpose* of these dialogues allows us easy ignorance regarding the true discontentment of college (and high school) students in traditional classrooms.

The further we reach into the twenty-first century, the less our dependence becomes on face-to-face communication in all aspects of our lives; consequently, the physical presence of the teacher within the educational system is also minimized. In many cases, the lessening of that teacher's presence means his or her intellectual standing—and intellectual immediacy as part of the learning process—is minimized as well. I do not aim to argue that clinging to teacher authority is the retrograde ideal, but I do aim to illustrate, as a larger project in this book, how educational systems—including teachers themselves—are in denial of the myriad extra-institutional activities that seek to shape students' educations far more aggressively than classroom activities, including teacher–student exchanges. The continued, often blind embrace of liberatory pedagogies illustrates this denial in quantifiable ways.

THE LIMITS OF LIBERATORY/CRITICAL PEDAGOGY

Liberatory pedagogy, adopted for the purpose of giving students authority in their own learning processes, is perhaps best known by sociologists and cultural anthropologists in the person of Paulo Freire, and is most often employed (or attempted) in the of teaching first-year writing in its current incarnation as a "gatekeeper" course designed to introduce students to the discourse of the university and its intellectual values. Liberatory pedagogy first rose to prominence in English studies during the 1980s; one of the first articles focused on Freire's work as applicable to composition and rhetoric appeared in 1983 in *Rhetoric Review*. Between 1978 and 2002, no fewer than sixty-six articles, books, and dissertation topics in the field of composition and rhetoric included Freire in their titles. Clearly, Freire's revolutionary theories and principles struck a chord for those teachers and students working in reading and writing classrooms, particularly first-year composition, a course whose curricular aims are frequently misinterpreted and even co-opted by public individuals and groups for social or political purposes, and whose students are therefore caught in the crossfire of debates regarding the perceived successes and failures of writing pedagogy in American colleges and universities.

Liberatory pedagogy, as informed by Freire's teachings, seeks to overturn the traditional systematic assumption in American schooling that teachers are in charge of the classroom, and students are merely passive participants within it; furthermore, it resists the notion that teachers should simply "fill" students with knowledge (Freire's well-known "banking concept") in order to make these students better citizens of the state. In contrast, liberatory pedagogy calls for acute social and political awareness on the part of the student, which promises to lead to a greater democracy populated by leaders and independent thinkers rather than "empty vessel" followers. Within this paradigm, the teacher-figure is a guide, but not a central authority; he or she should challenge the students to overturn their own assumptions about learning and mediate their negotiations while those challenges are in play.[3]

The teacher in liberatory pedagogy is decentralized, yet still present as a facilitator in the revolutionary process of being (actively) versus becoming (passively) educated. This pedagogical structure seems to function best in intimate classroom settings (i.e., smaller classes) and can be most readily enacted through acts of literacy, or more broadly, in classrooms teaching the humanities, for therein we see explicitly present our dominant cultural values in the form of literary texts and student and teacher responses to these texts. Already English studies, and the subfield of composition studies in particular, has wrestled with the best ways in which to impress upon students the value of reading and writing about humanistic texts; as such, the reading- and writing-intensive classroom, particularly first-year composition, is a ripe setting for pushing that struggle into more progressive arenas, even attempting to (seemingly) flip the roles of teacher and student, such that the student learns but also teaches, and the teacher teaches, but also learns.

Owing to this attractive paradigm—in which students take an active role in their own educations and become more intimately and politically involved with the texts they are reading and writing—liberatory pedagogy has a number of high-profile composition studies scholars among its converts. Ann Berthoff, an historical champion of Freire's theories, notes that Freire "has the audacity to believe that teachers must be learners, that they learn from students in dialogue . . . [he] encourages us not to defer change until some propitious moment, not to waste our substance on getting people ready for change, ready to learn, ready for education" (363). Berthoff's admiration for Freire stems from his call to action, his insistence that the classroom is not only an appropriate but a fundamental site for social action and, to an extent, class warfare. In the setting of school, students should be "liberated" from their oppressors, made cognizant of their own social value(s), and be inducted into the larger power structure of their culture, in order to become fully conscious as participating, political individuals. Berthoff's interpretation of Freire's theories centers on the dialogic space that the classroom must necessarily become in order to enact these changes in students.

In Berthoff's reading, and in most readings of Freire, the teacher is not only part of this important dialogue, however, but is the primary *instigator* of it. Without the teacher, there is no learning, let alone dialogue. While the teacher learns from the students, in Berthoff's view, the students also are still directed to learn, and directed to discover their own political beliefs and social roles, vis-à-vis the teacher-figure. Berthoff points out that in liberatory/critical pedagogies, "What we do is teach—what we provide occasions for learners to discover—is THAT they are so doing, THAT they can re-cognize and re-present and re-name, THAT they can make the world" (365, emphasis in original). Berthoff's emphasis here on action—as well as her linguistic parsing of "recognize" and "represent"—drive home the central role that the teacher-figure plays in Freire's paradigm. In Berthoff's estimation, this role is highly evolved from the traditional role of teacher as passive giver of knowledge and classroom controller, wherein learning follows Freire's "banking" method of storing, recalling, and dumping, systematically and from course to course.

Even in this evolution, however, the teacher still must *exist*—and in many ways, takes on a heightened structural importance in the classroom, as a political voice and organizer of men (and women), rather than simply an instrument of the state (or educational system). Such increased social value placed upon the teacher-figure inevitably leads to increased *moral* value as well, elevating the classroom to a status that becomes vaguely spiritual, nearly holy. As Berthoff observes, "Freire is both a Christian and a Marxist" (362); such an observation allows her exaltation of the power of his pedagogical approach: "When people learn that their misery and suffering are not necessary, that they are not God's will or the inevitable pattern of Nature, their liberation has begun" (366). Thus, the liberation is not simply book-smart intellectualism, but higher self-spiritualism as well. Certainly in Freire's original teachings, this spiritualism was important in order to liberate the peasant class and provide for them a greater inner awareness of their own plight.

In order for this spiritual and intellectual liberation to take place, however, there must be in place a second underlying assumption: that the act of teaching is always and already a *liberal act*, a left-leaning enterprise in which teachers struggle to curtail their own personal beliefs while still imparting what they believe to be sound values in their student bodies. Granted, the democratic/left view is often a predominant one on many college campuses, but in Freirean-influenced pedagogy, such a view is elevated to not only a faulty enthymeme (the act of teaching is a liberal profession; therefore, no teachers can be liberal/teachers cannot be conservative), but also a basis for designing the classroom as a similarly democratic space. In other words, unlike other professions wherein political beliefs may not be visible, or even important, to the completion of the job itself, the human-centered, ideology-driven profession of teaching calls upon us to negotiate our political beliefs on a daily basis. By recognizing and even celebrating this reality in the enactment of Freirean pedagogy, however, we call attention to the very class lines that such teachings aim to erase. Namely, our colleagues who explicitly work *for* others (whether it be on the assembly line or in the restaurant kitchen, on the sales call or in the retail management meeting) typically do not have the freedom—or luxury—to propagate their political beliefs as part of their profession. Teachers are privileged in this respect, but only insofar as they can weave the political and the professional in reasonable and productive ways.

Patricia Bizzell makes this political, and concomitantly class-based, assumption clear in the opening of her article "Power, Authority, and Critical Pedagogy," in which she articulates the unifying principle of liberatory pedagogy's roots for readers:

> Let me begin by assuming that many of us teaching today feel caught in a theoretical impasse. On the one hand, we wish to serve politically left-oriented or liberatory goals in our teaching, while on the other, we do not see how we can do so without committing the theoretically totalizing and pedagogically oppressive sins we have inveighed against in the systems we want to resist. (54)

Because Bizzell's article appeared in the *Journal of Basic Writing*, one could argue that her audience allowed for her predisposition in assuming said readers were liberals. This is because the typical (or typified) readership for basic writing studies is a readership involved in students' rights, specifically the defense of marginalized students who have been placed in preparatory, remedial, or "pre-college" courses, depending on the lingo of the institution, and as a consequence have been regarded as holding a lesser status than even "mainstream" first-year writing students, who themselves are often marginalized from the wider, intellectual conversation of the university vis-à-vis the perception that all introductory writing is "repeat" work from high school. Basic writers, in this paradigm, are doubly negligent and thus even less a part of the university's intellectual community. Bizzell's article therefore builds on her own situated ethos as a speaker to this community of teachers, who are themselves bound by a more-than-liberal agenda in the writing classroom.

I agree that basic writing teachers may, in fact, be more "liberal" (in a variety of meanings) than other university writing teachers, in large part because this population arguably has a percentage of its whole more students from less-privileged sites of education (community colleges, adult education programs) than do other writing-centered classrooms. But Bizzell's assumption still draws attention to the assumed status of the teacher-as-liberator, without consideration for the possibility that members of this community might (a) be more conservative in their viewpoints, or pedagogical strategies (and if so, may come to her article with a willingness to be convinced otherwise), or that (b) basic writing is a *de facto* site of liberatory pedagogy because its students already represent the *most* oppressed group within English studies, or the university, and/or are always found at the least-privileged institutions, or among the lowest class groups of individuals, which, simply, is not the historical truth.[4]

Bizzell's embrace of critical pedagogy comes through a particular historical lens, specifically by viewing "the history of composition studies as a series of attacks on classroom uses of power" (55). Indeed, in Bizzell and many other scholars' views, the teaching of writing is at its core a semester-long study in critical thinking vis-à-vis reading and writing, with the express purpose of bringing students to consciousness at the close of the term, to build a stark contrast to the earlier classrooms guided by current-traditional pedagogies, or grammar-based instruction and grading stemming from responses to canonical literature, taught by faculty with little to no investment in the literacies of student writers. When built into a writing course as a methodology, this counterstatement to the historical legacy of writing instruction can be reasonably successful, as a model for educating students beyond simple surface correctness or adherence to outdated forms. But when lain onto a course as a prime *subject*, in contrast, this approach can, in less-experienced hands, eclipse the act of writing instruction altogether, especially for particularly eager graduate students who know less about writing, revising, and critical reading strategies than they do about student-centered discussions and general responses to ideas and theories presented in texts.

Bizzell argues that critical pedagogy may be "brought to bear on the design of composition curricula" (55) as teachers select readings that are "politically engaged in a variety of ways" and that they "try to get students into these texts even if they initially seem very uncongenial" (67). Yet the characterization of writing *as* political act, including political content, in this case, has its limitations when set forth as a generalized ideal, apart from specific strategies of language facility and development also necessary in the first-year classroom and without recognizing where and when students may simply choose to disengage from this politicized process in favor of their own collaborative learning environments not authorized by the teacher.[5] I admit, additionally, to being wary of characterizing the writing classroom as a primarily political space. As Bill Johnston notes, in his review of the limits of liberatory pedagogy, I agree that the act of schooling is "political in nature" but also hold Johnston's belief that "teaching is not primarily about power or politics" (560–61). Like Johnston, I find the frequently used terms in liberatory pedagogy scholarship such as "*struggle, emancipation, liberation . . . revolutionary* and *radical*" to be problematic in terms of my own teaching strategies and in terms of what I believe students expect and gain from first-year writing instruction. But more importantly, I agree with Johnston that such terms mostly "seem intended to make readers feel like romantic rebels," even as that rebellion is mostly an idealized one, fought by students under the guiding of the rebellion-seeking teacher, who "must necessarily be a political creature" in the world of liberatory pedagogy, as Bizzell's work certainly reinforces (558, 561).

Bizzell's design scheme ultimately calls to mind the very power structures that liberatory pedagogy seems to seek to overturn, and which students seek to escape when going online and joining other extra-institutional communities of fellow students who are engaging in educationally relevant electronic discourse and activity. Although liberatory pedagogy's ultimate goal is to empower students and raise their critical consciousness, Bizzell argues that in order to accomplish this goal, students must necessarily surrender some of their own implicit better (or less-developed) judgment to the teacher, in order to reap higher benefits in return. Bizzell spells out three types of power within this paradigm, designating "authority" as the highest/most enlightened and "third kind of power," against the less-attractive options of "coercion" (power given without consent) and "persuasion" (power given with consent, after deliberation), the first and second powers, respectively ("Power" 56–57). In employing "authority," Bizzell imagines this paradigm at work, with "A" representing the teacher-figure and "B" representing the student:

Authority is exercised over B instrumentally in the sense that sometimes B must do what A requires without seeing how B's best interests will be served thereby, but A can exercise authority over B only if B initially grants it to A. . . . In a writing class, this might mean that the teacher A can require the student B to try to argue in a certain way, to enter into a particular audience's point of view, or to give credit to another writer's reasoning, even if these activities seem very uncongenial to the student at the time. . . . The student agrees to attempt these activities [as] the student has decided to trust A's assurance that some good will come out of it. ("Power" 57–58)

On the surface, this paradigm seems relatively benign as a call to action—as it is not visibly different than what we might envision taking place in a nonliberatory/traditional classroom. The teacher asks the student to complete an activity or task; he or she is unwilling but ultimately agrees, because there is a "good" to come of it—the grade, mark, or simply the general appreciation of the teacher him or herself, which will trickle down to the student in positive ways at that moment and hopefully throughout the semester. In a traditional classroom, certainly there is "surrendering" in a variety of forms, including the initial principle that the teacher is in charge and the students are subject to the authority of the teacher inside the classroom and outside of it (as represented in tangible ways, such as homework, and intangible ways, such as the social authority of the teacher-figure over the student, as allied with the parental figure, in the home community as a whole). Certainly this is the traditional, lamented aspect of authority exchange—or lack thereof—that sends students online and to other extra-institutional communities to exercise their own power in learning without the oversight of teachers, parents, or other socially controlling figures. In online student-led communities, the move from coercion to persuasion to authority is multivocal in its negotiation, and triangulated between students, rather than passed from individual student to teacher, and back again, for eventual resolution.

In a liberatory pedagogy paradigm, in fact, this A–B relationship carries a much greater expectation of an *ideological* good; the "reward" is not a grade, or even a teacher's appreciation, but an intellectual, political, or even moral (insofar as it is difficult, I would argue, to separate morality from ethics from politics in an educational setting, or in the culture more generally) outcome that benefits the student. As a result, it actually bears more authoritative weight in a classroom setting than might a more passive teacher–student exchange in a traditional classroom. Advocates of liberatory pedagogy would say this is the signal achievement—the implementation of an unease, a discomfort that enables the student to come to consciousness and thus *truly* learn. These advocates would also argue that displacing the grade as a reward is another realization of a learning ideal—deferring the work-for-evaluation system that characterizes our classrooms.[6]

A reticent student seeking to develop his or her own voice, however, may find such diffusion of traditional awards appealing (if the classroom is indeed able to eschew these entirely), but also may see this type of pedagogical strategy as a further hindrance to her own classroom agency, and thus be more likely to withdraw to an extra-institutional setting, wherein beliefs and values are more freely negotiated without the higher stakes of morality or ethics lessons from the teacher figure. As Karen Kopelson argues, the further composition theorists move into cultural-studies focused approaches, the more

> student resistance has evolved from a rudimentary resistance to the writing course per se into resistance to the writing course as "inappropriately" politicized. Indeed, many of our students view the increasing pedagogical focus on "difference" as an intrusion of sorts, resenting and often actively rebelling against what they may experience as the "imposition" of race, class, gender, sexuality, or (more generally) cultural issues on to their "neutral" course of study. (116–17)

This may be an intractable consequence of liberatory pedagogy: In order to exemplify for students the range of political viewpoints that can be represented by or employed in the act of writing, that exemplification may cause some students to desire the "neutral" position of instruction, even if that position is accompanied by less-critical methodologies, leading to less-complex student tasks. When students go online, they avoid this paradox, represented by the politicized (or not) teacher-figure, entirely.

Importantly, in the liberatory A–B paradigm, there is visibly present the element of *trust*, something that is therefore implicitly absent in other types of pedagogy and which thus aims to justify the transference of power from teacher to student. In liberatory pedagogy, the student *trusts* the judgment of the teacher; he or she *trusts* that the teacher "knows best" in larger aspects of the student's education that go beyond the simple mastery of material or the achievement of an acceptable grade. This two-way street relies heavily on the teacher being a leadership figure in ways that transcend the simple classroom lesson; he or she is a trustworthy figure that does not coerce, but gently guides the student to the "right" way of thinking (e.g., point of view, reasoning in Bizzell's framework). Again, if the student ends up in the "right" frame of mind, mission accomplished. But when dissonance occurs, what does the critical pedagogue do with the gentle coaxing required for the transfer of authority? What does the openly conservative student—or other marginalized student in a particular classroom's context—do to engage in the "right" way of thinking? Here, I am not criticizing the politics itself, but rather the implication that the teacher as classroom leader and intellectual overseer has both the best judgment and the best *choice* in values and beliefs to both use and give over authority to his or her students. Displacing institutional/grading/evaluative authority via moral/ethical/political authority does not seem to me to be as ultimately empowering as it aims to be: The teacher is still in control of a significant component of the student's learning process, one against which she may easily rebel.

In fact, if James Berlin is correct in his assertion that Freire believes "language is at the center of our knowledge of ourselves and others" and that "without the language to name our experience, we are the instruments of the language of others" ("Freirean Pedagogy" 415, 417), then a true enactment of Freire's pedagogy would necessitate a value-free classroom, insofar as the teacher would need to be ideologically if not physically absent from the discussion and the direction of that discussion, else they "become a part of a dehumanizing status quo" ("Freirean Pedagogy" 416). Such a classroom is not completely possible—at least not in the current configuration of schooling that we abide by in the United States. So even as Berlin's theory of the social-epistemic pedagogical approach, or transactional rhetorics, in first-year writing, is based on this idea that truth is created as a mediation between language and the speaker/writer (student), and that only through this mediation can meaning be made for any individual, the teacher figure is still at the center in Berlin's interpretation of liberatory pedagogy.

Scholars who have adopted Freire's theories as a model for their pedagogy certainly fall into the social-epistemic category within Berlin's taxonomy. But even as I myself subscribe to the social-epistemic view in broad terms, I take issue with the celebration of what I call "control acts," a core move that Berlin describes and sanctions (without naming) in his articulation of the teacher's responsibilities within liberatory classrooms:

> It is at the moment of denial that the role of the teacher as problem poser is crucial, providing methods for the questioning that locates the points of conflict and contradiction. These methods most often require a focus on the language students invoke in responding to their experience. The teacher attempts to supply students with heuristic strategies for decoding their characteristic ways of representing the world. Here we see why the teacher, the expert in language, is at the center of education in a democratic society (and in this case not because English studies has historically been used in U.S. schools to reinforce hegemonic ideological positions). The methods of questioning that the teacher poses are designed to reveal the contradictions and conflicts inscribed in the very language of students' thoughts and utterances. ("Freirean Pedagogy" 418)

In my view, it first seems ironic that a pedagogy based on student empowerment would describe the teacher as an "expert" in anything, let alone language, framing him or her as an interpreter, guide, even translator for the students. Here is one point at which Freire's description of educating Brazilian peasants may not translate fully to the American classroom (and its various levels of literacy within student populations). Second, any "decoding" that a teacher employs is necessarily unique to his or her own world perspective, and relationship with/to language. I am skeptical of the ability to universally "decode" a language experience across an entire classroom, but more importantly, I see the "decoding" aspect as the most problematic where student agencies are concerned. This "decoding," in fact, currently takes place online, within the sites I profile in this book, without the supervision of teachers and without the framing of language "experts." As such, this decoding process seems to me at best considered a control act, wherein teacher authority is primary and student acceptance is assumed. This type of relationship—unavoidable though it may be, to some extent, in *any* classroom, and certainly preferable to a completely passive learning paradigm, in which students have no voice whatsoever—is the very kind of seemingly "helpful" structure that students rebel against when moving their educational experiences into an online commercialized setting, assumedly to participate in a "free" market over which, as consumers, they believe to have control.

Although it is difficult to imagine a sanctioned educational space that does not draw on *some* authority—similar to the principle of group dynamics that states that in the absence of a designated leader, one will emerge organically—the discourse within these student-driven and regulated online sites begs the question, does that authority always have to be the *teacher*? Is there an alternative to teacher-centered practices, liberatory or otherwise? For a critical response to these questions, I now turn to the work of Richard Miller who has voiced arguments against the ultimate viability and effectiveness of liberatory pedagogy within our current educational system.

RICHARD MILLER AND LIBERATORY PEDAGOGY: AS IF LEARNING MATTERED

Miller is an iconic, if sometimes polarizing, figure in the field of composition and rhetoric today. His essays, such as "The Arts of Complicity" and "Fault Lines in the Contact Zone," have been widely anthologized and frequently are assigned to graduate students in composition studies (including my own), particularly those beginning their careers in English departments as teachers of first-year writing. Miller's theoretical stance on teaching and learning, and his willingness to call for a near-confrontational style of pedagogy in the writing classroom in order to effect meaningful learning, casts aspersions on the idealized practices that composition studies has embraced, including liberatory pedagogy, in the last twenty-five years of its institutional history. Miller questions the previously comfortable relationships between students and power, and teachers and institutions, as well as the possibility that writing, and writing studies as a field, can enact social change.

Miller's recent turn to the ways in which world events necessarily and undeniably enter into our classrooms, in *Writing at the End of the World* (2005), extends his larger question of where and how "schooling" actually takes place, and under what social and material conditions. But it is Miller's earlier book, *As If Learning Mattered: Reforming Higher Education* (1998), that I believe encapsulates many of his concerns about the limits of liberatory pedagogy while also providing salient historical examples that offer degrees of local context for his overarching arguments about teaching, educational systems, and power.

One of Miller's earliest statements in *As If Learning Mattered* is that "there are *no* ideal teaching situations, because all institutionalized learning occurs under conditions shaped by contingencies beyond the control of any of the individual actors" (5). This assertion underlies Miller's core examples in his book regarding attempted educational reform, both historical and cross-continental. Miller argues that he sees "every educational program as being the product of a series of complex, contradictory, compromised, and contingent solutions whose permanence is never assured" (8), especially given that any attempts to reform the practices of higher education are limited by not only the material conditions facing reform (costs, infrastructures, physical spaces, and geographic boundaries), but also by "the people who have been captured and rewarded by those practices" (201). Miller is glaringly forthright about the "if only" mantra that pervades higher education today:

> [T]hose interested in radically altering the bureaucratic delivery of higher education are left with very few options beyond wishful thinking: if only all the people in the system could be retired or "re-educated," if only an alternative educational regime could be established . . . beckoning toward such lofty goals without developing and then acting on a plan serves an important institutional function: it reinstates the critical intellectual as the academy's moral conscience. (203)

Even in the "Great Books" curriculum, for example—one of Miller's key illustrations in his book, and an interesting parallel to modern attempts at critical pedagogy—the attempt to provide (motivated) students with a highly dialogic, deeply intellectual curriculum becomes a struggle to "unite an 'aristocratic' content with a 'democratic' teaching principle" resulting in mass education in canonical texts and their accompanying ethical principles (88). Although the approach itself was revolutionary, as Miller argues, the ability to replicate this structure across institutions and with an inclusive set of texts (beyond the traditional Anglo-centric, male canon) has kept the core principles of the Great Books initiative (small classes, engaged discussion) from being more widely implemented across academe, again recalling the if-only paradigm that limits more revolutionary change from taking place at the curricular level (or beyond). As Miller notes, the proponents of Great Books "still aren't listening to what those on the outside have to say" in terms of who or what should appear on the reading list (119), and the public line on Great Books thus becomes about the ways in which the curriculum fails to be inclusive, rather than the ways in which the methodology itself is a sound attempt at bringing out students' voices in the classroom.

As Miller describes, the Chicago Great Books initiative was modeled on John Erskine's work at Columbia in 1919; Erskine's course aimed to "wrest control of the Great Books from [the] scholarly specialists so that the reading public might use the books as they pleased" (89). But in practice, Erskine's experiment required a discussion "[that apparently functioned] best when a homogenous group of male students from a prestigious university was led by a male teacher who would ensure that certain godless approaches would not intrude on the seminar's discussion of the male-authored texts" (91). Still, such an approach, in Miller's analysis, was counterintuitive to regular instructional practices, the hallmark of which was the academic lecture, because the Great Books plan provided "students with a social space to work out their responses to the books with each other," additionally "asking teachers to speak *with* the students rather than lectur[ing] to them," which upended the process for "circulating both knowledge and texts" (91), even if the participants were still all-male, and were still all part of the intellectual and cultural elite in the United States.

The latter version of this model, which is now widely associated with its implementation at the University of Chicago, continued the practice of engaging motivated students in a discussion of canonical texts, importantly grounded in, as Miller notes, metaphysical training that "offers the study of the Great Books as the antidote to the social and curricular ills that beset society" (97). George Hutchins, the instigator of the Great Books project at Chicago, worked against "many factions opposed to this project: the vocationalists, the specialists, the representatives of the textbook industry, the relativist sociologists and the cultural anthropologists, and those who believe in scientific progress" (97). In short, Hutchins' Great Books plan called for the exchange of ideas for the sake of scholarly exchange, assuming a student who, like Erskine's Columbia student, already had some knowledge of these texts' traditions, rather than a use of the classroom to inculcate "useful" knowledge for the purposes of obtaining even higher social or economic standing. In layman's terms, we would call this learning for the sake of learning.

Miller holds up this Great Books pedagogical initiative as an unrealized practice in today's higher education, noting its infrequent institutional adoption. He champions the Great Books core pedagogical *principles* in arguing that such principles show

> an evolving commitment to the image of the student . . . as an ordinary, common reader who can nonetheless establish a meaningful and productive relationship with a wide range of immensely complex texts. This flies in the face of prevailing assumptions about average students, who are regularly constructed by the textbook industry and by the professoriate at large as needing to start small, slow and easy, and who somehow are never seen to be quite ready to fully participate in or understand discussions about ideas, great or otherwise. (119)

Here is where Miller's criticisms of liberatory pedagogy as a cure-all for the ills of academe become most salient: In Miller's ideal classroom, students are not only included, but appropriately *challenged*, which would seem to exist in opposition to the liberatory pedagogy principle of relinquished authority and/or the teacher-as-expert. Miller's "liberated" classroom calls for a free exchange of values and ideals, but also a curriculum that assumes students carry with them some modicum of knowledge prior to entering the classroom. As empowering as most of the Freirean models in first-year composition seem to be, they do not, as a rule, assume a great deal of knowledge on the student's part prior to entry. Part of this is undoubtedly due to the frequent positioning of Freirean pedagogy in first-year composition, a course that is always and already "introductory," regardless of the institution in which it is taught (or the names that it may be given at more elite schools, such as "first-year seminar"). But another factor in limiting the assumed knowledge of students in composition, and paradoxically then elevating the teacher-figure's own knowledge base, is the convenience of using graduate student and other contingent labor to staff the course, thereby eliminating the visual representation of "authority" in the form of a tenured, staid professor in the classroom, but also reinforcing the "introductory" nature of the course—wherein basic principles must be taught (and learned) before enlightenment can take place, and where no *true* authority figure wants to spend his or her time inculcating students in these principles.

Indeed, Miller sees first-year composition as a paradoxical site in this way because it often is the subject of debated labor reform, but far less frequently the site of tenured faculty instruction. He singles out Cary Nelson, president of the American Association of University Professors, as a key player in promoting this paradox by noting that despite Nelson's prominent position in academe, "we see . . . horror arise in Nelson at the very thought that he might be required to descend back into the business of composition instruction, which, with its incessant circulation and assessment of student work, is from his perspective the equivalent of being returned to the secretarial pool" (202). In Miller's view, Nelson and those who invoke Freire are the strongest agitators in the "melodrama of educational reform" have a stake in being separated from the day-to-day "highly bureaucratized world" that keeps this reform from ever actually happening (202).[7]

Still, despite his own radical calls for reform, there remains skepticism regarding the picture of higher education that Miller paints in his work, including the intellectual and political characteristics of its faculty. Two prominent reviews of As If Learning Mattered—originally published in Rhetoric Review and College Composition and Communication, respectively—illustrate sample individual critiques of Miller's viewpoint. In his review of As If Learning Mattered, Joe Hardin asserts that Richard Miller's central purpose in writing this book was " to make us realize that we are bureaucrats whose primary institutional usefulness is exhibited in our role as functionaries who grade and sort students" and "to provide a realistic means of addressing the disillusionment that comes from that realization" (206). Hardin also notes that according to Miller, such "disillusionment and revulsion begin when graduate students are lured by theory and by the promise of a life of the mind into a system that primarily needs them as workers to staff the composition sections—work that is considered "disreputable" by tenure-track faculty" (207). Hardin characterizes Miller's book as carrying a "cynical tone" and "universaliz[ing] teachers and graduate students as profoundly disillusioned and self-deluded" (209). In particular, he finds fault with the book's approach and underlying assumptions, arguing ultimately that

> Miller's book is certainly a tonic for educators who believe that critical practice can transform the classroom into a student-centered, egalitarian utopia where the authoritarianism of Western education can be swept away and who imagine that teachers and administrators can change the structure of education by spreading the emancipatory practices of radical pedagogy. Miller's tale is also a caution for those who believe that higher education can be saved by a return to the imagined traditions of some more enlightened time. Still, I wonder how many educators subscribe to such naive assumptions and labor under the type of "false consciousness" from which Miller seems to believe most of us suffer. (208)

In contrast, John Brereton's review of *As If Learning Mattered* opens with a discussion of the relative dearth of composition's history as located in publications on educational reform; such observation is logical given Brereton's own scholarly focus and the publication venue for the review (*College Composition and Communication*), which itself frequently spotlights historical and/or retrospective pieces on the field. Brereton remarks that the historical focus in Miller's book is a "breath of fresh air . . . a book about reform that is grounded in genuine knowledge of teaching and learning" (495). Brereton agrees that Miller's core assertion is that "reformers are usually blind to the fact that they work in constrained circumstances," echoing Hardin's reading, yet focuses his review more closely on the historical components of Miller's study, including his chapter on the British media studies experimental course in the 1960s; the University of Chicago's Great Books initiative in the 1930s; and of course the paradoxical work of Matthew Arnold (495–96). Brereton then locates a key argument of Miller's, one that is comparatively somewhat glossed in Hardin's reading: "The failure of reform to base its efforts on real students and real teachers in an institutional setting" (497). Despite his apparent admiration for this goal, however, Brereton concludes his review by lamenting that in Miller's eyes,

> professors are not revolutionaries or spellbinding preachers but functionaries, educational bureaucrats concerned mostly with credentialing, policing the bounds of knowledge, and passing on information and skills. This modest vision will not win Miller wide approval. Is this all we are, lecturers and graders? Sure, Miller says; we need to find our fulfillment in those narrow parameters, not in earth-shaking pronouncements about the value of the liberal arts or in revolutionary discourse. (497)

Although I can appreciate these readings of Miller's book in the sociohistorical context(s) in which they were written—including the publication venues *for* which they were written—I believe that Miller's theorems about the position and role(s) of teachers in the system of higher education do, in fact, accurately reflect the current climate in which we busily, and sometimes at cross-purposes, attempt to undertake massive, standardized educational reform, particularly in the twenty-first century and its student-centered technology and extra-institutional resources. To address Hardin's concerns, I would argue that perhaps those of us who have been teaching writing for a number of years are, hopefully, less "naïve" about the utopian vision promised by liberatory pedagogies, but that for new teachers—such as doctoral students training in English departments, and especially in rhetoric and composition programs—the promise of liberatory pedagogy feels very real, and entirely possible.

Hardin is concerned that Miller overemphasizes the presence of "false consciousness" among writing teachers (or educators in general) in his work. But in fact, rhetoric and composition studies is in many ways built on the building and rebuilding of the self-aware student writer, one who rejects the formulas and linguistic limitations of past generations and who embraces first-year composition as instead a site of liberation, an entrée into the intellectual smorgasbord of the university. If this does not create some level of "false consciousness" among teachers—that their course and pedagogical approach is/will be unique among other subjects and introductory curricula (such as math, for example, the most widely required university subject behind introductory English), then I believe I have been observing a parallel universe in my sixteen years of teaching writing and working in English departments and composition programs. Rhetoric and composition, sometimes for good and sometimes, perhaps, for ill, bills itself as a very *different* sort of intellectual experience for students, one that in liberatory pedagogy will produce not only more confident writers, but also more confident citizens, especially in those programs that emphasize the tenets of classical rhetoric, such as my own. This is partially in response to rhetoric and composition specialists working and writing in a field that is consistently marginalized both inside and outside the institution; appropriated by various publics who need to assess and reassess the "fundamentals" of education found in its first-year course; and widely misunderstood as a skill-based field of remedial teaching that has no real depth within which its faculty might produce interesting or even intelligent scholarship. As such, "false consciousness" takes on many layers within liberatory pedagogy as a desirable methodological stance—and often works at odds against other similar utopian-framed models of critical awareness found in "beauty-and-truth" models of literary appreciation/teaching, or "artistic development" models of creative writing programs and curricula, each of which may find more or less purchase among career-minded, technologically savvy undergraduate students, depending on the particular institutional context.

To address Brereton's criticisms, therefore, I find myself voicing a similar response as to Hardin, but with different ends. Yes, we faculty are in fact very much "graders and lecturers," at least in the eyes of our undergraduate students, but we believe ourselves to be something far more than this. It is not really within the realm of secondary public education, for example, to position the teacher as a "revolutionary" figure; this is precisely why Freire and those who have adopted his pedagogical theories are so very invested in the revolutionary position.[8] As postsecondary teachers, we are under the distinct impression that owing to our academic freedom, our professional circumstances, and our social positioning—among young adults and those "of age"—we have a greater power to liberate young minds (and the writing produced by those minds) than do our secondary school counterparts. Secondarily, we who teach first-year composition believe it is the ideal location for enacting this liberation. But our perceptions of the teacherly act, if you will, versus the perception of our students regarding that teacherly act, are quite divergent. It would be ideal if this paradigm shift could occur for students when they enter college so that learning becomes more about empowerment and less about fulfilling particular goals and milestones in order to complete a degree. But that ideal is not the reality for most college students studying, working, and purchasing in today's highly interactive and competitive economy. Students typically do not leave first-year composition classes saying, "Wow, that was empowering," even if some of them have, in fact, absorbed the finer points of our pedagogical methods—and I say this not only based on my own teaching experiences, but also on several years of observing and reading end-of-term reflections and evaluations by students in other faculty and teaching assistants' first-year writing courses. Instead, students typically leave saying, at best, "that was a really interesting course. I learned a lot about writing," to, at worst, "glad that gen[eral] ed[ucation] requirement is over. What's next on the list?"

I do not mean to sound overly pessimistic as I map this problem that we face in the teaching of writing specifically and in teaching undergraduates generally, but I do aim to very openly situate my reading of Miller, and my theoretical position in the chapters to follow, in *terra firma* insofar as characterizations of writing, teaching, and learning in the university are concerned. Miller's vision of higher education is not entirely dystopic, in my view, but it does raise legitimate questions about what happens when liberatory pedagogy is *not* the grand solution to the problem of student disengagement and higher education's move toward ever-increasing assembly-line values and curricular standardization. As such, Miller's work serves as a fitting theoretical jumping-off point for looking at online student discourse about teaching and learning, as this discourse occurs in a deliberately teacher-less space, self-liberated from the classroom.

For Miller, the call for educational reform is not only falling on deaf ears, but has also been historically denied as a viable option due to the extreme entrenchment of the higher education system in the United States. He focuses his research in *As If Learning Mattered* on the documents and perspectives less-frequently cited in our research into writing and education, such as textbooks, course evaluations, and teacher's notes (21). Miller also explicitly constructs his research as a focus on "how the student has been figured both rhetorically and pedagogically by specific institutional practices within specific educational systems" (21). In doing so, Miller notes, "educational systems do not have a 'fundamental nature.' Rather, they have assumed a historically produced character that manifests itself in our time as an immensely complex bureaucracy with an inherent resistance to structural change" (23). If we take Miller's pronouncement as truth—or at least entertain the notion, based on our aggregate observation of the slow road to change that typically affects our home institutions and even our state legislative bodies on matters of education, especially higher education—then we must necessarily consider where and how to proceed with the mission of "liberating" our students within the confines of the classrooms that are part and parcel of this bureaucracy.

The solution is not automatically to throw up our hands and return to less-enlightened pedagogical methods—especially because the tenets of liberatory pedagogy certainly give *promise* to the notion that harkens back to the principles of rhetoric, namely that to teach a student to be an informed writer and thinker (and, we hope, careful reader) is to introduce him or her into the joys and true benefits of civic discourse. But it is also not enough to cling to seemingly radical pedagogies while being blissfully unaware that far more revolutionary work is taking place *without* teachers online. As Miller himself observes, despite faculty's (i.e., intellectuals') known distaste for organization and/or collective consciousness of the realities of the world outside of academia, they can, in fact, participate in collective action once they "become disenchanted with the allure of themselves as free-thinking individuals whose mental work escapes the logic of the marketplace" (28). Therefore, I do not suggest throwing out the Freirean baby with the bathwater. But I do suggest that given the ever-increasing bureaucracy that Miller notes, combined with the advent of student-driven and student-led extra-institutional technologies, we should be honest and readily educate ourselves about what the teacher *can* accomplish, and what may be better accomplished—even as we speak—outside the confines (physical and virtual, in the case of online courses) of our reading and writing classrooms.

TECHNOLOGY WITHOUT TEACHERS: MOVING PAST LIBERATORY PEDAGOGUES

Given the pros and cons of liberatory pedagogy and its extreme popularity in the English studies classroom, if we take this pedagogy's central variable—the teacher figure—and *eliminate* him or her entirely in student online discourse communities, what then happens to this highly regarded approach to teaching and learning? In particular, what occurs in courses such as first-year writing, wherein the relationship between the dominant (the university; to a lesser extent, the English department) and the dominated (first-year students) is historically critical?[9] If there is no teacher, or teacher-figure—and thus no authority against which to position oneself in the educational hierarchy (and within the broader agencies of the academy, and its complex power structures)—what is the pedagogical result? To again paraphrase the work of Peter Elbow, what happens when one not only "writ[es] without teachers," but *learns* without teachers as a standard, accepted practice? Even in Elbow's paradigm, we must recall, the teacher is *there* as a leader, a traffic director, an arbiter for the collective writing muse—depending on how expressivist-leaning the classroom is and how deeply it ascribes to Elbow's methodologies. Even if knowledge is to be found within the writer him or herself—the attractive and approachable notion of epistemology as residing internally, clamoring to be released against the noise of the normally authority-driven classroom—the teacher still *exists,* in Elbow's theories, to offer the prompts and guide the student's writerly growth, marginalized though his or her classroom evaluative powers may be.

Researchers in fields outside of English studies—for one example, sociology—can provide us with some insights into the consequences of students' rebellion against classroom structures and authority. As these studies show, resistance can, in fact, have greater outcomes than the simple loss of teacher authority in the given moment, or in the class across one semester, and students can be more significantly affected in the learning process—especially where participation is concerned—by their peers than by their instructor or the physical classroom space. These studies provide us with interesting possible applications to a discussion of why even the most progressive elements of student inclusion present in liberatory pedagogical methods do not preclude students' migration to teacher-less spaces online. Simply put, if the teacher is not as critical as previously thought, his or her specific teaching methodologies may have less impact on the students' learning process than do other socially based groups, either in person or online.

First, one can consider the consequences of rebellion as affecting the actual structure of the classroom, beyond simple teacher authority. As sociologist Daniel McFarland notes, although "everyday forms of active [student] resistance are combative claims (or counter) made in an effort to change the social situation of a classroom" in some cases, these challenges "can alter the classroom situation for good" (613). McFarland thus characterizes moments of student resistance as "windows into social processes that construct, maintain, and permanently alter social settings. Hence, the study of disruptive student behavior relates to topics . . . that are well beyond the domains of classrooms and schools" (613). We can apply this observation to the emergence of online technologies that enable students to act openly in defiance of teacher or institutional authority (such as online paper mills) or, in more dialogic cases, in consort with the learning aims of the classroom, as reinscribed through student interpretations (as in the case of Pink Monkey.com). In these cases, students are certainly "permanently alter[ing]" the social settings in which teaching and learning take place, and are doing so "beyond the domains of classrooms and schools."

In another survey-based study, sociologist Polly Fassbinder argues, "important differences between professors' and students' perceptions of discussion have yet to be uncovered," especially given that there exists "little information about professors' perceptions of classroom interaction" (25) in the field of sociology, and, I would argue, in the field of English studies—even in the classroom-based research that pervades a segment of composition studies scholarship. Fassbinder surveyed students across fifty-one courses of approximately twenty students per course at a private liberal arts college, in order to gauge their viewpoints on classroom interaction, focusing not on general attitudes, but on observations about the class in which the student was enrolled, and was completing the survey. Fassbinder's survey findings revealed that "peers significantly shape classroom dynamics," in that "students' reactions to a class may have more to with peers' behaviors than with course structure or a faculty members' actions" (29). Additionally, Fassbinder's survey respondents noted that students are even more affected by—and more aware of—student passivity than are instructors (30). Fassbinder recommends that faculty help students to see themselves as "part of a community, not merely as isolated individuals learning with the assistance of an instructor" (30), an admonition long-ago voiced by those in composition studies, and in particular put into practice by most faculty who employ liberatory methods.

Fassbinder's findings are especially interesting in light of the socialization that is primary on sites such as Pink Monkey.com, and even Rate My Professors.com (in that this site functions as a "referral" service of sorts, wherein students rely on the judgments and comments of peers in order to make choices about their education—i.e., teachers/professors—and in order to provide their own sometimes competing commentary on that teacher/professor). Because the students on these sites have afforded themselves situational authority in order to make the dialogues and exchanges as democratic as possible—with rarely a moderator's interference—the need to defer to the teacher is eliminated, and the situational behavior among the student participants is heightened so as to be the primary factor in gaining true, reliable information. Fassbinder's notion, therefore, that peers shape classroom dynamics seems critically obvious in the case of these participatory, advice-based, solution-seeking student Web sites because peers are the beginning and end of the discourse that drives the educational outcome(s).

Given these glimpses into sociology's work on student perceptions of teaching and learning, what can we in English studies and first-year composition in particular take away to understand the realities of "teacher-less" spaces that exist online? As previous noted, while liberatory pedagogy provides a solution within a system of problems that is instruction in higher education, it still relies, as a methodology, on the acceptance *of* the teacher as some kind of authority figure, however diminished or retreating. In ideal terms, liberatory pedagogy "frees" students to think for themselves and resist the dominant ideologies of the oppressive class. But in order to do so, such students must be paradoxically *directed* to free themselves; thus, the teacher-figure plays a central and perhaps inextricable role, ironically, in reshaping student consciousness. If we *eliminate* that teacher-figure from the learning equation, as these sociologists imply is already in part the case in students' perceptions of the classroom learning situation, then we necessarily redistribute the resulting authority among the students as agents. When that happens, are the principles of liberatory pedagogy still applicable? More pointedly, are these tenets of liberatory pedagogy, which somewhat paradoxically rely on the presence of an institutional authority figure (however "decentered") still *necessary* to ensure the actual liberation—or freedom—of students and their developing agencies?

First, it's helpful to parse out this critical notion of "freedom" as it may be envisioned by students in the classroom versus in online student-directed settings. Jeffrey Ringer, in his 2005 article in the *JAC*, questions what "liberty" truly means in the context of liberatory pedagogy and additional post-process views of liberatory pedagogy by composition scholars such as Sid Dobrin. Ringer notes that critical compositionists' discussions of liberty "privilege liberation as primarily individualistic endeavor in which someone is always being freed *from* something" (763), which necessarily limits how students can themselves see the empowering aspects of liberty as a call to action. Additionally, such emphasis on individual freedoms, especially as envisioned in post-process paradigms, directly contradicts the community-based values of liberatory pedagogy, which are "community, collectivity, and cooperation" (762). Ringer proposes that we therefore clarify what liberty is *not*, specifically "just freedom from constraint," or the road to anarchy, which Ringer believes "produces oppression, not liberty," as "to be completely free of constraint could serve to be more constraining—and more oppressive—than to live within the bounds of just laws and principles" (769). Additionally, Ringer reminds us that liberty is "incomplete if it entails gaining or sustaining one's freedom at the cost of another," again hearkening back to the values of Freire and collective good (769). Finally, Ringer notes that given the sometimes-confusion of "authority" and "authoritarian" in the implementation of liberatory pedagogies, liberty may be "understood as at best a suspicion of all authority, and at worst, a dismissal of it" (771).

This interrogation of the linguistic root of liberatory pedagogy are highly applicable to the linking of its possible shortcomings and the concomitant rise of online student discourse communities in which "authority" is dislodged entirely from the teacher-figure and taken back, in an explicit power move, by the participating students themselves. As Elizabeth Ellsworth has observed, in her often cited essay on the "Repressive Myths" of liberatory pedagogy, the very tenets of liberatory pedagogy—and here she lists the terms *empowerment, student voice, dialogue,* and *critical* (298)—serve to "perpetuate relations of domination . . . produc[ing] results that [are] not only unhelpful, but actually exacerbate" the conditions that liberatory pedagogy hopes to combat, including "racism, sexism, classism," among others (289). Ellsworth couches her observations in a discussion of a graduate-level course on "Media and Anti-Racist Pedagogies" at the University of Wisconsin, taught within a liberatory pedagogy framework. Ellsworth found that many of the students in her course had participated in movements outside the classroom or institutional setting that opposed these very racist viewpoints, but that "these movements had not necessarily relied on intellectuals/teachers to interpret their goals and programs to themselves or others" (311).

I find Ellsworth's observations to be quite parallel with the move on the part of faculty and, importantly, institutions, to bring student-led technologies—which exist effectively without such institutional oversight or interference—into the classroom space. At worst, such employment of these technologies looks like simple pandering to students, hoping for a return nod that the faculty are, indeed, worthy of inclusion in these student communities (e.g., Facebook, an essay about which has been included in the first-year composition reader, *Composing Knowledge*).[10] At best, these technological interferences serve to reinscribe the discourse of and within the sites in the context of the institutional status quo, as Ellsworth found with her activist students' discussion of their own resistance movements within the University of Wisconsin course structure. I would argue that the harder we try to co-opt these teacher-less spaces—and by "teacher-less" here I deliberately extend the definition to include social and political spaces that do not involve the oversight of the college or university intellectual authorities—the more complicated our own claims to developing truly *independent* student voices, student writers, and student thinkers becomes. It's hard to say that we are "liberating" students when we are, in fact, de-liberating their own spaces for institutional study and classroom appropriation.

In Kopelson's view, "composition's 'critical pedagogies' fail to meet the challenges posed by today's specific formations of student resistance and that they fail particularly, and most ironically, because of their inattention to differences among classroom rhetorical contexts and among teacher subject positions within those contexts" (118). Kopelson's solution is to experiment with this desire and engage in a "performance of neutrality" (118) as the teacher. Although such a position certainly addresses the concerns of scholars such as Ellsworth, and accurately reflects the paradox inherent in liberatory pedagogies, I think that it is prudent now to move beyond the teacher's presence entirely, and consider the imminent landscape of schooling without teachers.

CONCLUSION: "WORLD HAVE YOUR SAY"[11]

The current romance between online education and American universities is an example of the lessening dependence on student–teacher exchange; the romantic draw is chiefly related to financial savings and lowered dependence on human labor (read: diminished faculty lines). I realize that at this point, although some readers may be willing to consider my argument that online student discourse represents a movement away from teacher authority and even a counter-statement against progressive methods such as liberatory pedagogy, these same readers also may argue that such issues of student agency and lacking dialogic communication among and between student learners are solved—presto!—by the advent of online learning. Although distance/online education seems to de-center and render invisible the physical presence, at least, of the teacher-figure, we must recall a few facts. The online course, however minimally, *still* depends on the teacher as a guide and controller of information; even worse, from a liberatory standpoint, the course software licenser is usually the ultimate controller of pedagogical design, if and when the system is not owned by the institution itself. The faculty member rarely "owns" his or her pedagogical content, and so the overarching curriculum as well as the individual lessons themselves are truly state-administered, quite anti-Freirean in nature. The online learning communities constructed by and for students—in conjunction, quite frequently and admittedly, with corporations or entrepreneurs—have no such need for teacher-gatekeepers. Although the design of the web sites are usually in consultation with a for-profit organization, the exchanges themselves are neither dictated by those organizations nor limited in their reproduction, retransmission, or cross-participation by a nameless entity. They are upfront commercialized, to be sure, but they do not commercialize under false pretenses, as one might argue is the case with some course management software employed in online instruction.

Additionally, the online course simply takes the physical, on-the-ground classroom, and repositions it physically in the world of cyberspace. Online instruction certainly opens up myriad possibilities for otherwise disenfranchised students—including but not limited to those in rural populations who cannot come to the campus; those who are differently abled such that being in a traditional on-the-ground course is a physical hardship; and those who wish to "attend" a class that is a great distance from one's home community, but that serves a particular educational need. But online education does not put the *control* of the course itself in the hands of the students; indeed, when students falter in online courses, it is often because of this precise misconception—that the course will be more "free" and "easier" to complete, and that the teacher won't really be "in charge" of the situation as he or she would be in an on-the-ground setting. As much as I freely admit to *not* being an expert in the realm of online course management, I have taught online, and have observed the effects of online teaching on both student success and curricular construction, and I stand by my assertion that simply moving a course online does *not* solve the various problems associated with students' perceptions of their own agencies in higher education. In fact, it is a little insulting to think that students might feel "liberated" by technology alone. The perceived liberation on the student-led Web sites profiled in this book, in contrast, use technology to enable greater student dialogue and educational agency through online communication, as opposed to simply being "new" ways of presenting the same old class.

Instead, I would encourage readers to consider how both faculty and students alike are already headed down the slippery slope of a system of higher education without teachers fulfilling this heretofore critical role of leader, guide, manager—the qualifier here dependent on the particular institutional context and classroom situation. How long will it be before that need, due to the availability of technology and the increased facility on our students' part with information gathering, becomes obsolete, and how will we, as faculty, necessarily recast our roles as teachers when that time comes? This is the multifaceted question that I ask readers to consider across the next three chapters, beginning with Chapter 2, in which I discuss the concept of reading without teachers (or not "reading," in a traditional sense, at all) and the alternative practice of student communal textual interpretation that is one core feature of the popular web site PinkMonkey.com.

2

TO READ OR NOT TO READ

Online Literacy Interfaces and PinkMonkey.com

Faculty frustration with students' reading habits and practices is a reliably popular topic of discussion among those who teach first-year college writing, given the role of this course in transitioning students from the reading and writing practices and expectations of the secondary school classroom to those of the university. One illustration of how faculty view this vexing problem is apparent in an extensive discussion thread posted to the Writing Program Administrators' listserv in January 2009, which focused on the problems for, and solutions to, the ability of college students to complete required readings and to comprehend and/or engage in what they have read. One listserv participant noted the myriad problems as delineated by faculty at his institution:

- [Students will] only read material directly connected to grading;
- Will not read before class;
- Skip difficult material; if they don't see the relevance, they won't read it;
- Form an incorrect hypothesis of the meaning and misread;
- Decoding problems;
- Unknown vocabulary;
- Expect to read only once;
- Take everything at face value;
- Highlight everything;
- Can't understand written directions;
- Egocentric, can't see another point of view;

- Unable to reserve judgment until an argument has been completed;
- Lack of reading practice;
- Limited range of ability, can read textbooks, but not other books;
- No background schema to take in learning;
- Can't understand irony or understatement;
- Believe everything they read. (https://lists.asu.edu/cgi bin/wa?A2 = ind0901&L = WPA-L&T = 0&F = &S = &P = 14545)

The listserv poster also provided insight as to one key *process* problem behind these issues, specifically that students do not like to read difficult material "cold," and that they feel most comfortable discussing a book following a discussion among their peers. Following this proposition, another listserv participant responded that social interaction in the reading process is indeed critical, such that teachers might consider "using a blog where students talk to each other about what they have read" (https://lists.asu.edu /cgi-bin/wa?A2 = ind0901&L = WPA-L&T = 0&F = &S = &P = 14769).

Two important issues arose in this listserv dialogue, which involved at least twenty other faculty participants across the span of more than one week's time. First, as the participants just discussed note, college students fail to "do the reading" for any number of reasons, not limited to simple noncompliance (i.e., blanket, nonspecific refusal to engage with any sort of text), and in ways not always immediately addressable in the classroom setting. In other words, students come to texts with all sorts of motivations, or lack thereof, and these are not always intimately connected to the classroom or the course itself, or even the particular text at hand. Second, students' reading problems, whether stemming from a lack of ability, a lack of motivation, or a lack of deeper understanding/comprehension of the material, each stand to be aided by making the reading process a more socialized, collective—or collaborative—peer-based endeavor.

The idea of "discussing" (explaining, foregrounding, historicizing) a text *before* reading it, however, flies in the face of what most faculty know and believe about "comprehension" as an individual act, a testable measurement of knowledge. But students are desiring, and for some time now have needed, these collective engagements with texts, before, during, and after the act of reading—so as to understand, interpret, and make more meaningful what is being read, and how the text under discussion is viewed by one's peers. As noted in a 1982 issue of the University of Michigan's English Composition Board newsletter *FFORUM*, for example, what students bring—or not—to the text is the key because

[In] the reading of literature . . . it is assumed that the students adequately comprehend the material they are reading. Unfortunately, this

assumption is unwarranted. High schools and colleges have large numbers of students who are unable to understand literary text. This inability is usually not due to students' lack of intelligence or basic skills; it
is rather due to the fact that they lack appropriate background knowledge. (Stander 82)

Although this observation is now more than twenty-five years old, it seems
that little has changed for students, and that the issue has become only
more visible, in part as a result of the resources that students now seek out
in order to combat this lacking background knowledge, resources not readily available in the setting of the classroom. This lacking background affects
not only the reading at hand, but also the writing based on that reading—
a factor that inevitably leads to less confidence on the part of the student
writer that he or she can complete the writing assignment, as examined
more thoroughly in Chapter 3.

Despite our best efforts, students often struggle to complete assigned
reading, and yet we cannot *make* a student read anything on his or her
"own"—no more than we can make the student write in a similarly isolated manner—without invoking the language of sanctions and punishment,
which run counterintuitive to the values and pleasures associated with literacy that we hope to impart on our students. The continued uncomfortable, sometimes hostile, relationship between English studies and collaboration certainly rears its head in any deeper consideration of student reading practices, as does the question of what reading or writing "on one's
own" *means* to students in this networked century in which we live.[12]

As the romantic vision of reading as a solitary activity engaged best on
a quiet, rainy day remains supreme in the vision of faculty, the modernized
version of reading as a communal, online activity simultaneously emerges
as the preferred vision of students. As Patrick Sullivan posited in the
January 2009 issue of *Academe*, in his "Open Letter to Ninth Graders," the
qualities of students who are "ready for college" include a "love for reading," as well having read "some *important* books," implicitly those that are
drawn from the canon (7, emphasis in original). Anyone who has taught
today's range of first-year college students would likely dispute that such
qualifications exist as a hard-and-fast rule (or even common traits), especially when one considers the possible successful avenues for college students who are heavily invested in other nonliterary reading practices, areas
of study where reading exists more for information than for interpretation,
or who disliked reading in secondary school but in college, have developed
a greater appreciation for it. Nonetheless, the "love of reading" and moreover, reading "important" literature remains clearly the public—and publicized—ideal as a tenet of literacy acquisition.

Given these faculty perceptions, and institutional expectations, about
the engagement of students with texts and the act of reading, it is my con-

tention that more exploration into why, how, and whether students read in academic settings must include the actual *student* viewpoint toward the institutionalized (academic) act of reading, which aims at the heart of faculty pedagogical principles. Namely, students question whether it is *important* to "do the reading" in the ways that teachers intend it to be done in a classroom setting—which necessarily presumes the student's solitary struggle aided only by necessary teacher mitigation/interpretive assistance.

When students opt out of traditional reading practices in favor of those that collaboratively bypass this isolation, followed by teacher mitigation, then, what does it mean to "do the reading" at all? One possibility is that in fact, reading is not only more desirable to college students as a social endeavor, but in fact is more *intellectually successful* as a social practice, and that technologies that enable this socialization of reading practices allow students to achieve greater "reading" successes than they experience in the traditional classroom setting, especially the general education, mix-and-match student community of the first-year writing classroom. College students are already well versed in social networking sites such as Facebook, MySpace, and Twitter, each of which allows them to interact with peers (whether across town, across the country, or any other part of the world) both synchronously and asynchronously, and provide one another with "updates" about their personal, educational and/or school, and professional lives. Of course, these technologies—particularly the mini-burst information punch of Twitter—do not provide for extensive conversation or dialogue between and among participants. Nor do these sites open up their discussions to the "public" in the sense that one must "friend" someone in order to communicate with them on Facebook, for example, or "follow" one's feeds on Twitter in order to receive all, true updates on status. But the social networking that brings together students (and others) on these sites is, in fact, methodologically replicated in more discussion-based, education/school-focused sites such as Pink Monkey and, as I discuss in Chapter 4, Rate My Professors. These socially driven sites additionally bring together students to discuss readings, and the act of reading texts generally, within voluntary discourse communities online, wherein the physical classroom and the teacher-as-mediator are replaced by extra-institutional student discussions on topics and texts chosen by and the students, for the purposes of better understanding what is read, and thereby conquering the challenge of "doing the reading" for the teachers who assigned the text within the institutional setting.

Part of the problem with talking about student reading habits, or the ways in which they exhibit these habits in the high-stakes setting of the college classroom, lies in faculty's tendency to see the terms of academic reading (and the academic writing that stems from that reading) in blanket, traditionalized terms. David Jolliffe raises the question of what reading "means" in a recent issue of *College English* when he asks the following:

[Composition students] need to read the assigned books, articles, essays, and chapters (don't they?) because their compositions involve their interacting with these texts in some way (don't they?) . . . I've heard time and again the same complaints about student reading in composition courses—students often come to class without having read the material and are therefore incapable of "participating in a discussion" (whatever that phrase means); when they do complete the reading, many students cannot understand the assigned texts with a level of insight that goes beyond the transparent and superficial. ("Learning to Read" 471–72)

Jolliffe's questions challenge faculty to consider if our views on "reading" in an academic setting in fact more deeply rely on our predispositions to seeing reading as the automatic precursor of "good" writing (or any writing at all). Furthermore, Jolliffe challenges faculty to define the terms of art that so frequently are bandied about without qualification; "participating in a discussion," for example, is implied to mean taking part in some significant way in an analysis of a reading, as opposed to simply nodding or occasionally raising one's hand when a simple question might be answered without even having read the text in question. Online technologies here again allow faculty some insight into how students see "discussion" as a model of civic discourse, wherein individual participants are responsible for raising and defending viewpoints in the context of the larger community involved in the discussion. In student online communities such as Pink Monkey, there is no teacher-moderator to either privilege certain participants or redirect the discussion. Similarly, to be silent is to be invisible—but without academic penalty. To observe, or "lurk," has no negative consequences, and with discussions archived for later reading, observation/silence can be, in fact, "participating" in a much more beneficial way than being observational/silent in the traditional teacher-led classroom. But the roadblocks to accepting these technologies as useful for students in developing and growing their relationships with texts, and with reading itself, often come from the faculty themselves, those who are the greatest voices for classroom change and who desire a resurgence in academic literacy practices among their student populations.

For example, while we have on the one hand Jolliffe's thoughtful parsing of what it means to read and be part of a reading community—the perhaps critical distinction between how students "read" a text and how teachers expect that text to be not only "read" but internalized, and publicly valued—we also have other negative competing views on students' reading abilities and attitudes present in the punditry of scholars such as Mark Bauerlein, professor of English at Emory University and director of research at the National Endowment of the Arts.[13] Jolliffe aims to question the accepted components of pedagogical practices that lead to misreading and nonreading among certain student populations, thereby shifting the focus (and blame) away from students alone to students, teachers, and the institutional conditions under which academic reading gets done. By comparison, Bauerlein, on his Web site, "The Dumbest Generation," points directly at students and asks them to bear the weight of this problem, as he sneers that even though the current generation "has more schooling . . . more money . . . and more leisure" than previous generations, it also chooses to "download, upload, IM, post, chat and network (9 of their 10 top sites are for social networking)." What these students do *not* do, according to Bauerlein, is "read, even online (two-thirds aren't proficient in reading)" and as a result, he laments that "cyber-culture is turning us into a nation of know-nothings" (www.dumbestgeneration.com).

In the simplest terms, Bauerlein does not raise questions, but instead presents practices as de facto *facts*: Going online makes students dumb, and these dumb students don't read. Online student communities become an easy target when Bauerlein, and other faculty who subscribe to his views, artificially divide social networking and other collaborative technologies from staid academic practices. When scholars such as Bauerlein, who *additionally* have nonacademic, public cache, make this equation, technologies such as Pink Monkey also become publicized as "dumb" resources by default. Bauerlein explicitly links student socialization patterns online to his "dumbing-down" of the college population; online social networks of all kinds become negative spaces that suck energy and intellect from students' brains, rather than possible sites wherein meaningful exchanges about reading, texts, or even just conversations about schooling might take place. Putting aside how students must feel when individuals such as Bauerlein—who likely do not engage with any of the youth "cyber-culture" so vilified here—label them in these pejorative terms, his vitriol toward the position of the Internet as an interference in students' literacy acquisition forces into public discourse a critical point of debate. Do students go online to *avoid* the constraints of classroom-based reading (and reading practices associated with academic traditions), as Bauerlein claims, or do they go online to *augment* or *reify* these practices, in terms that reflect a displaced position for the traditional arbiter of literacy, the teacher?

I argue that the latter is the case, and that sites such as Pink Monkey illustrate specific examples of how and why this reification works, and what it says about our classroom traditions and expectations where "reading" is concerned, particularly in an age in which the digital text holds its weight against the print text, and student readers can easily connect with peers who live far outside these readers' own home communities for discussion and interpretation of texts. Pink Monkey allows students to subvert, and reify, the traditional values and mechanisms of literacy acquisition as present in critical academic (i.e., teacher-led), reading practices. Pink Monkey augments, and for some students, perhaps, supplants, the traditional writing and literature classroom as the authoritative space for learning, creating an online community that crosses spatial as well as temporal boundaries, and which offers an alternate space for literacy acquisition, as defined by college student reader/writers. Pink Monkey, as one example of an extracurricular online student community, has immense potential power in shaping both negative and positive conceptions of the English classroom, and of reading and writing as acts of intellectual agency.

Therefore, I argue in this chapter that a serious consideration of the role played by online student communities, such as Pink Monkey, in literacy acquisition is critical to furthering our understanding of when and why students reject traditional literacy opportunities as historically presented by the "system" of professors and institutions, and as sanctioned by the increasingly vigilant, education-valuing public, a public that both blames the educational system for the literacy levels of its children, yet simultaneously endorses and champions sometimes arcane reading and writing practices, and philosophies, within that system.

READING WITHOUT TEACHERS: DEFINING THE TERMS

If we accept the premise I submitted in Chapter 1—that in higher education today, and in the acquisition of literacy skills in particular, the teacher matters far less—or not at all—than he or she did even a generation ago—then our attention next may shift to the positioning of the text *itself* rather than the teacher-mediator of that text as the subject of primary importance in studying how students do or do not read. In order to engage with the text, whether in print or on screen (including visual texts), faculty usually argue that it must be "read"—either in the traditional sense (i.e., the written word on the page) or the alternate sense (i.e., film or media semiotics). One must "read" a text to begin a meaningful encounter with its subject matter and/or message; the reader may take a variety of forms, but we endorse the notion, as faculty, that the reader must initiate the relationship in order for meaning to be made, at the same time that we acknowledge the text as a cultural artifact with many historical and social purposes that change from reader to reader.

The relationship between reading and writing, and the direct bearing that comprehension of and compliance with assigned reading has on a student's written work, is perhaps for these reasons an underexplored area of composition studies; to examine this aspect of literacy is to engage in a complex dialectic centered on highly broad terminology and theories of readership, and requires that one dislocate traditional terms from their traditional settings. Faculty typically assume that terms of art in the writing classroom, as illustrated in Jolliffe's point about participating in a discussion, have uniform properties and stem from uniform requirements, such as the careful reading of a text *prior* to class and the ability to talk about that reading experience (and in some cases, reading process) as key to effective and successful writing. But such uniformity is rarely found across all student reader types and all student-to-text relationships. Additionally, the notion of "comprehension"—what the reader truly understands, and at what level—has not been codified across various sites of learning. We know even less about how much of that comprehension is "translated" into written analyses of a text, even as we study the evolution of that writing through drafting and revision processes. As such, faculty cannot say without qualification that we agree on the exact *definition* of what "reading" is in an assessment-based situation, including in the critical introductory space of the first-year writing classroom.

Faculty *do* recognize, however, that students often fail to complete that first critical and seemingly incontrovertible step—actually *doing* the reading. Jolliffe's questioning of the consequences of "skipping" that step in the context of first-year composition likely sets off many alarms for writing teachers in particular. How can students write without reading? How can students read without writing (about the text, as well as *to* the text)? Students in the twenty-first century have access to a plethora of media beyond the physical book or article, as presented via multiple technological devices (both personal and institutional, portable and stationary). These presentations of and venues for "text," as well as their capabilities for synchronous and asynchronous interaction, result in decidedly different views of what "participating" and even "reading" truly mean. As with other steps toward literacy acquisition, college students use nontraditional, and extra-institutional, means to achieve the goals of their first-year writing classrooms. This is in large part because of their stance on the relative sanctity of the reader-to-text personal experience. These nontraditional methods supplant the communal "discussion" of texts, prioritizing instead the extracurricular study session and information sharing as it occurs online, outside the authority of the textually based writing classroom and its embrace of the personalized author–reader relationship.

PinkMonkey.com is one online venue that allows students to participate in a type of free-trade, barter-system that challenges our school system's mediated view of reading and relative classroom-based relationships with texts. The name of the site is eye-catching, but has a potentially deeper origin as well. The term *pink monkey* is, in fact, apparently shorthand for the unusual/atypical student—often in educational circles cited as the "gifted" child—who is like the monkey taken from his or her tribe, dyed pink, and then rejected by the other monkeys when returned to the group.[14] As such, the site's rhetorical positioning lies outside the "usual" methods of teaching and learning offered by the traditional schooling process, making a nod to those students who feel, in whatever context, "different" and thus want something tangible that addresses their particular learning needs. Even though such rhetoric may cause its detractors to see the site as anti-school, however—lumped in to the same category as, for example, paper mill Web sites—the site's "about us" overview lays claim to a far different, and more culturally noble, purpose:

> Unlike most of the other sites that attract teenagers on the Internet, PinkMonkey is very proud of the fact that we are a "G-rated," child-safe, and teacher-approved site. We have made it our top priority to only carry content that is suitable for all ages. Parents and teachers can be comfortable in recommending the PinkMonkey.com site to anyone, as we do not and will never feature the adult language and sexual themes that are so commonplace today on almost all teen and college sites. That unique commitment, along with our enormous content, sets us far apart from most of the other "education" sites on the Internet today. (http://www.pinkmonkey.com/compinfo/comp_info.asp)

Indeed, the content on Pink Monkey is distinctly framed as advice-centered, teacher-friendly (in that it welcomes teacher referrals), and additive rather than resistant or antiestablishment.[15] This content includes broad categories such as "study guides," which include basic background information on a variety of subjects, similar to a pared-down online handbook; "student smart," which includes a large number of lessons on how to study, how to take notes, and how to improve one's memory; and "parents' tips," which includes advice for parents on helping their children with tests and college application essays. Pink Monkey also provides thousands of "book notes" online, as well as numerous textual notes and study guides, each of which circumvents traditional (i.e., singular) reading practices. Although Pink Monkey's book notes are neither a new nor underground genre—they are descendants of CliffsNotes and other similar publications, and are backed by the corporation of Barron's Book Notes—putting these notes in conjunction with other discussion-based "help" forums allows online students to complete reading and writing assignments completely *outside* of the classroom structure, within a virtual, networked environment of their peers.

But what draws the greatest amount of participation, aside from patronage of the online book notes, and also provides the largest amount of data with which to study students' attitudes toward reading, is Pink Monkey's discussion forum. Within this central feature of the site, students participate in hundreds of discussion threads centered on a particular text (or occasionally a type of text, such as Shakespeare's plays). Therein, students propose exchanges such as "I'll give you a quote from *Beloved* for your paper, if you give me a summary of *The Handmaid's Tale* for my exam tomorrow." Students also ask general questions about interpreting specific texts; analyzing specific characters; or situating texts within a larger framework (e.g., "What do you think *Gatsby* tells us about capitalism in America?"). These forums are free and open to the public and significantly, but not exclusively, focus on topics related to literary texts. Because the threads are free and open-ended, they may span only a number of days, or may go on, intermittently, for a number of months, or years, as I illustrate in a later discussion.

Despite its friendly tone and apparent endorsement of teachers and parents in the educational process, however, Pink Monkey as an extra-institutional site functionally serves to pit the school "system" (as both a physical infrastructure and as a bureaucratic methodology) against those who question the requirements and accompanying values of that system. In this context, I posit that Pink Monkey represents the oppositional, yet potentially productive, divide between the reading practices and literacy values of extra-institutional online communities and "regular" classrooms led by an authority figure who abides by accepted rules of another authority figure as a representative of his or her institution, and as the arbiter of all reading-related activities therein. Key questions raised by this opposition, as well as Pink Monkey's success in growing a community of readers-without-teachers, are as follow:

- Do we (students) need them (teachers) to guide us through texts?
- Do we need to view reading as a singular enterprise?
- Is the "text" a comparative model for our own writing, or an object with which we can only interact in limited ways?
- Do we need to "read," in the traditional sense, in order to write well, and to be "literate"?

In order to answer these questions, it is first helpful to examine scholarly views of reading practices, including those of teenagers (an age group that includes high school as well as first- and second-year college students).

READING METHODOLOGY AND COMMUNITY PRACTICES

If we momentarily return to Jolliffe's interrogation of the current divide between student reading practices and faculty expectations of (and assumptions about) how those practices might be positively modified in the college setting, we see that he also asks critical questions in pursuing the roots of this seemingly unsolvable problem. Among these questions:

> Shouldn't students . . . have mastered careful, critical reading by the time they get to college? . . . Yes, high school students should have had more experience learning how to read texts, particularly nonfiction prose, carefully and critically in high school. But, no, it's not reasonable to expect they have "mastered" the process by the time they come to college, simply because the material they're now reading demands that they modify, ratchet up, and rethink the ways they read the material they're assigned. And maybe our assumptions . . . actually occlude a consideration of other factors that affect student reading in college courses. (472–73)

Jolliffe does not explicitly include online student communities in his categorization of "other factors" affecting student reading, yet such inclusion is not only valid, but also critical in this analysis. The concept of "modify[ing], rachet[ing] up, and rethink[ing]" reading material obviously is not an individual or isolated (noncommunal) process; if it were, secondary schools and colleges would keep all discussions of written texts *out* of the classroom, focusing instead on other subject matter related to, but not *about,* the text itself. Most high school teachers rely on traditional, and seemingly reasonable, means of dissecting texts for and with student: small-group work, large-group discussion, reading quizzes and take-home study guides, many of which involve some version of "close" readings of particular passages within works.

But as Don Bialostosky argues regarding the traditional reading methods in English classrooms—which he sees as unlabeled inheritors of the New Critics' pedagogies—"close reading" in its institutionalized New Critical instantiation, has "created the habits and expectations of reading literature that college English needs to resist and reform, or at least articulate and examine, not the habits and expectations it should uncritically cultivate" (112). As Bialostosky practically observes, "Paying close attention doesn't guarantee even minimal understanding or response" to a given text (112). If we consider previous points in this chapter about students' lack of background knowledge being a detriment to reading comprehension, it is clear to see how, indeed, "close attention" for such students may result in nothing more than apparent/physical compliance with teacher directives. Given this and other problems with current reading pedagogies, Bialostosky ultimately calls for a new definition of "best practices" between secondary and college teachers, in order to more clearly understand the relationship between reading and writing, and between readers and texts, in the classroom.

Similarly, Faye Halpern argues that "critical reading is not a neutral description" as it "performs crucial work for English departments by assuring skeptics that what we do is very hard, although teachable" (552). Halpern argues, in her defense of other types of "identification" with fictional characters as a viable reading process for students, that the concept of critical reading "differentiates [English teachers] from those reading amateurs out there, which is what our beginning students are. This phrase carries an aura, and it is not in [English faculty's] interest to pick it apart" (552). Halpern goes on to argue that the "high valuation of prolonged questioning" in the reading process, in which a reader takes a critical, oppositional stance—and frequently a politicized one—"reflects the current thinking about the pedagogy of writing (and reading) in composition studies: exploration over assertion, process over product" (553).

Such a delineation between exploring the ramifications of a reading and simply asserting (or reasserting) content/subject—the difference between being an "expert" and an "amateur"—seems also to describe the fault lines between high school and college readers, or the fault lines that English faculty believe may be transgressed by virtue of the first-year writing course. But the differences between reading practices from high school to college are typically not so dramatic as critical reading pedagogies may aim to achieve. In Jolliffe and Allison Hurl's study of a group of 100 first-year students at the University of Arkansas, they found that students reported reading about 7.6 hours per week in their senior year of high school, "70 percent of which was for their classes" compared with "12.9 hours per week [in college], 84 percent of which was for their classes" (605). To contrast this with students' nonacademic reading, Jolliffe and Hurl found that students not only read an *equal* amount of time per week outside of school, but that this reading consisted significantly of online texts, including "Facebook profiles, emails, instant messages, [and] Internet sites" (606). Their study seems to echo the widely perceived notion that "neither high school nor college students spend much time preparing for class, the central activity of which we presume to be reading assigned articles, chapters, and books" (599), and also emphasize the fact that students "read" online texts regularly and integrate them into their daily living patterns. If the reading habits of college students do change little in their first year, during the critically framed required course, then it is difficult to argue that such pedagogies in themselves—and as delivered via on-the-ground traditional methods—are causing much revolution in the depth and breadth of student canonical literacies, especially when the methods often eschew the very extracurricular technological spaces that students most comfortably and voluntarily inhabit.

Just as there is no universal method for ensuring that students critically absorb, or "get" a reading (whether it be expository or literary in nature, or for that matter scientific, humanistic, artistic, and so on through the scholarly categories of texts), there also is no universal rejection of a particular methodology for reading analysis, even when it repeatedly fails. Scholars such as Glynda Hull and Katherine Schultz have noted the dearth of research into nontraditional literacy practices, those that might provide alternatives to, or substitutions for, the less-successful, traditional in-class practices that English teachers repeatedly reinforce in the literature and writing classroom. In their 2001 article "Literacy and Learning Out of School," Hull and Schultz survey the existing research on literacy in "out-of-school settings" (575). They come to the conclusion that future research into this area must prioritize "an examination of the relationships between school and non-school contexts," including "how might out of school identities, social practices, and the literacies that they recruit be leveraged in the classroom?" (603). Certainly in the general discourse posted on Pink Monkey, one can see how having anonymous, nonschool identities—as is the case on most listservs or in most chatrooms—frees participants to more liberally posit their opinions about a text or texts, which in turn certainly has the potential to allow for extra-institutional literacy values to better emerge.

The suggestion to more closely link out-of-school and in-school literacy practices, as well as to consider the impact of larger cultural shifts on the reading and writing habits of students, is the focus of James Paul Gee's article "Teenagers in New Times," in which he argues that students' perspectives on literacy are shaped in large part by "new capitalism" (412). Gee first argues that in his paradigm of "New Literacy Studies," situationally specific language is "fully integrated with specific ways of thinking, believing, valuing, acting, interacting, and, often, ways of coordinating and being coordinated by other semiotic systems, other people, various objects, tools, settings, and technologies" (413). As such, literacy is never "self-contained," especially across different social classes, including social classes within teenage populations. Gee puts his New Literacy Studies model in the context of "new capitalism," in which

> hierarchy is flattened (there are no "bosses" and "workers", only "partners"); the business becomes a network of interacting units (a distributed system). In the ideal new capitalism business, then, local units (both individuals and small business groups) control their own actions, combining and un-combining in flexible ways project by project. . . . There are no discrete stable individuals, only ensembles of skills stored in a person, assembled for a specific project and shared with others. (414)

Furthermore, Gee argues, schools are aiming to prepare students for the three "slots," or types of workers who will emerge from this new economy—namely the "symbol analysts" who are the designers and transformers of networks, and who possess expert knowledge; the "enchanted workers" are those on the front lines who must be flexible in designing and redesigning their work, although they are paid meagerly, surviving on bonuses; and the "backwater workers" who are at the lowest level of the chain, and have the least amount of knowledge but the greatest amount of "brute strength" ("Teenagers" 414–15).

Gee ultimately argues that an analysis of teenage literacies in the context of this future capitalist structure (and, because he was writing in 2000, one might argue that this is consequently an emergent-present structure today), it is no longer enough to classify literacy as "the ability to read and write" (419), but that we must see literacy as intimately tied to cultural and social practices that students both bring to the classroom and that which they thus become trained to do, through their continued employment of these practices in school-based situations, as future workers. Gee notes that given the "future without a stable working class," the working-class teens in his study will especially suffer because they see authority as the embodiment of "facts, rules, and laws," rather than a force with which to interact dialogically, as opposed to the upper middle-class teens, who were "deeply interpenetrated by the social languages and discourses of professional families, schools, and public sphere institutions, which they see as making them worthy of success" ("Teenagers" 419).

I include Gee's work at some length here because I believe it raises issues that are directly relevant to my argument regarding how student online spaces contain and harness valuable dialogic interchanges on reading, writing, and the superstructures of higher education. The new capitalism that Gee describes exactly mimics the principles of sites such as Pink Monkey, wherein hierarchies are, in fact, collapsed and erased, and individuals are given over to identities based on sets of "skills"—in the case of Pink Monkey, literary knowledge or interpretative abilities—that serve a greater collective purpose for the group in the end. There are no "bosses" (teachers) and as such, individuals "control their own actions" within the dialogue and among their peers. Additionally, as Gee has shown in his research, the ways in which this capitalistic structure both affects how students are implicitly trained to join the workforce (one thinks here of earlier efforts mimicking such goals, e.g., ability-tracking) although it is routinely neglected as a subject within higher education's discussions about the definitions and uses of literacy, and student socialization into various literacy communities. Sites such as Pink Monkey take up this neglected discourse *outside* the institutional structure, but do not improve what continues to take place *inside* it.

Deborah Brandt, in her seminal work "Sponsors of Literacy," certainly takes up some of Gee's charges, examining how and with what effects out-of-school settings work to codify alternate uses for, as well as evolving definitions of, literacy. Brandt heavily focuses on the workplace setting and the demands for reading, writing, and critical thinking skills that arise outside of the traditional classroom setting. Most importantly, she identifies the concept of "sponsorship" as key to literacy practices, arguing that traditional schooling is not the only site for promotion of particular literacies, nor is it always the most influential site for literacy acquisition. Brandt declares sponsors of literacy as "a tangible reminder that literacy learning throughout history has always required permission, sanction, assistance, coercion, or, at minimum, contact with existing trade routes. Sponsors are delivery systems for the economies of literacy, the means by which these forces present themselves to—and through—individual learners" (167).

Elsewhere in Brandt's scholarship is an attention to the other external forces that shape literacy practices. In "Remembering Writing, Remembering Reading," Brandt postulates, specifically in the case of parent–child relationships, that "what motivates and brings meaning to acts of reading or writing may not always be texts. Instead, much of learning to read and write involves learning the possible attitudes that can be taken toward these two activities—which are often more separate and competing than we may sometimes want to admit" (460). In Brandt's ethnographic study of the childhood learning experiences of several Wisconsin residents, she finds that "writing develop[ed] in situations and out of psychological motivations that are saliently, sometimes jarringly, different from those surrounding reading" ("Remembering Writing" 464). Brandt further notes that even though in these households, the "messages about the prestige [were] sent to children early and often," in school, "where reading and writing are most explicitly connected in official tasks, unofficial literacy lessons occur, and, as in the home, mixed messages may occur about the consequences of reading and writing" (476–77). Such data mirrors Gee's general findings about upper middle-class students and their ability to advance socially via literacy acquisition.

What is most applicable about this recent literacy research in the context of online student communities is the interface between school and home, and between conceptions of reading and writing that do not always reinforce the tried-and-true mantra that better readers make better writers. In Gee and Brandt's work, as well as in the studies surveyed by Hull and Schultz, it is clear that home life—as well as peer groups and their socialization processes in home communities—has a significant influence on how students develop as readers and writers. It is common knowledge that children who are read to, encouraged to read regularly, and are supported by family structures that reinforce the importance of literacy practices are much more likely to succeed in school than those children who do not possess these resources. But what studies such as those discussed here also highlight is the powerful influence that nonschool-based attitudes toward reading and writing have on lifelong *attitudes* toward those activities, and the uses of literacy, regardless of what kind of success the students have in the actual tasks of reading and writing.

In this context, a closer look at student-to-student online communities that exist outside the more socially accepted sites of learning (i.e., school and the workplace) is both merited and timely. Some might term these communities as "underground" sites of (anti-)educational system discourse, and they exist and operate without the explicit oversight of any authority in determining their practices. As mentioned previously, Pink Monkey has a primary corporate sponsor—Barron's Book Notes—but the sponsorship here is purely economical, and as such, nonjudgmental and nonauthoritative, educationally speaking, and in terms of the majority of the site's content (save the advertising). Barron's is, theoretically, one element of Gee's "network of interacting units" that enable the Web site to operate. Such online student-run communities are logical extensions of what Robert Brooke first labeled *underlife* in the college classroom, wherein a secondary discourse takes place beside (or below, or above, depending on the context) the "official" discourse of the classroom.

Brooke defines underlife as "those behaviors which undercut the roles expected of participants in a situation" (141). He then translates this into the setting of the writing classroom, where

> both students and teachers undercut the traditional roles of the American educational system in order to substitute more complex identities in their place. On the one hand, students disobey, write letters instead of taking notes, and whisper with their peers to show they are more than just students and can think independently of classroom expectations. On the other, writing teachers develop workshop methods, use small groups, and focus on students' own "voices" in order to help students see themselves as writers first and students second. Both sets of behaviors are underlife behaviors, for they seek to provide identities that go beyond the roles offered by the normal teacher-as-lecturer, student-as-passive-learner educational system. (141)

Brooke illustrates how students can turn the sanctioned topic of conversation or study in a given classroom setting into a tie to other related discourse of their own, without necessarily being seen as "off-task" and without completely undermining the official, teacher-led discussion at hand—yet also redefining what their roles in learning may be, particularly because they want to show themselves to be independent, "more than students." Brooke's theory also allows for a turning of tables by *any* participant in the classroom, including the authority figure who gives up his or her leader ethos, in part or in whole, within the classroom structure.[16]

Although some may argue that Pink Monkey is not a valid example of Brooke's underlife because it exists *outside* the physical classroom structure, I argue that as an open, online communication venue, wherein students are visibly and forcibly transgressing the boundaries and values of the teacher-centered classroom, Pink Monkey indeed serves an "underlife" function in its role as a venue for students' alternative reading practices online. First-year courses are beginning to embrace similar online *structures* in their pedagogies (e.g., Blackboard and other similar discussion-based forums included in course requirements), however, this does not make the extra-institutional version of these structures any less subversive. And because these extra-institutional versions are controlled largely by the students themselves, rather than an instructor or similar authority figure (save the webmaster, who remains essentially invisible in relation to the dialogues and exchanges), the "underlife" transgression is still that which rejects the dominant educational discourse in favor of allied, and often more thorough and self-sustaining, than that found in the regular reading and writing classroom.

Consequently, it is not enough to simply mimic these online structures that subvert academic literacy values, including reading practices, in institutionally sanctioned online course programs; we must also recognize the power and viability that the extra-institutional systems have in further defining the shape and tenor of our classrooms, beyond the simple introduction of like technology into our teaching methods. As Jeff Rice argues in *The Rhetoric of Cool* (a book that I explore further in Chapter 5), simply acknowledging a technology's presence in our teaching is not enough; we must also understand how and why it should cause our methodologies of writing (and, arguably, reading) instruction to change. As Rice argues, composition studies' "very specific assumptions and ideological associations with print" and print-based writing instruction have been consistently and doggedly reapplied to new media technologies, even though new interpretive frameworks beyond these systems are necessary in order to fully understand the rhetoric strategies present in these new media technologies (8). I similarly argue that simply promoting the use of a discussion board in a reading and writing course at the first-year (or any) level does not mean that we are sufficiently or even accurately replicating the "work" of student online discourse on sites such as Pink Monkey. Instead, we are using old frameworks to cannibalize new ones—without understanding the very particular conditions under which these new media frameworks operate, especially the highly social, student-centered frameworks that allow for their operation in the first place.

Therefore, as we examine sites such as Pink Monkey, in addition to noting how students view the process and product of reading (whether it be "close" or casual, inside or outside the classroom), it is important to also remember the relationship between the text itself and the reader who is charged with its interpretation, especially when there is no authority figure mediating the text *for* that student, the expert who encourages that students transcend reading for plot and story and elevate their practices to those of analysis (and meta-analysis). We should consequently seek to understand Pink Monkey as not an "anti-school" site, wherein students speak and write without this supposedly necessary oversight of teachers who might challenge the students' "unthinking obeisance to [the text's] powers" in their reading and writing practices (Halpern 553), but as a site wherein the teacher-figure has no significant role in the process of interpreting a text for students or making any student "literate," as defined by the institution. This desire to *minimize* role of the teacher as central to learning on Pink Monkey is a desire that is antithetical to classroom pedagogies. Such classroom privileging of the text, and student resistance to it as teacher-interpreted and institutionally read, at least can be partially traced to the history of literature as a sanctified category in the classroom, as well as the shifting role of student voices (and student authorship) within that classroom throughout the twentieth century.

TEXTUAL SANCTITY: ONLINE INTERFACES AND COMMUNITY-BASED READING ANALYSES

Ultimately, the resulting casualty of the public influences on student reading practices is the text itself, or more precisely the traditional *nature* of the text as an object tool in the schooling process. With some rare exceptions, the structure of schooling demands only that any given student's knowledge of any particular text be only as the course assignment requires. Over the course of a semester in an introduction to literature class (or in a first-year composition class that regularly engages with published or outside texts beyond the students' own writing), a college reader/writer will encounter a good deal of textual material (e.g., in my own writing program, an average of 200 to 250 pages of reading per term is assigned) of which he or she will likely meaningfully absorb very little, given other readings and requirements in other courses, as well as the student's extracurricular obligations. Or at least that is how our typical college curriculum is structured—with rare meaningful interface between texts, across courses (and disciplines), except in extremely thoughtful major course work sequences or interdisciplinary seminars that require students to truly *use* what they have learned to demonstrate exit competencies in the field (i.e., senior capstone courses, cumulative portfolios). To students, reading a text or texts in a manner approved by the teacher is a hurdle that must be cleared, like any other, in order to obtain the degree. Whether a particular student is economically minded (the degree as commodity) or, in rarer cases in our troubled new economy, aesthetically or intellectually minded (the degree is a mark of edification and personal growth), certain texts must be read. These texts are then the subject of tests or other quantitative and qualitative measurements doled out by the teacher-figure. Then the student moves on to repeat the process in other disciplinary contexts, and with other teacher-figures.

This systematic approach to textual analysis, as well as the distanced relationship between reader/writer and the text itself, is a distinctly modern practice, as Dana Harrington illustrates. Harrington notes that our current practice of treating the text as an aesthetic object that cannot (and should not) exist in a comparative, dialogic setting with student texts, stems from a giant shift in the eighteenth century away from texts as rhetorical models and toward texts as "products of superior genius" (251). Prior to the eighteenth century, student and published, or externally authored, texts were viewed in consort in the classroom, as classical rhetoric "did not distinguish between 'literary' or poetic modes of invention and those that students used," therefore "reading and writing were mutually reinforcing" (252). Harrington argues that in this more productive era of instruction, reading practices "allowed students to invent their own discursive authority by helping them master the rhetorical strategies and conventions that they would need to enter into the various discourse communities in the public sphere" (253). Subsequent practices (from the eighteenth century forward) that separated and sanctified the literary text from the student reader thus "not only drove a wedge between student texts and literary texts but also drastically shifted the relationship of the reader to the text" (256). Two consequences of this shift that persist in the twenty-first century classroom were 1) a clear division between the acts of reading and the acts of writing, resulting in a skewed view of student authorship; and 2) an emphasis on literature as the "supreme civilizing agency," serving a social role and sometimes moral function in educating students (258).[17]

Harrington's observations illustrate the historical precedent for the rise of nonschool-sanctioned reading practices on sites such as Pink Monkey. The existence of extra-institutional sites of student discourse seek to streamline and even re-codify the process and product of college reading, in partial response to the supreme edification of literary texts as they are presented in the writing and literature classroom. As a site that brings students of like-minded practicality together to tackle such matters, Pink Monkey provides a viable communal outlet for the required moves related to "doing the reading" for college coursework. Its unique position as not only an extra-institutional site, but also as a nationally networked community, give it serious leverage in subverting these accepted readings of, and uses for, literary texts in the college classroom. Although the text may be the impetus for a discussion thread, as the text is traditionally the core of the writing to be assigned or test to be completed, the discussion of said text typically reaches far beyond simple reader response or factual regurgitation in the Pink Monkey forums. Frequently, the forums exhibit a cross-temporal, multilayered set of responses to a simple query, which not only extend the life of the query itself but also breed allied queries and problem-solving tasks, expanding the definition of "reading" to include a variety of personal and political perspectives that may not otherwise be found in a 50-minute, three-times-weekly classroom consisting of a more heterogeneous population set on performing a specific teacher-centered task.

Examining two sample threaded discussions from Pink Monkey helps illustrate these core principles of the site, which may be summarized as (a) a rejection the supremacy of the teacher–text relationship, (b) an investment in authority for interpretation and reading of texts in the students (or their online personas) themselves, and (c) a sincere desire—at least in means-to-an-end terms—to achieve an *understanding* of the text at hand, through collaborative discussions and shared perceptions of the text, or parts thereof critical to holistic appreciation, or an understanding of the larger forces at work when *reading* the text—including the difficult position of the student within a classroom community of sometimes unwilling readers/learners. Such community investment in peer authority is an example of Kristie Fleckenstein's assertion that in cyberspace, ethos not only is a concept attached to a particular rhetor, but also a *system* by which the continuum of speakers and actions determines ethical behavior in a virtual environment, because the speakers cannot "read" one another. As Fleckenstein notes, in an online environment

> *ethos* does not construct itself in response to the dictates of a solitary displaced actor. . . . Instead, it evolves on the basis of the flow of information, enabling rhetor, audience, place and language to create each other mutually through the establishment of relationships called prudence, virtue, and good will, adapting to one another as a means of maintaining the constancy of those relationships. (7)

Fleckenstein asserts that ethos in cyberspace is the result of an "ensemble performance," a flow of messages that "is the system and constitutes the system simultaneously" (8), because "cyberethos and pathways are mutually constitutive, both cause and effect at the same time" (9).

Fleckenstein's cyberethos theory accurately describes the interactions that take place on Pink Monkey. This is a community built significantly on *trust* (i.e., the advice I am going to give you, as one student to another, is sound and good and true, and I believe that you will give me like advice in return). Returning to my discussion of liberatory pedagogy in Chapter 1, the trust that liberatory pedagogy requires on the part of the students toward the teacher is intrinsically different than the trust required on Pink Monkey. Whereas liberatory pedagogy requires a trust rooted in moral and ethical mirroring—your (the teacher's) values are good, I will accept them as substitutes for or amendments to my own—on Pink Monkey, the ethos is situated, built on a mutual goal: achieving success in the educational system, on noncompetitive, cross-institutional grounds. In other cases, students participating in Pink Monkey discussions are simply trusting of their peers as fellow *readers* who have a sound sense of the text—on their own terms—and thus bring valuable (or arguable) points of view to the table. In either scenario, the "pathways" of information, and the manner in which they are received between the online rhetors, are inextricable from the rhetors themselves.

Unlike in a standard classroom environment, where a variety of motivations that may affect academic performance in general may be at play—personal animosities, competition over achieving the highest grades, like or dislike for the teacher—Pink Monkey's online environment, with its anonymous or pseudonymous representations of self, negates such motivations. Additionally, without the authority figure of the teacher or professor presiding over the space, as is the case in networked or computerized classrooms, or even practically speaking in Blackboard, or class blogs, the students themselves are both responsible for maintaining good order and good will, and for testing and judging the veracity of participants' claims. As such, Pink Monkey is an "ensemble performance" in reading and literary/textual interpretation, which may in practice bear little resemblance to that same work as done within a traditional classroom space, at least in terms of rhetors' ethical motivations and actions, not to mention the atemporality of the actions (responses) themselves.

The first topic thread on Pink Monkey that I discuss, "Why Iago Hates Othello," began in fall 2001 and continued through May 2008. It deftly illustrates the range of responses and interchanges that take place between students in this extra-institutional community.[18] The original poster, "Bob," starts the thread with a simple text-based question: "What are the 'reasons' given by Iago in Act 1 for his hatred of Othello besides the rumors of him sleeping with his wife?" The next day, another poster, "Treefrog1000," replies with an extensive explanation/response:

> Othello has passed over Iago for promotion, preferring Michael Cassio for the post instead. Iago particularly resents this as Michael Cassio is a mathematician who has "never set a squadron in the field"—i.e., has no direct experience of the battlefield, unlike Iago. He admits later that Cassio has a "daily beauty," which makes Iago appear "ugly"—this hints that he is jealous of Cassio. Iago claims that Othello has slept with his wife, but the audience finds this highly unlikely. There are lots of possible motives behind his hatred. . . . Marxists have claimed that Iago is the victim of a classist society—i.e., his behavior is the result of being treated as being of a lower social status than Othello and the other characters. He is an "outsider" in a way, as a soldier, and there-

fore more coarse and vulgar than a courtly Ventian gentleman like Roderigo or Iago. You'll have to look more closely at the text.

Following this more traditional response, another poster, "Zac," responds— three *years* later—with an alternate theory:

> Dude, Iago is gay. He is infatuated with Othello. Why else would he get Othello to kill Desdimona? Why wouldn't he just do it himself? Why does he keep referring to getting his revenge on Othello, when it was Cassio who took his place? Iago hates him to thoroughly to only hate him. There has to be some fancy there. There has to. Othello hasn't done enough to him to make him as insensed as he is, and I don't thing any one is racist, conservative or insecure enough for that. It also explains his view on women, that they are all whores and only good for one thing. Remember "Make the Moor thank me, love me and reward me"? Or "they are all but stomaches, and we all but food; they eat us hungrly, and when they are full, they belch us." Not what you would get from a loving husband's wife.

A few days later, another poster asks "Zac" what *proof* there is that Iago is gay—and questions whether Shakespeare would have wrote the character deliberately this way. Zac responds:

> iago loves othello because Shekespeare once loved a prince, (ever wondered who all those love sonnets were sent to? well now u know) and Shekespeare wanted to have a character to explain how he felt. Well, i dont think he would be as bad as iago, unfortunatly shakespeare never left any insite into his night life so we will never know . . . But iago cannot possibly hate othello so abomnbly without a reason other than "it is thought abroad that 'twixed my sheets / He's done my office." "done my office," where? In his job, that was cassio. In marrying Desdemona? Iago thinks all women are whores, why should this one be different? "'twixed my sheets"? I detect a shakespearian second meaning there. It's hugly complex but you're rite, you should never use it in an essay, unless of corse you have 3 hours to spare and lots of paper. But as an actor i use it as his primary motive in the play, it works, trust me. It cannot be proven, as you said, but it's there, oh it's there.

One month after Zac posts this rebuttal, "Elle" posts her own take on Iago's sexuality, this time invoking the academy/classroom to prove the veracity of her theory:

Um . . . I think the gay conspiracy is a very powerful theory, actually. I recently got 98.75% using that argument in my senior year. . . . One must remember Act 3 Scene 3 where Iago frequently declares his "love" for Othello, saying that he is "bound to (Othello) forever" by "heaven's light." . . . This is like a wedding vow, a sacred event where two people confess their eternal LOVE. Also, Iago is an intelligent man skating on thin ice. He knows that he has to stay subtle, or he'll get caught. He can't cause suspicion. Why then, does he go so overboard declaring his love for Othello? If it was simply a reference towards brotherly love to convince Othello that he (Iago) was worth trusting, he wouldn't be so passionate and repetitive. Furthermore, at the beginning one of the key motives of Iago is that there are rumors Othello & Emilia slept together. Iago is a misogynist, who evidently doesn't love his wife—so why would he get so upset about the rumor? Being seen as a cuckold is an easy reputation to remedy. . . . One can read this as 'Iago is jealous that Emilia slept with Othello, especially as Othello just married Desdemona & appointed Cassio lieutenant, because now Iago feels like everyone's gotten a piece of Othello, except him.

In these exchanges, there is clear evidence of Fleckenstein's assertion about the "ethical depth perception" of cyberspace where students' interpretive readings are concerned (18). Fleckenstein argues that "good character and good action are situated in actively shifting pathways, the behavior of which yields an ethics of performance constantly morphing between doing and judging" (18). We see this in particular between Zac and Elle, who debate the theory of reading Iago as homosexual using not only textual evidence, but in Elle's case, the ethos of her classroom experience ("I recently got 98.75% . . . in my senior year"). Not only does Elle demonstrate in her reply to Zac that she is intelligent (i.e., she receives high grades), but also that her take on Iago has *backing* within the value system of the on-the-ground classroom, evidenced by its reception including a high grade. Zac, on the other hand, builds a different type of situational ethos in cyberspace by referring to himself as an "actor," implying that those in the theater arts have a particular insight into the plays of Shakespeare. Thus, he not only relies on the text, but on his legitimate *interpretation* of the text, to assert his theory that Iago is *not* a homosexual. Instead, they must commit the "ethos of performance" that requires they momentarily judge the credibility of one another while employing their own good reasons and building their own virtual ethical identities, identities that, in a traditional classroom space wherein the players are face to face, may be less rhetorically effective, and less pertinent to the greater purpose of the classroom that day (e.g., a test on simple comprehension).

Neither Zac nor Elle can claim to have the authoritative response to the original query, however, especially because their readerly interpretations pit the "real world" of the theater against the closed world of academia and in doing so, further open the debate beyond a simple question of what is *written* to how one *reads* a text, in a more general sense. Each of these readings are individually valid, and none is incontrovertibly "true." Additionally, this collective and collaborative act of reading extends far beyond one course or one semester, as is the case in the regular on-the-ground classroom. Because there are no institutional limitations on how, when, or even *why* rhetors can respond to this or other posted queries, the Pink Monkey forum allows the student to engage in a singular interface with the text vis-à-vis the larger Pink Monkey community. The response to reading becomes a validation of self, and a rejection of the dominant discourse, or dominant pedagogical approach, within the home classroom. To be "right" in this sense is to transcend the desire to achieve a "good" grade or institutional validation, or even to "do" the reading as a simple requirement. Instead, the motivation of such a query is to engage in a more humanistic way with other extra-institutional readers and writers, in order to reclaim a readerly agency unavailable to the student while at school.

For example, "Ebsi" claims in his/her October 2006 response within the Iago thread:

> Shakespeare did not intend to create Iago as a homosexual. There is no proof, and I've been told that if anyone was to even try and prove this in an essay, they would fail miserably.

However, "Amee" disagrees, noting that:

> people should not be critized for how they interept Othello if people want to believe Iago is gay and can prove it so be it. you dont have to agree with them and if you don't it doesn't make them wrong

"Callahan," who presents himself as a fellow actor/acting student, then some five months later responds:

> I am going to think more about it, but at the very least, from an acting point of view, it provides density, complexity, and in a way, because the turmoil is so intractable and so much poison gets thrown from it, a kind of despairing human vulnerability, especially in his quiet monologing moments when he might be at his most cacklingly evil.

Kayleigh, writing in March 2007, seconds Callahan's openness to the claim regarding Iago's sexuality:

> Hmmm . . . i think that everyone is entitled to their own opinion, and
> their own interpretation of the text. There's a massive amount of sup-
> port for the claim that Iago is gay, and as for the people that argue that
> the text has been taken out of context, that's not strictly true, for
> Shakespeare himself was in fact gay . . . there are so many ways that
> Shakespeare's work can be interpreted, and there is no right or wrong
> way, as long as ideas can be justified, and people who have different
> ideas to ourselves, does not mean that they're idiots. chill out guys,
> we're free to think differently, that's what makes us interesting!!

Callahan's response—specifically that "we're free to think differently"—
illustrates the entrance of what we might see broadly as a "teacherly"
impulse (i.e., to calm down the students who risk getting too far from the
subject at hand). Callahan's insistence that "there is no right or wrong way"
to interpret the play/Shakespeare's work, however, is a claim that would
typically ring false in most traditional literary-focused classrooms. The
insistence that *all* readings are fine if "justified" likely would be met with
temperance in a traditional classroom, wherein the text has both larger and
smaller purposes: to inculcate students in the principles of canonical literature and also the trajectories of literary discourse through analyzing the
play, as well as to provide students with the cultural capital associated with
knowing and appreciating Shakespeare's work. But the purpose at hand, at
least the one of which students are typically most readily aware, is to
understand the "right" interpretation of the text, the "right" way to frame
a discussion, and the "right" answer to questions about said text, both in
the classroom and outside of it—in high-stakes testing situations, typically
precollege admission. Within many classrooms, the freedom to be "entitled" to one's opinion is often subsumed by the larger impulse to "cover the
material."

Thus, one might argue that the virtual identity of these and any forum
participants—the "'I' of virtualized discourse"—is always "subjected to the
discourse invented for it" (Sosnoski and Macallister 130). In their home
classrooms and even home communities, these students may or may not
have an opportunity to voice their opinions about a debate such as Iago's
sexuality—although it is highly likely that most, if not all, secondary school
students pass through one or more of Shakespeare's texts in their schooling and some of these students go on to enroll in writing and literature
classes that also will read and analyze Shakespeare and his work. But in the
Pink Monkey forum, with the list of literally thousands of threads on hundreds of commonly assigned literary (and occasionally expository/nonfic-
tion) texts, students may voluntarily augment their readerly identities by
virtue of participation in a forum of their choosing—and debating their
opinions about and experiences with said text as part of a virtual community that is bound by neither space nor time constraints. This virtual ethical

representation may be a contrary one, loyal to institutional admonishments about "straying" from the dominant teacherly interpretation (Ebsi), to a defiant yet receding self, who nonspecifically defends readers' interpretive freedom (Amee), to more measured, balanced rhetors who draw on their real-life experiences and readerly stances to call a "truce" between sides, and serve as mediators of polarized opinions (Callahan and Kayleigh).

Importantly, the students participating in the Iago thread also are reading the text in direct response to their peers' readings, without any need for the limits of teacher mediation. There are no "institutional" pronouncements of right or wrong, nor is there a teacher directing the "traffic" of the discussion; instead, the students choose how and whether to respond, and decide whether their own readings (or lack thereof, as it must be assumed that some Pink Monkey participants seek out the forum as a *substitute* for reading the text/s themselves) fit with what their peers have proposed. This is a dialogic that is *possible* in the classroom, but theoretically very difficult for a teacher to enact—particularly the teacher who has a lesson plan built on a specific agenda or curricular goal, whether at the secondary or postsecondary level. The discussion on Pink Monkey is somewhat analogous to the example of a self-directed choir; in both situations, the group must lead itself and keep its own "time" to the discussion, without the oversight of institutionalized/sanctioned leadership. Such freedom can be problematic—and certainly there are threads on Pink Monkey that devolve into distractions and/or gather little participation. But occasionally, there are threads that not only raise legitimate questions and answers about the text at hand, but also engagement in interesting meta-issues related to students' reading practices.

Another Pink Monkey thread entitled "I Hate This Book!" exemplifies such a meta-discussion, this time stemming from the text *Crime and Punishment*. The participants are (self-declared) high school *and* college students—something again impossible in a traditional classroom, whether inperson or online—and represent both positive and negative views of Dostoevsky's work, in response to the original poster's exclamation. Additionally, the responses in this thread evidence an attention to the *methodologies* of reading, as well as the difference between reading on one's own, and reading "for" the teacher or within the classroom setting. Finally, the posters raise the question of how a book is presented—and how students are asked to respond to it, taking into account personal/social perspectives, including a reader's age.

The thread begins in March 2002 and continues through October 2007.[19] The original poster, "Argh!," asks whether anyone else on Pink Monkey finds *Crime and Punishment* a "very boring and depressing book." The next poster, "Annoyed W/School," succinctly agrees that the text is boring, but the next poster, "T-Bone," takes a different approach, in his September 2002 response to the original query:

I assume you're both students at a high school. I personally enjoyed it. Dostoevsky adds in a few parts I don't agree with, but on the whole, the book is definitely a thinker, and I enjoyed it. However, younger, less mature minds, tend not to grasp concepts and want to read about action stories and *Goosebumps*. Perhaps as you age you will read CaP again, and enjoy it for the classical piece of work it is. It really is intriguing and insightful. And nothing really good happens in chapter 5, short of the killings. The good stuff happens later on. Young people, always so impatient.

"Scarlet_Spider" responds, in December 2002, in implicit disagreement with both T-Bone and Argh:

I read it this year in high school and it is now one of my all time favorite books. It really depends on how the teacher presents the material. . . . I can see how it can become dull and boring, but I love looking into the mind of Raskolnikov . . . aren't we all a little insane sometimes??

"Skyreaper" then adds, in January 2003:

I'm a junior in high school and we're required to read it. Like always, I've pushed reading to the very last minute, but reading about 150 pages last night (we have to read it up to part III) I really enjoyed it. It's quite strange, and I learned so much. I concluded that the author had to have murdered somebody. Just kidding, but really, he sure knows the complexity and regression that follows murder.

"Student 109897" chimes in, in August 2003:

Okay. I have to admit until I found this site the book was really dull. However, if you read a chapter of the book, and then read the Pink Monkey summary things are a lot better. I'm not sure if it is because you understand the book better or because it helps you analyze the "deeper meaning" but it's not that bad if you can make it to Part Four.

"Spiderbite 99" then comments, in December 2003:

Dostoevsky has written a very good STORY inside of this book. In my opinion, his writings ramble incessantly, and a certain tone in the characters voices is needed to understand the twisted dialogue completely. A knowledge of the mid-1800s history would also be helpful to make this book more enjoyable. Myself, I enjoyed the book much more after i had read it, re-read it, read a comprehensive summary, and then re-read the book again. HaHa! Some people might not have time for all that reading but trust me, the book does become MUCH better after an in-depth knowledge is acquired. The STORY is much better than the BOOK itself.

"Crusin Thru" adds his perspective in January 2004:

i am a senior in HS and i have to write 7 seperate short essays for this mad book. Our teacher assigned it over our 3 weeks christmas holliday, and it has snowballed into an out of control assignment for me. i just went and bought the **********.... that helps a lot . . . raskolnikov IS a freak, indeed.

And finally, "Sammy," "Kiri," and "MalibuBarbie0526," finally acknowledge, respectively, in August and November 2004 the outlier position of "T-Bone," posed two years prior:

I think it is really close-minded to look down on younger people. At least these people are READING the book, which is more than lots of even adults would do. The fact that some people don't like the book doesn't really have to do with someone's age. The only two possible ways I can think of that would have to do with age are: 1) the person is not old enough to understand it (at least literally) or 2) the person is too young to relate to the subject matter. For instance if the book deals with having children, obligation to pay bills etc. In this case neither applies, so please do not say that it is because they are young. Even if one or both of these things did apply, there is no reason to look down on people because they are young. It would be fine just to say that they might change their mind when they get older. (Sammy)

It's quite unfair to base intelligence and such on age. I just read CaP this last year, as a senior in high school, and I loved the book. At times, I did find it a bit tiresome, but the majority of the book was wonderful. I wrote my theory paper for high school on the book, and all in all, I love the book. Alas, I'm often finding myself likening it to life, especially the dreams. Well, that was my two cents. (Kiri)

It is so stereotypical to say that a high schooler would hate this book. So what? I bet many adults, if they even read it, would hate it. It's a matter of opinion, not age. And though some environmental determination, like age and maturity, have to do with understanding some of the themes in this book, it doesn't mean that just a certain age group is bound to dislike or not comprehend a book. As a sophomore, I'm offended at the thought that someone would look at me and immediately say that I'm too ignorant for a good piece of literature and hand me Goosebumps. (MalibuBarbie0526)

There are many points of interest present in these student exchanges. First, the primary motivation (at least as it appears) for the original poster is a basic one: to get a general opinion from his online peers of the novel *Crime and Punishment*. His query is neither specific (i.e., "I need a quote for my paper") or seemingly directed toward fulfilling an assignment (unless the assignment were, "why is this book boring?" which seems unlikely). Instead, his request is an open one, and is not responded to for many months. Once the responses start to roll in, they focus first on the nature of the book itself, but then quickly move to the ways in which the book might be *read*, including high school versus more "mature" frameworks (T-Bone). Although three posters—Sammy, Kiri, and MalibuBarbie0526—leap on T-Bone's hypothesis with fairly specific counterarguments, other posters relate the book back to the classroom itself (Crusin Thru), whereas still others discuss the habits of reading—and reading strategies—that result in a more positive experience with *Crime and Punishment* (Spiderbite 99, Student 109897). Present in these exchanges as a *group* is a distinct attention to the position of the reader in relation to the text itself; none of the exchanges mentions a particularly positive experience with the book inside the classroom (Crusin Thru emphasizes the amount of *writing* required to complete the assigned book within the larger lesson plans/curriculum; Skyreaper emphasizes the "last-minute" reading practice frequently found among students toward assigned reading—or other school-related tasks—that are not immediately appealing to them).

Given the complex contents of the book itself, one might anticipate a discussion thread for the text to instead focus on the recapitulation of plot points, the analysis of character, or other immediately "useful" points of interpretation that students might bring back to their classes. At least this kind of query and subsequent responses would be the "expected" thread on such a site, from a critical point of view that assumes students seek out peers only for useful help and immediate answers to assigned questions. But instead, the *Crime and Punishment* thread illustrates a higher-order type of response, one that admittedly begins from a benign, nonspecific query (i.e., "anyone else bored with this book?") but that results in a much richer discussion of how and why students read, and under what conditions—a discussion unlikely to take place in a classroom focused on reading and digesting the book as required text. The rather passionate responses from Sammy, Kiri, and MalibuBarbie 0526 additionally illustrate a defense of students as invested, viable *readers*—particularly MalibuBarbie 0526's dread that a teacher or other adult might "say I'm too ignorant for a good piece of literature and hand me *Goosebumps*," a popular fiction series often touted as successful for middle and high school-aged readers. MalibuBarbie 0526's response to T-Bone indicates that, indeed, students not only are capable of, but also interested in, what Patrick Sullivan calls "important" literature, earlier in this chapter. But more than this, her response, along with Sammy and Kiri's, would seem to be counterintuitive to the prevailing notions that students *won't* read whole books, or even attempt to; instead, the aggregate responses here reveal a need to read in better, more feasible *contexts* than the traditional classroom and its well-intentioned apparatuses.

Although the bulk of the threads on the Pink Monkey discussion forum are of this nature—students talking with students, about literature as assigned, or as chosen (e.g., readings that are not part of the curriculum but are of interest to students, such as the Harry Potter books)—there also are two other types of threads that I briefly spotlight here. These are what I call the *teacher-interference* threads, and the *"How's my writing?"* threads. These threads illustrate additional negative and positive ramifications for employing Pink Monkey as an extra-institutional site of student exchange and discourse about literacy practices, specifically the act of reading.

In contrast to the typical/dominant text-based, student-initiated threads on Pink Monkey, occasionally teachers (whether high school or college-level) will initiate a discussion thread as part of their class activities, which in my terms are the *teacher-interference* threads. I label these threads as such because they would seem to interrupt the student-led spaces of Pink Monkey with teacher-figure interference, co-opting the site—intended as an extra-institutional venue—for classroom purposes. Of course, the sponsors and webmasters of Pink Monkey are friendly toward teachers and other educational authority figures, as mentioned earlier in this chapter. The main import of Pink Monkey, however, is to provide a teacher-free zone for students to discuss, ruminate on, and critique texts and various reading practices as applied to those texts. Thus, although the aims of these teacher-interference threads are surely good—to capitalize on student interest in the medium, and to engage students in electronic discussion and writing—the resulting discussion is frequently far less successful, or thoughtful, than other student-led threads.

For example, "Houston 415," who very quickly unveils herself as a classroom teacher—Mrs. Houston—of students at an unstated level, directs her students to "Discuss the significance of the numbers used throughout *Inferno*. Think specifically of the number of circles, cantos, total lines in the poem." The student responses, and Houston 415's replies, posted between April 3 and April 18, 2006, are as follows (with poster names/screen identities in parentheses following each post):

Like mrs. houston said in class, the number 3 pops up a lot. In catholocism three represents the holy trinity (father, son, holy spirit). In wicca it represents the phases of the goddess (mother, maiden,c rone), and the whole mind, body, spirit, and beginning, middle, end thing. oh, and the nine circles, nine is considered one of the perfect numbers because its THE perfect number (3) 3 times. (kerryann)

Very good Kerry Ann. Can anyone give any other examples from the text where the number 3 pops up? (Houston 415)

There are 3 beasts that chase Dante from the hill. He ventures through Hell for 3 days. Beatrice sends the prayers of 3 saints, Virgin Mary, Saint Lucia, and Rachel. Dante notices 9 people in the second circle of Hell, and 3¥3 = 9. Cerberus has 3 heads. (But I dont think that one counts) 3 Infernal Furies threaten Dante and Virgil. Also, there are 3 lines in every stanza too. Thats all I could find though. I'm sure I missed some. (G-Man)

Wow . . . very good! If you find more, continue to post them . . . I'm sure you will. Of course Cerberus counts! Why wouldn't he? Who is G-Man???? (Houston 415)

And there were three furies. Edit: Ah wait, that was already posted. Oops. (Katinar)

-In-fer-no = 3 syllables; -3 levels of after life- Purgotory, Ante–hell, Hell; -9 circles of hell = 3*3; -My book # has a 3 on it :[]; -Each canto has lines that are multiples of 3; -pg 265 the illustration of the ninth circle(this is deep) the Italian world for the ninth circle has three sylla-bles(co-cy-tus); -Three is a lucky number. I realize that 3 is used a lot more than 1, 2 , or 4.........baseball 3 game series tournament next week 3 game elimination. (Katinar)

I think that this book is what made three a frequently used number when i think about it. (I really liked this topic.) —"Inferno opens on the evening of Good Friday in the year 1300."—"The sun shines down on a mountain above him, and he attempts to climb up to it but finds his way blocked by three beasts—a leopard, a lion, and a she-wolf." (Katinar)

Virgil leads Dante through the gates of Hell, marked by the haunting inscription "abandon all hope, you who enter here" (III.7). (Luis M)

(Quoting Luis M): "I think that this book is what made three a frequently used number when i think about it. (I really liked this topic.)"

Actually, the number 3 has been used forever. It's symbolic in Christianity, Catholicism, Mythology . . . everywhere. Dante just continued with that tradition. It's considered the divine number. (Houston 415)

As in Inferno, Hinduism also accepts the number 3 as being holy. It stands for the 3 worlds (the Earth world, the Inner or in-between world, and the World of Shiva {the world of the gods.}). The number 3 also represents birth, death, and rebirth, and also the threefold deities, Brahma, Vishnu, and Shiva. (tRiNiBoi108)

Hmmm . . . you've given me an idea. Anyone who wants a few extra points, do some research on different religions (or mythologies) and find out the significance of the number three in those different cultures. Just type up a paragraph of your findings. You can post it on here or give it to me in class. (Houston 415)

There are numerous problems with this thread on Dante's *Inferno* when it is set in comparison with the types of exchange and thinking available and present in the other two sample student-led threads. First, the dialogue takes shape not as led or directed by students, but as directed by the instructor, Mrs. Houston. Her acknowledgments of the "right" or "good" answer, as illustrated in her first post, move the dialogue in a direction motivated by confirming the teacher's lesson goals, rather than by a critical, independent reading of the work. Second, by questioning "who is G-Man?" Mrs. Houston obviously wants to give the pseudonymous student credit for his or her response—in her class records—but in doing so, violates the typical framework of Pink Monkey and other discussion forums, in which posters do not, in fact, typically use their own names, so as to gain a virtual freedom not found in the classroom. Third, the threads are allowed to meander in sometimes ridiculous directions (e.g., the numerology attempt by Luis M.) that are not acknowledged at all by Mrs. Houston, other than the end of the thread, which she contradicts. Luis M. may, in fact, simply be babbling to see if he gets her attention—which he does not, and as such, his post is assigned little value in the discussion. Finally, when another student (tRiNiBoi108) mentions the use of the number 3 in other religions, Mrs. Houston does *not* tie this back to the text, but instead takes the student's idea as a prompt for offering extra credit, to be given to students if they "type up a paragraph" of their findings. We have now steered completely away from the Dante discussion at hand, and shortly thereafter, the thread ends.

I do not mean to sound overly critical of the pedagogy of this instructor (even if I do find the thread's oversight, as it were, severely lacking in organization and depth); instead, I aim to illustrate how the use of Pink Monkey not only does not *add* to the quality of the discussion, it may, in fact, detract from it instead. The interference that the teacher runs serves only to create a back-and-forth between herself and a few select students—and even these exchanges are sorely lacking intellectual depth. To put this thread in the context of Jeff Rice's argument about the use of new media technologies, this instructor is simply taking a regular classroom discussion—including the existing power dynamics and rules of exchange (as well as rules of avoidance, where off-topic responses are concerned)—and laying it into an electronic environment, here an environment where teachers are not necessarily the most logical or beneficial participants. I thus include this sample teacher-interference thread to exemplify the *caution* that faculty must exert when attempting to co-opt these student technologies for their own use(s).

Finally, I want to briefly mention a contrasting and certainly more positive, if still alternative, use of the Pink Monkey site, the thread-type that I will call *"How's my writing?"* Of course, readers know that online writing centers and other similar technologies have existed for the past two decades. Purdue's Online Writing Lab, or "OWL," is one such example of a site wherein students may submit their work and within a set period of time (usually twenty-four hours) receive a response from a tutor, designed to provide generative feedback and suggestions for improvement of the piece. Pink Monkey seems to have its own version of such online assistance, in the form of these "How's my writing" threads. Students typically post short pieces of writing—most often poems—and ask for peer critiques. Unlike a creative writing classroom, wherein the identity of the writer is inextricably tied to the "identity" of the poem—even in classrooms that shuffle such work anonymously, there is little difficulty in telling whose writing is whose, at least by the middle of the course—on Pink Monkey, students are submitting work from across the country and their online peers are reading it "blind" to authorial identities. One such thread focuses on a student, Samwise Gamgee, who posts a poem entitled "The Message" and asks for feedback, both good and bad.[20] Samwise Gamgee's poem receives many immediate (within two days' time) responses, and accumulates eleven respondents posting nearly twenty messages about the poem. Many offer words of support—as the poem is about child who died of cancer—whereas many others offer specific, detailed critiques. Throughout, Samwise Gamgee asserts that he or she wants actual feedback—not just positive responses.

I include this note about the poetry/"How's my writing" thread to illustrate yet another facet of reading practices present on Pink Monkey: the peer-to-peer reading directives that take as primary text not a piece of published literature, but a student-written text put up for critique. There are a significant number of such threads within the Pink Monkey fora, although in comparison to the discussions of published texts, the numbers are small. For students to want to engage in extracurricular readings of student work seems to indicate a security in textual analysis that is separate from the questioning of literary techniques or interpretive readings they are doing in support of their home reading and writing-based classrooms wherein these canonical texts are being assigned. Peer review, as a practice in composition studies, has certainly been studied from a variety of angles in the field's literature, but less frequently do we consider the connections between a student's willingness to read a text in a classroom setting and his or her similar willingness to read peer work in that same setting, let alone outside of school. The visibly apparent inclusion of such peer-text threads on Pink Monkey might give us pause in our blanket assessments of student engagement with the abstract notion of "text," if indeed they are motivated to engage in textual analysis of not only assigned readings, but also peer writing, outside of the institutional setting.

ADDRESSING THE GAP: TECHNOLOGY
AND LITERACY IN THE CLASSROOM

Regardless of how a student exercises, or simply represents, his or her own reading practices and/or attitudes toward textual analysis, broadly speaking, that student's presence as a rhetor on Pink Monkey critically bypasses the authority figure or figures who typically controls text-based discourse: the teacher-figure. On Pink Monkey, the participants may roughly be classified by levels of need in relation to textual interpretation and reading practices—but not all of these needs are necessarily school-related. Participants may engage in the forum discussions simply to get information about a text or texts in order to complete an assignment; certainly these queries are abundant, and usually labeled as such; student Bob's original query about Iago, for example, could have fulfilled such a need, although he does not explicitly say so (nor does he return to the thread to thank participants for their input, probably because the thread does not end within a timeframe anywhere near his posting).

Other participants, however, particularly those who respond to original queries, are *not* necessarily fulfilling an institutional need. Rather, they are fulfilling a personal need or committing an intrinsically motivated act of response that fulfills either their need to represent themselves as agents within this large virtual community, or to engage in a dialogue about a text or texts using terminology, experience, insight, or general discussion parameters not permitted or available in an institutional setting. Additionally, participants might be engaging in the reading–writing process using their own or peers' texts as starting points. Each of these varied readerly (and writerly) needs, under Pink Monkey, are collected under an advice-based umbrella that does not explicitly undermine the school experience itself, but purports to complement and enhance it, all in full view of the authority figures so visibly absent on the forum's various exchanges.

The existence of Pink Monkey, and the likelihood that it is but one of many future Web sites of its kind, calls our attention to the vast online network of extra-institutional discussions about literacy acquisition. Pink Monkey also highlights a clear desire among a diverse group of high school and college students to circumvent the practices of reading and writing as guided by a central authority figure or larger institutional structure. Even though teaching with technology—both in computerized classrooms and via course management systems, blogs, and wikis—has become so commonplace as to be the "norm" rather than the exception on many college campuses (and in some progressive high schools), faculty still generally devalue or significantly discount the electronic spaces that students frequent when not in the classroom. Examining a site such as Pink Monkey, which serves both a social and nontraditional educational function, allows us to better imagine the ways in which students can and do work outside the classroom (or teacher-sponsored online) boundaries to make their own meanings of texts, through collective discussion, negotiation, and ethical re-interpretations online. Adding the atemporal, nonlinear, and nationwide potential audience elements of forum responses available to Pink Monkey participants only broadens the possibilities for students to draw from extra-institutional sites of educational discourse in growing and developing their own reading practices.

This student use of the Web also illustrates a deliberative impulse among students—namely, an impulse to extend and reframe text-based debates across multiple rhetors and myriad rhetorical motivations. As Amy Kimme Hea argues, even Web-based instructors themselves "must interrogate the contradictions and ambiguities of cultural narratives about the Web" in order to create "more democratic learning environments" in this type of classroom (332), echoing some of Rice's concerns about the lack of new pedagogical theory present in sites of new media-based instruction. I argue that Hea's theory can be extended to on-the-ground instructors who certainly address the use of and interaction with online environments and/or sources in their students' work, if not in their own pedagogies. As Hea argues broadly that "looking at the 'normalized' ways we incorporate the Web into our classrooms can help us uncover underlying expectations and values associated with the roles of Web-based technology, literacy, student–student and student–instructor relationships" (333), her proposition need not be limited to those faculty who teach with technology. Hea posits teaching the theory of the Web as a "global village" (335); employing this theory, instructors (here graduate student teaching assistants) can shape their "edentities"[21] as learners as well as teachers, including the employ-ment of "resistant material instantiations" that "reassert the technological context as primary in determining possible uses for that technology. In other words, the environment, persons, and situations affect the technolog-ical integration rather than placing primary emphasis on the technology itself" (343).

Hea's concept is directly applicable to re-seeing Pink Monkey as a legit-imate extra-institutional learning tool. By prioritizing the participants with-in the forums, as well as taking into account the environment in which these participants negotiate and renegotiate not only their understanding of texts, but their own reading practices as relevant to their ethical identi-ties and the identities of other participants, faculty might indeed be reminded of context over technology, of the highly situational learning tak-ing shape within an online space that rejects, in many ways, the tradition-al elements of the teacher-led classroom.

Ultimately, reading, writing, and general literacy practices have not his-torically and will not in the future be exclusively limited to the institution-ally sanctioned space of the classroom. As we freely recognize sites of learning that occur beyond the course space—in workplaces, homes, and other community gatherings—so, too, should we recognize the power of student-led spaces that make use of opportunities to speak outside the range of authority, or beyond the reach of our faculty hearing. In the next chapter, I explore one such out-of-range site, namely the online paper mills run for economic rather than educational gain. Although these sites sharply differ in their surface goals, their core shares with Pink Monkey a funda-mental aim to provide an alternative, albeit a negative one, to the system of higher education, in the case of paper mills, to best the system by eschewing both its rules *and* its moral authority.

3

NEGOTIATED IDENTITIES

Online Paper Mills, Student Authorship, and First-Year Composition

As complex and layered as student reading practices may be, especially when allowed the freedom to be augmented outside the limits of classroom-based authorities and methodologies, the effort to record, review, and revise one's ideas in writing gives rise to even more complex pedagogical issues, both in terms of the students' writerly identities and their relationships with authority and *authorial* figures who also inhabit the educational system in which "academic" writing takes place. As students increasingly go adrift from the influence of the teacher-figure while acquiring their critical sense of literacy (and multiple literacies), they become more disengaged from the values and traditions of the system within which the teacher-figure "knows best." Paradoxically, however, they continue to be *bound* to that teacher-figure and his or her authoritative stance in the classroom, specifically to his or her grading power and, in higher stakes situations such as high school or college graduation gates, his or her true "gatekeeper" status.

Although the system of literacy education purports to be evolving—via new methods of course delivery, increased online and distance education, and other atypical methodologies designed to "speak" to Generation Y students—there has yet to be a lasting and viable alternative to evaluation and grading across and among course subjects at the college level (with the exception of institutions such as Hampshire College, which does not assign grades at all). As discussed in Chapter 4, this system of evaluation is ripe for extra-institutional commentary and public debate, specifically on teacher ratings sites such as Rate My Professors. Although first-year composition, as one such subject in which evaluation must take place, has moved in some arenas to a greater emphasis on holistic assessment, such as portfolios, it would be naïve to say that teachers did not still have a great deal of power in controlling the overall academic fates of students. Such power (frequently) breeds contempt, and such contempt breeds fear and avoidance—in the case of first-year composition, avoidance of the root problem to be circumvented: the act of writing itself.

Students are largely led to believe that they are "only" students writing within this highly structured enterprise of evaluation (i.e., adhering and responding, in their written work, to the evaluative categories of praise and sanction). As such, these students do not perceive themselves to be *Writers*, let alone the loftier label of *Authors*. These students eventually come to accept their perceived lesser-status struggle to achieve by giving up the vexing quest to overcome this elevated status altogether. This critical decision to negate, circumvent, and essentially *avoid* the act of writing from the point of being a "lesser" self, rather than deciding to partake in some moment of criminal, evil-meaning, and criminalized behavior, is where and when plagiarism is born. In this paradigm, plagiarism is not conceived of by the erstwhile struggling student as a "crime," but as an alternative—viable and, in actuarial terms, with a good risk–benefit ratio— to lesser, clearly meaningless, attempts at student authorship.

The online paper mills—unlike Pink Monkey, which encourages *positive*, if academically counterculture, student online agencies as an alternative to classroom readerly practices—promote a negative, anti-ethos alternative to these students as they undertake the risky enterprise of writing. Online paper mills thus fill the neatly provided gap created by the seemingly insurmountable student/author binary at work in higher education's classrooms. Whereas Pink Monkey is centered on productive communication and the presentation of self as ethical rhetor, the online paper mills in contrast suppress and de-value any independent student effort at expression, communication, and learning. The suppression and devaluation of the student as ethical entity by paper mills is critical to the concomitant elevation of these sites—and our larger culture's—depersonalized, business-minded approach to education, one that promotes an efficient, economic view of authorship that purports to have greater "real-world" applications than do the traditional author-centered writing practices found in school.

In this chapter, I examine how, as a free public venue, the Internet therefore not only may allow for positive student agency-building within student-led discussion sites, but also for the negative mass student exodus from the pursuit of authorship within the online paper mill Web sites, which propose for student consumption a more attractive, if not simplified, version of what it means to "write" in our larger commodified culture outside academia. To illustrate this negative aspect of online student-centered discourse, I consider both theories of authorship and plagiarism as well as studies of student online behaviors, and revisit my student survey on academic dishonesty, originally conducted at my previous institution in fall 2001, both by reviewing my results from that original sample set and by replicating the survey with a similar student demographic at my current institution in fall 2008. What I argue within this re-examination is that despite a separation of seven years (or almost two cycles of four-year college student populations) between the two surveys, little has changed in student attitudes toward, and perceptions of, academic honesty. What remains is a significant disconnect between what students perceive to be "right" (i.e., ethical) and what students actually *do* when faced with the dilemma of whether to engage in acts of singular, ethically minded authorship in fulfillment of their academic writing assignments, specifically those assigned in first-year composition.

PLAGIARISM AND THE STUDENT–TEACHER–INTERNET DYNAMIC

The question of what truly *constitutes* plagiarism, let alone how to address its many permutations in this age of electronic cut-and-paste, continues to occupy the time and intellectual energy of many teachers and scholars both inside and outside composition studies. The scholarship on plagiarism has evolved somewhat in the twenty-first century, with more attention being paid to the intricacies of authorship and the ethics of detection devices, specifically illustrated in the growing skepticism of industries such as turnitin.com. Scholars such as Amy Robillard have deepened our understanding of the term *author* by introducing new variables into the authorship equation, in Robillard's case her work with Ron Fortune on "literary forgery," or one's authoring of a text that is then deliberately billed under another author or artist's name.[22] Still, there has been little attention paid to the role that the Internet plays as an *agent* in the process of plagiarism, despite the significant attention that the "cut-and-paste" generation has garnered from high school and college teachers who lament the ease with which texts may be located and lifted from various Web sites.

As I argued in 2005, and in 2006,[23] online paper mills are relatively prosperous in the absence of true critical reflection on their persuasive power, especially in composition studies, where definitions of authorship are the most contested and where student understanding of authorial agency is the most tenuous. But I would now argue that the paper mill sites are not the only player in the larger rhetorical framework that persuades students to plagiarize. Rather, I contend that the on-the-ground, concomitant classrooms in which student work is assigned and submitted, and sometimes in this process also plagiarized, bears some blame for this problem. This is not because faculty write bad/generic assignments (although we do), or do not pay enough attention to the drafting and revising process, especially in large classes (although we don't), or even because most faculty can't find enough time in the day to accurately and meaningfully respond to all our students' writing (although we can't). No, our classrooms are part of the problem because they are assumed to be the antithesis of the online paper mill sites; the physical classroom space is assumed to be truly dialogic, student-centered, and intellectually satisfying for those students who want to engage in it, for the sake of *learning*. Online student spaces of various formations, and within various venues, are assumed to be the anti-school "other," except in the case of online instruction (but even there, some faculty have significant collective doubt about the quality and integrity of student work produced without the physical presence of a teacher).

But what we overlook here is the ways in which academic writing, as an intellectual act and as embodied heavily in the first-year course, continues to elide student agencies altogether, even in liberatory pedagogy-aspiring classrooms. This is because writing, to students, is less about learning than about goal-meeting, future purchasing power, and effective information-centered commerce. In other words, although we claim to value our students as authors, there is little about the structure of higher education in particular that promotes authorship to these students as a truly agentic process, at least in the ways that online paper mills and other Internet commerce allow. Instead, the writing classroom is more frequently part of a cattle call of first-year requirements, process-driven though those requirements may be, on the way to a job—especially in a poor economy such as the one we are facing today. The consumer-driven discourse of online paper mills, and of our students' online communicative lives in general, must therefore be integrated into our research on student authorship and student–teacher relationships in the digital age. Understanding online paper mills as one significant and seductive corner of the online discourse communities discussing and critiquing higher education is critical to empowering first-year student writers (and readers), and to bridging the gap between teacher and student where conceptions of authorship are concerned.

Unlike faculty, who in their secondary and postsecondary student years *may* have idealized—or at least valued—the idea of "writing well" in an academic setting, first-year composition students today continue to alternatively and carefully weigh interconnected economic, academic, and personal needs when choosing whether to do their own college writing and research or purchase it elsewhere. Instead of consulting sources in a dialogue—or a "conversation," as writing teachers frequently term it—or even the less-adept activity of employing the World Wide Web to piece together a paper of their "own," these students often are seeking out already-finished, available-for-purchase papers by nameless and faceless authors, so as to meet their academic ends more quickly and with more certainty of success (i.e., a finished paper is a better bet than a pieced-together product of resulting unknown quality).

Without these students—who do not believe that they can or should be authors of their own academic work, but do believe that they can *and should* co-opt the accomplished authorship of others when necessary—the anonymous and powerful online paper mill industry does not exist; unlike more generally applicable student-led sites such as Pink Monkey, the paper mill industry is born of and dependent on the specific, lacking confidence of student writers. First-year composition students are the most likely group to fall victim to the rhetoric of this industry, as these students not only are unfamiliar with the university and its discourse, but also are enrolled in a required course that emphasizes the development of intellectual *identity* through writing. Anxious about the course and sometimes even angry that a new form of writing is being foisted on them, one that often contradicts or complicates what the time and space of their high school English curriculum allowed them to learn, first-year composition students quite literally may buy into the rhetoric of the paper mills. In the process, they shape their lifelong perceptions of what authorship in academia really means.

It is important to note that these students, by and large, patronize online paper mills not because of a desire to outwit the academic system of authorship—or their predilection to engage in so-called "criminal" behavior, as it is presented explicitly or implicitly in various honor codes and student handbooks—but as a result of their cultural and ideological disconnection from the system itself. The rhetoric present in online paper mills and in our students' support of them challenges our comfortable and traditional definition of plagiarism, which is predicated on academia's (and faculty's) intrinsic defense of authorship as an intellectual, creative activity. In order to truly understand how and why students continue to engage in this type of plagiarism in the composition classroom, we must seek to understand how and when students see themselves as authors and as *consumers*, not just in the purchase of a college education, but also in a society defined by anonymity, convenience, and privacy; and how students reconcile the warring concepts of author and consumer in the space of their own writing, and against their notions of where and when the teacher-figure is of value in their pursuit of higher education.

Although the composition studies community recently has engaged in more critical discussions of student authorship, as noted earlier, it has yet to fully answer two important questions that underlie absent notions of authorship on the part of these students, and which I posed in my previous published studies. First, what is the complicated relationship already in place between *student* authors and consumer culture that dictates the role that writing plays in one's college career? Second, how might this relationship explain why the online paper mills consistently, even exponentially, profit from patronage by students? To these two questions, I add a third based on the three years I spent being informed by additional published scholarship on plagiarism and authorship as well as the preoccupation with technology and teaching found on professional listservs and in other faculty groupings: How does the role of the teacher-figure—or the avoidance and clear negation of that figure in commercialized online communities—play a part in the unwitting negation of institutionally driven definitions of student authorship?

The further separation of students from faculty via commercial Web sites that have co-opted the terms and conditions of writing education increases the physical, as well as intellectual, distance of students from faculty, as writers and as writing mentors. Addressing these three questions thus begins a necessary inquiry into how and why students in the twenty-first century frequently see college writing—their own, their friends', that which is provided by the online paper mills specifically and the Internet commercial community generally—as an economic act rather than an intellectual one.

INVISIBLE AGENCIES: STUDENT AUTHORS VERSUS "REAL" WRITERS

Some scholars argue that authorship in the twenty-first century is about negotiating the giant collage of available information that undermines the authority of a single author in favor of multiple, combined identities; theories of pastiche and multimedia composition certainly point to this trend in the polyvocal, even if such collage work is typically undervalued and infrequently assigned in college writing courses. As Rebecca Moore Howard argues, studying the ever-shifting notion of author and text, and the way in which students inevitably "patch" together sources from their textual (and hypertextual) universes in the collaborative research act, is a more productive use of our time than focusing on the criminality of plagiarism via detection and punishment. In "Plagiarisms, Authorship, and the Academic Death Penalty," Howard states that patchwork comes from writers' engagement with "unfamiliar discourse, when they must work monologically with the words and ideas of a source text" (796), and argues that "it is . . . reasonable to revise definitions of plagiarism to account for the contingent nature of authorship" (798). In *Standing in the Shadow of Giants*, Howard further articulates the issue as stemming from a "new binary: plagiarist/author" whose premise is "Writers who are mimetic and who collaborate with their texts are not authors. They are, at best, students. If they fail to acknowledge their mimesis or collaboration with source texts, they are plagiarists. If they are both plagiarist and student, they are punished" (75–6).

As counterpoint to Howard's theories, Candace Spigelman argues in *Across Property Lines* that "for readers, the substance of a written work is always a kind of public property" (6) and thus true ownership of student writing comes only with a recognition of students as "the central authority, the 'authors' and the 'owners' of their texts" (54). This is in contrast to Howard's assertion that all sources are equal parts of a student's hybrid written discourse, as Spigelman believes that students can and do recognize their position as creators of knowledge that is vulnerable to appropriation by others, even as this stems from complicated notions of "property." In Spigelman's study of writing groups and their perceptions of authorship and textual ownership, she finds that

> most student writers do think of themselves as textual "owners" (at least to the extent that they can think of themselves this way, given the competing urgencies of teacher evaluation and appropriation) because they "know" that writers "own" their texts. They may feel the urgency to hide or hoard their thoughts, their ideas, in part because they feel fellow students will "steal" them. (23)

For Spigelman, this concept of ownership explains the reticence on the part of some students to participate in, or even attend, peer workshops. But what her assertion also evidences is a fear among students that information may indeed be "stolen" from one's paper and used by a classmate. Spigelman's research indicates a very real disconnect between how teachers seek evidence of intellectual exchange in student writing and how students resist that exchange sometimes entirely. This resistance, and confusion over who "owns" the text, may lead some students to abandon their authorship rights altogether in favor of obtaining a "good" piece of academic writing that better suits the teacher's needs. Particularly in the context of the often fraught relationship between students and teachers over classroom agency, as discussed throughout this book, and the resulting contextual reality of the grade as the site of permanent evaluative summary, the desire to submit a piece of writing that fulfills an assignment, and does so unquestionably well, is a strong one, far more so than the promise of a romanticized, iconic author label.

Spigelman and Howard's approaches to understanding plagiarism emphasize sound student-centered pedagogy over time-consuming out-of-class investigative work, and as such continue to influence other scholars working on issues of intellectual property within composition studies. Both Spigelman and Howard have acknowledged the fact that students often do not acknowledge their authorship in the context of existing and voluminous published works that serve as "sources" for student writing. But as I argued previously, these revisions in our discourse about plagiarism should *also* focus on the idea of authorship and the concept of "stealing" writing, as our students understand it, when pondering *whole-text* plagiarism such as that which occurs in the purchase of a previously authored paper. These occasions of whole-text plagiarism may fail to "patch" together source material, but they still show a lack of recognition on the students' part that authorship is valuable and that published writing is more than a product for the taking.

I suspect that we continue to dismiss, at least at the institutional and therefore the authoritative-classroom level, online paper mill patronage as a site of study because this type of academic dishonesty goes to the core of our popular, capitalist culture, itself predicated on the exchange of specialized, even personalized, goods and services, of which papers-for-sale are only one possibility. In Martha Woodmansee and Peter Jaszi's *The Construction of Authorship*, which interrogates historical notions of copyright, authorship, and text, David Sanjek points out that in one area of highly commercial exchange—music sampling—"it is a longstanding practice for consumers to customize their commodities, command their use and meaning before they are commanded by them" (343). Faculty frequently fail to see (or refuse to engage with) the complexity of the online paper mill structure that engages in this business of "customized commodities," and entices students to buy papers that are written *just for them* and delivered via the privacy of e-mail. In our zeal to punish students and protect the sanctity of intellectual property and academic scholarship, we overlook the complexity of the students' perceived academic needs, which sometimes are in unintended conflict with their own personal ethics and morals, and the complexity of the Internet as it has been embraced by not just our larger popular culture, but also the smaller intellectual culture of academia. This paradoxical embrace of the Internet as a resource, as evident in the discussion forums on Pink Monkey and other similar author-centered online exchanges, and the acknowledgment of the Internet as a site of dishonesty, in the case of the paper mills, is a concept with which academia cannot, ultimately, reconcile itself.

Howard has briefly addressed paper mills as a subject of study, arguing, "certainly, morality is the major factor in the purchase of term papers . . . and it may apply to other types of plagiarism, as well, depending upon the writer's intentions" ("Plagiarisms" 797). Furthermore, she has argued that submitting papers that are not one's own and engaging in patch-writing are "subsets" of plagiarism, such that "one is intentional, the other unintentional" ("The Ethics of Plagiarism" 80). For Howard, "unintentional plagiarism" is committed by students who are "ignorant of academic ethics . . . (the act is) unintentionally unethical" (80). The distinction is logical: When one pastes together sources, he or she *may* do so in ignorance of how to cite properly, or, as Howard hypothesizes, how to negotiate multiple authorships as relevant to academic discourse. To then claim, however, that the purchase of papers is by definition "intentional" and thus deliberately unethical because, by design, it does not seek to negotiate multiple sources in a dialogue is perhaps too simple a conclusion to draw. As Howard herself recognizes, "if the plagiarism was intentional, we then need to know motivations" (*Standing* 163).[24]

We cannot, however, dismiss the use of online paper mills as demonstrably different than typical, random acts of plagiarism, thus rendering the practice not worthy of critical study simply because on the surface, intent *seems* more clear and by extension the student's ethics seem more malleable (or altogether absent). Nor can we say unequivocally that those who buy papers from the online paper mills are savvy about authorship to the extent that they fully *understand* "academic ethics." If we do, we are indeed engaging in the time-tested practice that Howard describes of putting "the student writer (at) the bottom of the hierarchy. . . ." (*Standing* 138) in which intent is fixed and uniform among the population, and where ethical discussions do not apply to economically driven models of authorship. And putting students "at the bottom" is the core of the rhetoric of plagiarism— encouraging students to see themselves as *nothing more* than students, wherein the concept of "student" is the lowest rung on the academic hierarchy, as well as a liminal space, devoid of institutional authority. Such rhetorical positioning, in students' minds, mimics the position they believe teachers put them in when assigning limited-audience academic writing in the first-year classroom. If we ignore this perception as present in our students' overall online discourse about higher education and literacy practices, we consequently relegate the phenomenon of whole-text plagiarism to some back-street location where faculty dare not go. Such a perception stems from a keen attention to hierarchies of intellectual commerce, which delineate how and why our students critique the tenets of academic authorship against our more lofty, theoretical stances on the teaching of writing and the understood ethics and practices of the first-year writing classroom.

First-year composition students often have difficulty understanding the imposed and complicated ethical standards of writing in academe until they first begin to understand their own place in the economics and politics of the academy itself. In "Students, Authorship, and the Work of Composition," Bruce Horner argues that the "author/student writer binary" is what keeps composition students from receiving agency in the academy (505). Horner asserts that until students understand the binary and its classroom construction, they may not overcome the limits imposed on them as aspiring authors:

> Efforts to teach students to establish rhetorical authority risk bracketing the work of the classroom from the social and reinscribing the sta-

> tus quo of the "author," naming *as* the social a uniform official view of
> the classroom, unless they are accompanied by students' critique of
> the conditions of the various practices by which types of "authorship"
> are socially produced, as well as those producing its opposite, the "stu-
> dent writer." (520)

Horner specifically takes issue with the conflicting messages that composition teachers send to students about their ability to be authors, and
emphasizes the liminal status of the dreaded "student writer," the majority of whose work/aggregate textual production is, admittedly, of little use
to the outside world beyond the university. Horner cites Nancy Sommers,
who, as an advocate for the merging of students' personal and writerly
identities and their academic written products, argues that we should
respond to the content of student work, rather than correcting it, as often
we unintentionally "sabotage our students' conviction that the drafts they
have written are complete and coherent" (qtd. in Horner 511). Horner's
emphasis on the message that Sommers and others send, and that
Spigelman has proven students do in fact receive, is crucial to our understanding of how and why first-year composition students, skeptical of their
own abilities as new agents in academic discourse and aware of the prestige that published authors gain in the academy, might seek out these
"complete and coherent" products elsewhere: They simply are unable to
achieve the desired status of completeness, of perceived *perfection*, that
authorship seems to require. Even strategies such as process pedagogy,
which clearly privileges the trajectory of work toward a more cohesive end,
may backfire in debunking the myth of "perfect" writing, as students
inclined to distrust their own writing abilities may see, in a cumulative portfolio, a history of mess and failed attempts rather than a positive record of
progress—or may expect an automatic "A" for effort, even when the aggregate writing does not merit such an assessment. When these same students visit the bookstore (or virtual sites of reading online), there is no such
mess: There is simply finished "perfect" product, validated by visible readerly consumption.

Such ready consumption is a factor, according to Horner, in first-year
composition, as it is a course often driven by commodification, limited by
institutional working conditions, and taken by time-conscious students
who strive to be "cost-effective" and thus seek to make writing a *product*
they must produce in order to get "more bang for their tuition bucks while
having less time to devote to their writing" (522). When we consider these
two elements of Horner's argument in relation to online paper mills, it
becomes clear that the paper mills by design play on the new college writer
and his or her perception of the author/student writer binary, sidestepping
issues of plagiarism by sidestepping notions of the author, from whom to

"steal," altogether. Add to this a very quick "bang for the buck" in the fast and easy access that students have to these papers from their home or school computers, and it becomes plausible that the success of online paper mills stems from the desire by students to *succeed* through false or purchased authorship, particularly when that authorship comes vis-à-vis faceless online exchange.[25]

PERCEPTIONS OF PLAGIARISM: TWO INSTITUTIONS, SEVEN YEARS—LITTLE DIFFERENCE

I weigh the utility [of cheating], then decide.

—University of North Carolina-Greensboro
survey respondent, 2008

When I originally published an earlier version of this chapter's material in *College Composition and Communication* in June 2005, my survey findings were based solely on my English 101 students at my then-institution, Southern Connecticut State University (SCSU). As discussed elsewhere, these SCSU students represented a fairly typical first-generation, commuter-student college pool, working significant hours at part- or full-time jobs, and often attending one or more institutions before SCSU (our transfer population numbered approximately 30% at the time of this study). Additionally, SCSU students were, and still are, predominantly female (65%) and overwhelmingly enrolled (or with intentions to enroll) in the schools of nursing, business, and education.

In order to both update my findings and test the applicability of these findings on a new student population—one that resembles in some ways the English 101 students at SCSU (in percentage of female students and the overall popularity of pre-professional majors, in particular), but in other critical ways represents a more varied sociocultural cross-section, specifically of working and middle-class families in the South—I re-employed the same survey in English 101 classes at my current institution, the University of North Carolina-Greensboro (UNCG).[26] I received 247 responses to my original SCSU survey, for a compliance rate of about 30%; to replicate the raw number from this data set as closely as possible for the UNCG survey population, I asked the thirteen teaching assistants in my graduate composition pedagogy seminar, each teaching a twenty-two-seat section of the 101 course, to distribute the URL to their students for the electronic version of the survey in fall 2008. Of the 286 possible responses from this group, I received 215, for a compliance rate of 75%. Because the available pool in

2008 was determined using tighter controls, the compliance rate was demonstrably higher, even though the raw number of responses was statistically almost identical. In my 2008 survey, the teaching assistants were asked, as part of our course activities and discussion on plagiarism, to direct their students to take the survey, and were allowed to give extra credit to students for their compliance, if they wished. In the 2001 SCSU survey distribution, compliance instead depended on faculty buy-in rather than student return because I asked all contingent faculty to distribute the survey in their individual classes, using class time, without explicit rewards for their students or their own participation.

Additionally, distributing the survey online in 2008, versus on paper in 2001, not only kept the survey from taking up regular class time (and thus affecting instructors' lesson plans), but also allowed for a greater degree of freedom in terms of timing and conditions of the responses. Students could take the survey at home, in the library, at a coffee shop, or anywhere else that offered Internet access, thus more accurately replicating the ways in which students use the Internet as a social and academic tool outside of the classroom, including their use of academic-based Web sites, like Blackboard, for homework and other course readings and writings. Additionally, students could take as long as they liked to complete the survey—although on average, based on the tracking data, most students took less than five minutes to respond. Finally, the promise of anonymity was greater because the students' instructors did not collect the surveys in class, and because there were no markers linking students to particular sections.

The online setting, as is the case with other Web-based communication sites discussed in this book, allowed students an invisible status wherein only their ideas/responses were in play, and not their personal, physical identities. Because I wanted to be assured of gathering unique responses as much as possible, I *did* ask the students to enter their e-mail address at the end of the electronic survey—and in my instructions doing so, I also alerted them to the importance of *not* taking the survey more than once, for the data's integrity. I decided on this somewhat unscientific method in lieu of other controls, such as limiting IP addresses, for example, given the problems that such limitations would cause for students using public labs. In the end, my instructions appear to have worked (although of course, I will never know if certain students "tricked" the system—yet I could not perceive the benefits in doing so), I received 217 responses to the survey, two of which were from the same e-mail address, and so I eliminated those and calculated the 215 remaining responses in the final survey results.

In terms of the course level and content, the SCSU and UNCG courses both coincidentally carry the course title "English 101,"[27] and both emphasize a degree of research-based writing, but in the UNCG course, the teaching precedes a companion course (English 102), in which research is more heavily emphasized, this time via instruction in writing as well as public speaking. Thus, the instructional aims in the two courses are not identical, but the nature of each course as both first-year and as required for graduation binds the two populations. As such, my analysis of their survey responses keeps in mind these students' common institutional positioning as often unwilling—and underconsulted—participants in the process of literacy acquisition at the college level, in this case instruction in the slippery/mutable skills of "research writing" and "source citation" as applicable to the acquisition of academic literacy.

As apparent in both sets of survey results, these first-year composition students *could* see themselves as authors in some writing situations outside academe, but fail to see how multidimensional the definition of authorship may be in the academy and in our culture at large. When students were asked what "being an author" meant to them, the choices provided deliberately complicated the idea that authorship may be only one thing.[28] The most frequently recognized "type" of author was reflected in the 45% of respondents of SCSU respondents and 46.5% of UNCG respondents who said that being an author is "Writing something for which one may become famous or well known." In addition, 58% of those surveyed at SCSU and 71.2% surveyed at UNCG—the only notable increase in percentage of responses within the survey as a whole—recognized that "Writing anything, whether it is academic or not and whether it is published or not" constitutes authorship.

This increased percentage *may* indicate a slightly more liberal stance toward the breadth of definitions of authorship. Only 39% and 46% of the students surveyed, however, said that "Writing material for the Internet (either a personal or business Web site)" constitutes authorship—even though clearly the amount of writing that students do online, on sites such as Pink Monkey, but also on their own blogs, web pages, and social networking sites—is vast. This indicates that many composition students *still* do not see writing that is posted on the Internet as "authored" material, which may be due to the proliferation of anonymous Web sites and the ease with which anyone may create a Web site and thus become an "author" without having the writing screened for content or quality. Nonetheless, it is a slightly troubling statistic that indicates the immense amount of online writing that these students do is not considered "authored," at least not in the context of a survey about authorship as implicitly constructed by and within academia.

When this hypothesis about online authorship is extended to paper mill Web sites, it is clear that the material there, in addition to being offered up by nameless and faceless individuals, is truly "authorless" by design, which must further confuse students who already fail to see the Internet as a site of "real" authorship, a concept perhaps reinforced by some faculty or other teacher-figures whom these students encounter. This "authorless" paper mill writing would include the papers available for purchase, even though at least one of the paper mill companies, The Paper Store, sells papers listing the original author's name at the top and a warning at the bottom of each page which states, "No portion of this document may be reprinted without proper attribution to the Paper Store as a source" (Mohr-Corrigan, "Role of Women" 1). Even citing this quote for the purposes of this book, however, is complicated: Is Lori Mohr-Corrigan the "author" of this statement, simply because the Paper Store states that this is her paper for sale and includes the warning on her paper? Or is the Paper Store the legal "author," as the statement would indicate? This blurring of boundaries tells students that authorship, especially that produced and traded online, is generally up for grabs, and that, of course, none of the admonitions mean much because Lori Mohr-Corrigan was not involved *directly* in this sale of her work and because the Paper Store additionally claims that Mohr-Corrigan's paper was "Research [*sic*], Owned, and Published Globally" by them (1).

Based on the comparative responses in the survey, it appears that the majority of SCSU and UNCG students would not recognize Ms. Mohr-Corrigan as an author if she were also a fellow student, and would thus likely give over her authorship rights quite easily to The Paper Store. Although 64% of SCSU students and 52.6% of UNCG students surveyed (here, a noted and troubling *decrease* in this response category) said that "writing a book or academic article" constitutes authorship, only 35% and 40% of students, respectively, thought that "writing a paper or project for a college course" constituted authorship as well. So it seems that even though students may recognize that academia produces authors, the responses indicate that only a little more than one third of the students considered *themselves* authors, even though all were in the process of writing an "academic" paper for English 101. Additionally, these comparative responses show that even fewer UNCG students—nearly 12% fewer—considered the two hallmarks of writing in academia—"a book or academic article"—true acts of authorship. Herein we see a very serious disconnect between faculty and student perceptions of authorship, in that most faculty aspire to write in one or both of these genres in order to secure their intellectual position in academia. Students, on the other hand, either devalue these instances of authorship, or lump them into the category of "useless academic writing," not understanding what writing in these genres may mean to *faculty*, and consequently, to academia—of which they are, as students, truly a part.

Although the economic "collaboration" between a student and the online paper mills is obviously outside the limits of traditional notions of authorship as defined in this survey or in college courses, one might postulate that students see this collaboration as a profitable one, with both the original author and the "new" author (the student who purchases the paper) receiving some sort of marginal intellectual credit. But SCSU and UNCG survey responses contradict the notion that students believe *any* sort of co-authorship leads to a legitimately "authored" piece of work. Only 36% of the SCSU participants felt that co-writing a project constituted authorship, exactly identical to the percentage of UNCG students surveyed. An even smaller, yet identical, percentage—only 6% of both SCSU and UNCG students alike—believed that "Gathering different sources and pasting them together as a collection of writing, then putting your name on that collection" constituted authorship, seemingly contradicting the notion that students do feel "ownership" over cut-and-paste written products. In addition to the fact that this perception of collaborative authorship has *not changed* between these populations and after seven years between surveys, the more obvious conclusion apparent here is that collaboration or co-writing is viewed by students (and some sectors of academia) as less than "true" authorship. As a result, one might postulate that the process by which students purchase papers also is not seen a *merging* of identities to form a combined authorship (i.e., buy that paper but put your own name on it and it becomes yours), but instead a wholesale lifting of another's identity for a singular purpose—the completion of a college assignment. Such lifting would, in theory, meet all requirements, as most of the sites explain that the papers are fully "researched" and include citations and bibliographies/works cited pages. Such lifting, however, would also negate students' own writerly identities—which, as I argued elsewhere in this book, are already at least partially negated in the typical teacher-centered classroom, as opposed to within online spaces led and controlled by the students themselves.

First-year composition students occasionally may view themselves as authors, and by extension infrequently view the papers they buy online as "authored," because they also place so little value in the actual work that they produce as college students, for reasons previously theorized in this chapter. Of the SCSU students, only about one third agreed that, "Most of the papers I have written for college courses could best be defined as . . . material that has no use outside the particular course or area of study." By comparison, a nearly identical percentage (34%) of UNCG students agreed with this statement, indicating little, if any, increased positive view of academic work in first-year composition since the 2001 survey, and in other writing courses as universally applicable to their educational goals. Only 26% of SCSU students and 30% of UNCG students felt that their academic papers contained "material that may be used in other situations, such as job or professional applications." The most interesting statistic, however, comes from the small percentage of respondents (SCSU, 11%; UNCG, 14.9%) who felt that their papers were "material that in no way represents who I am as a writer." In contrast, the Pink Monkey postings, especially the "how's my writing?" threads, show that students *do* believe in the value of writing for themselves, and for the praise and critique of their fellow students, in these publicly defined, extra-institutional spaces.

Therefore, this survey data appears to indicate a mismatch between student self-conceptions of potential authorship (the work *does* reflect who they are) and the assignment for which this work was produced (the work *does not* have future value). Based on the comparative responses to these particular questions, seven years after my first study, I believe we *still* need to discuss openly and extensively in our composition classes whether what we promote—student originality in writing and research—corresponds to the scope and value of the work assigned, as frequently pieces of writing that are not deemed valuable may become opportunities for simpler routes to "authorship" (i.e., the purchased paper).

The idea of authority and experience may be at risk as long as students are taught from generation to generation that original authorship does not matter. These students have no concept of "mastering" sources when they are instructed to only use sources as a means of double-checking the work of others, or shoring up an incomplete paper acquired from another source, namely the paper mills. Our continued emphasis on illustrating the hybridization of source material within academic work apparently is falling on deaf ears, as students consider the grade-based value of the final piece of writing, even when well informed by the writing and research of others. The paper in this thinking becomes a product with distinct attributes of "correctness" irrespective of its intellectual value or academic quality; this perception, of course, perpetuates the myth among composition students that "good" writing is nothing more than clean prose that may or may not be intellectually engaging. The "real" writing they do in other venues— such as online student-led spaces—is free from such scrutiny, and not responsible to research citation or other intellectually framed collages like academic collaboration.

Exacerbating this juxtaposition of students versus sources, and the complex rules by which students incorporate and value the words and ideas of others in their writing, are teachers in the humanities—many if not all among us—who have contributed to the idea that the author is not a student, or even a "regular" person, but an entity to be studied at arm's length, historicized for the college curriculum. English studies tends to emphasize in its literature courses the importance of a great number of deceased canonical authors; these authors, for example Shakespeare, Faulkner, and Fitzgerald, rise to a near-mythic status in high school, and subsequently college, curricula. Students are left to believe that authorship is connected to fame and not accessible to the lowly student, who is only good enough to *study* these authors from afar. Such attitudes seem implicit in the construction of Web sites such as Pink Monkey, wherein students voice viewpoints about canonical authors and texts that may not be welcomed within a more traditional, author-centered curriculum. In the case of paper mill patronage as well, the recognized person-product is the true marker of authorship. As Margaret Price points out in her call for a revision of plagiarism policy so as to consider the various *contexts* in which a piece of writing is produced, this person-product concept is key to academia's heralding of the historical author and his or her moment of creation, in that sometimes there exists "the issue of whether authors create texts or whether, perhaps, it is the other way around" (94), a point that recalls the discussion in chapter 2 of Dana Harrington's research on pre-nineteenth-century reading practices and the subsequent near-mythical elevation of the author figure.

Do our composition students, therefore, understand this concept of authorship—and the relationship among author, text, and reader—too *narrowly*, such that they might only see an "author" as this sort of published or publicized person, from whom only to cite, borrow, or, in this case, purchase, existing and successful work? Do these students believe that authorship comes as a complete package that is at once "creative" and economically attractive to others—neither of which is available to those completing routine writing assignments for college courses? Perhaps this conception of authorship exists among many first-year writers because the authoring we ask them to engage in is in the service of a product that they see as neither attractive nor valuable.

As a way of examining this perception among students that class work is without value in the "real" world, Horner warns that the reification of student writing as "fixed object" allows "the work produced in the classroom . . . to be seen as no more than preparatory 'practice' for meeting the demands of a world somehow more real yet outside the classroom and so outside of the control of those within it" (512). Such a concept reinforces the notion that schoolwork, or that which is assigned and completed within the parameters of the institution, is highly irrelevant to "real-world" reading and writing practices. This perception, I argue, is present in many facets of American schooling, not just the writing classroom. Although liberatory pedagogy seeks to overturn the notion of student writing as "fixed," for example, by giving it potential sociopolitical import, the position of most general education requirements, including first-year composition, itself assumes a "preparatory" status for "real" subject matter and coursework forthcoming in the latter stages of one's college education. And if we extend this theory to include the whole of college coursework through the senior year, one could easily argue that college as an *enterprise*, to many students, is simply "pre-work" necessary in order to gain employment; ergo, all work done within this preparatory environment is of limited use value.

Teachers themselves may inadvertently validate this thinking when they present *themselves* as fixed-knowledge vessels, those who understand the singular "truth" of a situation, problem, or idea, within or without an academic context. As Nick Tingle argues, employing a psychoanalytic approach, the teacher must avoid being "ego-autonomous," or too divested from the passion of the subject at hand and the pursuit of it in relation to the self. Tingle believes that "If [a student's] self-relation to the role of teacher is informed by a narcissistic investment in the idea of the self off the horse of the passions, [the student] is not likely to present this position, in his embodiment, as an ideal" (62). In other words, students must see teachers, like authors, as human beings invested in edification vis-à-vis research, analysis, and ultimately authorship. Writing must not simply be an "act" designed to fulfill classroom requirements. Of course, many scholars in composition have emphasized and continue to emphasize the valuation of student writing; as such, this point in my argument is not a new one. However, in terms of the already-growing distance between teachers and students, this dispassionate approach is especially risky, and reinforces the teacher-figure as controlling entity rather than fellow scholar and academic traveler. These dispassionate presenters of material and concepts seem to the new college writer to be too far removed from the work, such that engaging in it in a personalized, truth-seeking manner would contradict the "ideal" representation of scholarship. In Tingle's argument, students take away the lesson that academic work is only practice-based, and not character-driven, or ethically important to the development of self.

A necessary valuation of the student as academic author *and* ethical rhetor, and of the given assignment as *real* writing, integral to the student's understanding of his or her own authorship and thus his or her intellectual *self*, is thus one initial step in combating the popularity of online paper mills and avoiding what Howard terms "a qualitative hierarchy" of authorship, calculating "who is best and who is worst" (*Standing* 41), as represented by pieces of writing. Students are employing that scale as they comb the Internet, finding whole papers for sale that seem to be sold to them as the "best" as compared to their own "worst" attempts at authorship.

EVERYTHING'S FOR SALE: ACADEMIA MEETS CONSUMER CULTURE ONLINE

When papers with absent authors are sold online, certainly students and professors agree that this is considered to be plagiarism in academia's eyes. So in order to understand why students would still *buy* these papers, we need understand the slippery presentation of ownership versus authorship not only within these paper mill sites, but in our own popular culture and its economic exchange system, including how faculty understand—or profess to understand—what it means to create an "original" and *quality* text to "own" as an author. In my own discussions of teaching materials and research findings with colleagues, particularly those new to the teaching of first-year composition, I often hear queries such as "can I *steal* that assignment?" or "do you think I could use that syllabus as a *model* (or a *template*)?" New graduate students teaching writing are often encouraged to use a standard syllabus, set by the program's Writing Program Administrator, and divert little if any from its trajectory; such also is the case sometimes at community colleges, where the sheer number of new adjunct faculty rotating in each semester leads to a standard syllabus for the first-year course, one that has no "author" but is appropriated by all.

Sometimes this practice is taking to confusing extremes, evidencing that even graduate students—whom we assume possess a more sophisticated definition of authorship—may not always understand the boundaries of textual ownership. A former teaching assistant of mine at SCSU, for example, took my first-year research writing syllabus wholesale—and then proceeded to present it at a local writing conference as her "own," detailing its construction from the position of *author*, not at all understanding the concept—even though I was sitting right there, in the audience, during her presentation. She had interned with me, but had not helped in any way to write the syllabus; apparently because she assisted in that course's instruction and delivery, she felt the syllabus was subsequently now "hers" for the taking in future courses in which she was the sole instructor, and was therefore also *authored* by her.

Similarly—although in a clearly more institutionally sanctioned manner—in creative writing courses, teachers often encourage students to "mimic" canonical authors so as to internalize traditional styles and to understand the value of voice and poetic form, even though the creative writing community in general fails to recognize this as formulaic or derivative once the story, poem, or play built of this mimicry is complete. Many creative writing classes—including my own—include some sort of exercise on "found" poems (built with lines from other published poems, without attribution), or an exercise on voice and/or persona, asking students to assume the vocal position of another author or public figure within their own writing. These are only select examples of how the creative, collaborative notion of intellectual production in the humanities often leads to "borrowing" ideas back and forth, between complicit and entirely well-meaning individuals, few of whom would consider themselves to be "unoriginal" in thought or practice, and none of whom would likely be construed as a "criminal," in the ways we readily construct students who plagiarize.

Certainly in other disciplines outside English studies, such as music, students understand the widespread use of electronic *sampling* as homage to other artists, with such samples melded seamlessly into one's own work in the studio. David Sanjek questions whether "anyone with an available library of recordings, a grasp of recorded musical history, and a talent for ingenious collage can call themselves a creator of music, [and if so] is it the case that the process and the product no longer possess the meanings once assigned them?" (345). Woodmansee more broadly argues that the "economic model" governing copyright "justifies protection only insofar as it promotes social welfare by providing an incentive to create and/or distribute new works" and builds on the "'natural law model,' in which copyright merely confirms a preexisting entitlement" to authorship ("Introduction" 5). How many of these words and supporting legal concepts are then retranslated in a different context, or with differing impetus, when a student seeks to complete a paper assignment but can't quite seem to do it "right?" Even when students understand that taking the intellectual and artistic property of others without acknowledgment or consent is *wrong*, they might not clearly understand why it is wrong when said product is for *sale* on the Internet. When students then make that final leap, as part of a consumer culture, to see writing as a "product" designed to fulfill a distinct purpose in a college course, how far must those students leap to arrive at the conclusion that like many other items in our culture offered online for sale, this product, too, can be bought?

Economic precedents for the commerce of writing, built upon existent writing-for-hire conditions in our larger culture, complicate notions of authorship. If a student logs on to an online paper mill and buys a paper that was put there by another student or *paid* contributor, thereby entering into a *business transaction* agreed on by both parties, the consumer-minded student, unable to distinguish authorship from ownership, might wonder, where is the "stealing" in this transaction? Consider taking this logic even further: A student who appropriates a published online article or similar piece of writing available on the Web without that author's permission is indeed both "cheating" and "stealing" because he or she seeks to defraud both his or her audience and the author who originally wrote and posted the work. But a student who buys a paper with the author's permission has *stolen* nothing; the student has appropriated another's authorship for academically dishonest ends—with the express permission (via payment received) of the author, or the agency (paper mill) representing that author.

This kind of logic obviously conflicts with attitudes in academia regarding authorship as an intellectual activity. As Alice Roy points out in her investigation of faculty attitudes toward plagiarism, often the definitions include "taking something that belongs to someone else," and "making something seem like your own" (58–59). But she also argues that the idea of the "fixed, immutable text" makes certain questions prudent in a broader discussion of plagiarism, including "Where is the text? Who's got it? Whom does it represent?" and, importantly, "who controls it?" (56). She goes on to argue, "plagiarism assumes the concreteness of texts, the reality of authorship" (56). Underlying the faculty definitions of plagiarism is a clear sense of when it is "wrong" to take someone else's work: when one is working in the intellectual parameters of academia, which values authorship. Students, however, in their quest to see college as an economic and "practical" (which here serves as the antithesis of "intellectual") enterprise, do not envision "authenticity" as a prioritized term of their discourse.

Andrea Lunsford and Susan West recognize this student discourse as they approach the issue of writing-for- sale in the context of a larger argument about intellectual property, and the risk posed to research and inquiry by proposed laws governing copyright and ownership of ideas. In their article, "Intellectual Property and Composition Studies," Lunsford and West question the long-term implications of recent copyright infringement suits, even under "fair-use" educational purposes (384–85). They specifically interrogate the acceptance of "possessive ownership as normal" and the way in which this idea leads to "student adherence to an increasingly strong protectionist view of copyright" while it "hinder(s) educators' use of the Internet to pique student curiosity and blunt its value as a research tool for everyone" (386). Lunsford and West argue that such government regulation of text "ownership" will limit students' and teachers' ability to dialogue with sources in their own scholarship.

But Lunsford and West also acknowledge the dangerous messages that this sort of legislation would send to composition students in particular as these students, new to academic discourse, must consider who "owns" ideas and from whom one can *acquire* ideas in a commercial rather than intellectual exchange. They argue such legislation demonstrates the following:

> [L]anguage can be owned, cordoned off and protected from tres-passers, *bought and sold like parcels of real estate*—whether by an autonomous and stable Romantic author/genius or by a multinational corporate author/surrogate who claims the absolute right to control of dissemination and use—must be scrutinized by teachers of writing everywhere. (390, emphasis added)

When we apply this hypothesis to the online paper mills, clearly the agents who are using students' trust in the rhetoric of student-centered Internet Web sites are selling papers "like parcels of real estate." The "multinational corporate author/surrogate" are the paper mill companies, which indeed "claim the absolute right" over the *original* author of the paper for sale, as examined earlier in this chapter in the example of the Paper Store and Lori Mohr-Corrigan. Mohr-Corrigan serves as a "work-for-hire" author in Lunsford and West's terms, much as they argue that English studies scholars must sell their work to journals in the form of copyright (390).

Although Lunsford and West make a direct connection between their ideas about intellectual property and the online paper mills, they do not extend this point beyond a mention near the close of their article, chiefly due to the relatively infancy of the Internet at the time of their writing.

They acknowledge that "Term paper mills (now available on the Web) have for many years been a thriving cottage industry . . . students buy academic essays in much the same way they would purchase a chair . . . as something they have paid 'good money' for and can now call their own" (399). The argument here, with which I strongly agree, is that as our culture increasingly privileges the property values of texts—including, perhaps, that which is bought and sold under unethical circumstances—students will increasingly see their own writing and the writing of others as nothing more than commodity itself. The critical point in our students' lives that requires further study is when the academic concept of authorship—as well as the everyday practice of authoring one's own words and valuing that process—is negated, and the economic concept of paper-for-sale takes hold. Additionally, when we reinforce with the students the idea that their academic writing is primarily and significantly assigned, read, and evaluated by the teacher-figure, from whom the student continues to be further and further disconnected, as this book argues, we risk negatively reifying academic writing as *only* a context-driven practice, susceptible to end-around completion strategies, such as authorship-for-hire.

Because current culture has constructed authorship in economic terms, students are not as troubled about the consequences of their paper mill patronage as are the faculty who assign the work for which papers are purchased. To faculty, plagiarism represents not only a violation of course ethics, but also a violation of teacherly *control*, in ways that are understandable and with which most can sympathize, especially given the traditional structures of higher education. As Robillard has noted, even though composition studies has researched issues of plagiarism and issues of emotion, these two strands have failed to come together to augment one another. Robillard argues that "the barriers to an understanding of plagiarism's affective effects are thick and invisible" ("We Won't Be Fooled" 10). She notes that "we cannot contribute to treat plagiarism as a writerly issue without also considering the role of the reader," as "plagiarism is a form of authorship to which readers respond affectively" (11). Robillard believes that "Because composition studies persuades teachers to enact a particular kind of emotional relationship to students and their writing, teachers who respond angrily to plagiarism or suspected plagiarism find themselves defending conflicting values of their institution and their discipline" (13).

This concern over public displays of emotion—specifically anger—as antithetical to "good" teaching also intersects with the perception that "good" teachers of writing—and particularly first-year writing—must respond to their students' work with a more humanistic approach than do other teachers within the academy. First-year writing (and reading) instruction herein again bears the tremendous weight described elsewhere in this book: Teachers in these classrooms must be authoritative, yet must emphasize the personal and personal–political connections found in the writing process. Teachers must also suppress their own classroom disappointments where students' writing integrity is concerned, such that when plagiarism occurs, the response is institutional, rather than emotional or personal.

This stands in sharp contrast to the kind of personal and even emotional reactions to writing and discourse that students receive on sites such as Pink Monkey, or even the emotional landscape on display in teacher evaluation commentary on Rate My Professors, which is discussed in the next chapter. Robillard's assertions regarding the *readerly* aspect of plagiarism is equally important to an understanding of paper mill patronage; she promotes the idea that students who plagiarize produce texts that *have no* readers, or that their readers are not *affected* by what these students produce/write—that such work is entirely invalid as a piece of writing if it violates the codes and ethics of academia. Such a perception—that the reader only exists for certain types of writing, and writers—is obviously not going to lead to generative progress in terms of helping students to become authors.

Many faculty—particularly, we may observe, *contingent* faculty who have far less long-term authority over students and courses, given their liminal status within the institution itself—obviously fear the clear and rising tide of plagiarism as a direct threat to their classroom authorities and the integrity of their instruction. Perhaps faculty have some reason to be concerned, although reports and statistics vary. As Mark Edmundson notes in a piece in *The New York Times*, a study of 18,000 students nationwide conducted by Donald McCabe showed that "38 percent of the students polled had committed 'cut and paste' plagiarism . . . 40 percent admitted to copying without attribution from written sources. In the last such survey [three years' prior] only 10 percent of students admitted to cheating" (A29).

If the survey results I collected are any indication, however, the *enforcement* of ethics, codes, and academic honesty regulations in the classroom have become more successful, or at least more prevalent—as students report. In 2001, 39% of students surveyed reported that their peers who cheated had been "Sometimes been caught and punished by the teacher or professor," compared with 51.2% of students in 2008 who reported that this was the case. Comparatively, in 2001, 83% of students reported that peers who cheated were punished by "Failure of the paper or exam for which the cheating was done," in 2008, 91% of students reported this to be the case. Finally, although only 14% reported in 2001 that students who cheated received "Higher disciplinary action (such as academic probation) or expulsion from school," 20% of students in the 2008 survey reported that this was the case for their peers.

But faculty who believe that a rise in enforcement levels are a positive indication of the lessening problem of plagiarism, whole text or otherwise, may be fooling themselves—much as law enforcement does when it equates more drug-related arrests to a lessening of drug-related crime over-all. Some faculty may concomitantly believe that using services such as tur-nitin.com to raise these figures regarding enforcement is a good use of one's time may be further compromising or even significantly altering their own pedagogy in favor of entering a lose–lose electronic universe, as many critics of this for-profit enterprise have noted. In addition to risking their own breaches of ethics,[29] faculty who use systems such as turnitin.com may be engaging in a process that mimics a dog chasing its tail, as Internet-based plagiarism shows no sign of dissipating simply due to increased detection efforts or other internal deterrence systems.[30] Furthermore, although the results of the survey may indicate a greater attention to *enforcement*, the other student responses show no significant change in *attitudes* toward plagiarism or academic dishonesty itself. Additionally, using electronic resources, especially Web-based ones, to combat electronic methods of plagiarism would seem to miss the larger point about how and why students interact online in the first place, as these methods assume the Internet, again, to be a site for negative capa-bility in one sense—in regard to student writing—and positive capability in another, in terms of available punitive technologies. Nowhere in this dichotomy is there room for *truly* positive, intellectual discourse in elec-tronic environments, even though it is clearly taking place within and among online student communities.

For example, even though only 4% of all SCSU students in the original survey reported never knowing anyone who had cheated in school, only 1.4% of UNCG students surveyed in 2008—nearly zero, in whole num-bers—reported the same. Regarding Question 4, ("In my opinion, it is acceptable for me to cheat in school if . . .") 73% of SCSU students also answered, paradoxically, that "It is never acceptable for me to cheat," whereas 81% of UNCG students responded in kind. Most alarming here is the decrease in the number of students who do not know anyone who has cheated in school, next to the *increase* in the number of students who state that it is "never acceptable" to cheat themselves. With these data, one might wonder where all these purported plagiarists are. Certainly, these surveyed students may allow cheating to go on around them but do not report it, or may be the students who themselves cheat in private, under certain circumstances, but recognize internally that their behavior is inap-propriate, even if it goes unreported or undetected. In either case, it seems highly unlikely that these particular survey respondents are among the tiny percentage of students who, in truth, have "never cheated" themselves. There is a clear lack of recognition among these students, who are only a representative sample, but a true, live group nonetheless, that the two responses are highly incompatible with the real-life academic dishonesty that we know, from our own teaching experiences, takes place within their academic and social peer groups.

We may hypothesize that such students—those "morally" ashamed of their cheating but also compelled to cheat if the academic situation warrants it—are those who may be the most susceptible to the online paper mills. The anonymous purchasing power that these students have circumvents not only the authority of the teacher and assignment, but also the ability of their friends to detect and report such behavior, and by extension the student's need to rely on others known to him or her (getting answers to a test, borrowing a previously written "A" paper) for the act of academic dishonesty. When working within the parameters of online purchasing, certainly there is no teacher-figure oversight, as there implicitly is within the school system and on-the-ground cheating. And with the advent of purchasing technologies such as Paypal (now accepted by sites such as Collegepaperxchange.com), students need not even have a credit card to buy goods online. The transaction is seductively seamless, without apparent harm to the buyer or the seller, and entirely outside the purview of teacher or other institutional authority.

Thus, students not only are conflicted internally about what constitutes cheating, and whether it is acceptable to police one's peers in the service of agreed on ethical academic standards; they also are clearly sent mixed messages from our consumer culture about what is acceptable to download, purchase, or appropriate, and are even fooling themselves, perhaps, that such purchasing/downloading/appropriation is not *really* happening, or that they will never do this kind of thing *themselves*. Given these internally persuasive discourses at work, it seems naïve to think that Internet-based cheating, including online paper mill patronage, will disappear if only we as faculty become technologically "smart" about cheating, employ similar electronic measures to police the patronage of paper mill Web sites, or continue dismissing the patronage of online paper mills as an extreme act of academic dishonesty that lies outside authorship or intellectual property discussions, or their students' general motivations and abilities, altogether. We should instead pay attention to these messages that originated in academia about the Internet, and which the online paper mills appropriate in their business-based discourse with students. These messages center on the ease of electronic information and the relative value of academic writing or "original" thought production inside this electronic universe. Although sites such as Pink Monkey positively incorporate the notion of free exchange, and thus paradoxically provide students with an intellectually driven site of discourse that deliberately eschews the student–teacher–classroom dynamic, the online paper mills capitalize on the concept of "sharing" as a mechanism for devaluing and erasing the origins of a text, as well as eliminating the speaker/writer/rhetor *behind* that text. Such sharing is far from "free," as its byproduct is the erasure of student agencies within and without the virtual environment in which the text is exchanged (for profit).

If the 2008 survey results are at all representative, students clearly continue to have a complex relationship with writing and authorship that can lead to the patronage of paper mills, or engagement in other academically dishonest acts, as they are neither interested in nor afraid of faculty or institutional detection methods rooted in such contradictory messages about intellectual property, recognizing at some level the push–pull between capitalistic notions of property and academic notions of reading, writing, and textual production. First-year students elect to take calculated chances in order to assimilate into a new, often overwhelming academic community, and are particularly willing to compromise their own agencies and risk their ethical reputations in order to achieve the singular end of academic "success" resulting from the submission and positive evaluation of a written product, even if it that product is not their own. These same students, however, *are* certainly interested in and persuaded by arguments put forth by the online paper mills, as these appeal to their own doubts about higher education, those lacking recognition as viable within the classroom setting. These are as follow: (a) college is a waste of time; (b) the written product (term paper, essay, research project) is indeed a *product* in economic terms, interchangeable by owner and authored by none; and (c) in the Internet age, with a variety of resources available online for the trade and sale of the written product, the author is more than dead—he or she never even existed. The paper-for-sale product floats in cyberspace like so many other products, on sites quite similar to those selling legitimate products to the same eighteen- to twenty-five-year-old target demographic.

Michael Pemberton has estimated that, based only on the number of customized papers purchased online per year (approximately 16,000), in the course of a four- or five-year college degree, one in seven hundred students will buy a paper from an online paper mill ("Threshold of Desperation" 144). This number does not take into account the number of papers *previously written and on file* with the paper mill companies, written on "stock" topics (from common literature assignments such as Shakespeare's plays to more general social topics frequently debated, such as gun control). Nor does the number take into account the growing number of free-exchange sites offered online, which serve as a virtual swap meet minus the monetary transaction. So the total number of students engaging in the commerce of online paper mill activity is undoubtedly many times higher than this one in seven hundred estimate, even if the profile of the sites themselves is low by comparison. The companies are operating for all intents and purposes anonymously (try finding the webmaster's name for any of the paper mill sites) but with the bravado of a high-profile corporation, as they hoodwink their customers into believing that cheating is "OK" for a variety of reasons. These include blaming professors for not creating new writing assignments; blaming universities for assigning too much work that students cannot complete without "help";

blaming the overall economic structure of the country for requiring students to be "well-rounded" in various careers, which leads universities to offer needless general education courses, for which they do not have time to write papers, for which professors hand out the same assignments again and again . . . you get the idea.

And this is exactly the rhetoric we use in our professional discussions of plagiarism and paper mills: We should write original, compelling assignments so that they won't be recycled; we should be sensitive to student pressures and stress when we assign work; we should think carefully about our general education requirements and work to "streamline" courses for budget needs as well as student interests. It is shocking to think that perhaps the instructors and the paper mill proprietors are having the same discussion; the difference is, the paper mills are using this reasoning to make money on student fears and insecurities related to writing in college. Paper mills run on this rhetoric of blame, and in the process, convince students that paying just a little—or maybe a lot—for a product that they really *deserve* to have, that will never be detected by this thoughtless, careless system, is not only acceptable but the standard means by which one completes a college degree. This is a powerful package that students buy into, lacking other compelling dialogues about authorship, ethical representation, or their own institutional authority—which could be enhanced through active intellectual engagement with community members and texts—within the system of higher education.

An examination of the paper mill sites reveals that their commerce with students is built on long-standing student suspicions of how much writing is ultimately valued in an academic setting, and how much trust one can actually invest in the teacher-figure as an authority on what is good, valuable, or worthwhile an enterprise within the larger pursuit of the college degree. For example, the rationale on Swaptermpapers.com, just one of several sites allowing students to trade in an essay of their own for another essay from the company free of charge (and also enabling those unfortunates without an essay for trade to purchase one from the database instead) is: "Every student has written term papers, essays and book reports that are lying around without any value. We put value on your work!" (www.swaptermpapers.com/aboutus.htm). The message being sent here is that only students can be trusted to make college work ultimately valuable, since the primary long-term function of academic work is to collect dust—as papers even as we speak are "lying around" the house, serving no *real* purpose once class is finished. Every time a box of unclaimed student portfolios sits in a departmental hallway, or a paper is handed back with summative evaluation ("good work: B"), or as I discuss in Chapter 4, a student evaluation of a particular course is dropped into the abyss of an office drawer, unread, we see this suspicion being validated by students *and* teachers, and the value-less principle thereby being enacted.

Another point of argument on the sites, drawing from student perceptions of the value of their own work, is that paper mills serve as deserved "assistance" in writing, a substitute for the tedious task of actual learning via research, in the absence of caring, dedicated teachers. Such declarations of proven assistance are put forward as 'true' in purpose, even while the sites, in their graphics and visual design, privately wink at the students regarding the falsity of this claim reliability for students facing academic distress. The sites' caring outreach to students sounds like any other consumer-driven business seeking a loyal customer base; in the case of paper mills, that customer base is made up of insecure, desperate student writers who do not feel their original ideas are good enough for the grades and course credits they hope to accumulate, and who distrust their teachers to be there for them in the writing process. Pink Monkey participants harbor similar suspicions—that some teachers are unable or unwilling to truly give students classroom authority in the reading and discussion of texts, let alone assistance in interpreting them in written assignments. But the paper mills use such suspicions to remove teacher authority from not only the discussion, but also the *evaluation,* of a written text, as purchased papers are advertised to be "A" level, or of "superior quality," thereby being *already vetted* for performative purposes.

Amazingly, some paper mill sites interrogate this very idea of doing "original" work in their online discourse, highlighting their "authentic" research papers as smart alternatives not only to doing one's own work, but also to the temptation of "cut-and-paste" that leads to *less professional, legitimate* papers. This ironic claim is likely in response to the proliferation of scholarship on and news coverage of the spread of Internet plagiarism, specifically cut-and-paste work that sites such as turnitin.com seek to detect. One site, AuthenticEssays.com, seeks to persuade students of the quality and "authenticity" of its work:

> Authentic is more than a word for us. When you order custom essays from AuthenticEssays, you can be 100% sure that you will receive *a truly authentic work*—we do provide refunds if our customers find even a couple of sentences in the paper ordered that came word for word from some outside source without giving proper references. . . . Customer satisfaction is our primary goal . . . *thus superior quality is something you can always count on* when you buy essays from us. Besides providing you with a money back guarantee in case you detect *copy pasted material* in your paper, we have prepared more treats for our clients. If you like the quality of our custom writing service, we have a lot of special offers and discounts, which means that *our customers can save money* ordering their custom written essays from AuthenticEssays. Besides, we can help even in the most critical situation—our staff writers are able to complete your paper within 12 hours if needed. (www.authentic.essays.com, emphasis added)

Obviously, myriad consumerist messages abound in this statement. First, the site speaks to student's fears of "quality"—a legitimate question when patronizing the paper mills. It assures "superior quality," assumedly as opposed to other paper mill sites that let the consumers/students down in this regard. Second, the site appeals to the "good bargain" of buying a paper online—emphasizing that "customers can save money" through special offers and discounts that come from *repeat* patronage of the site; this appeal alone points to the suspicion among faculty that once a student buys a paper, he or she is "hooked" until the point of detection/punishment occurs—if it ever does. Finally, AuthenticEssays offers immediate, time-sensitive help with assignments; in other words, not only can students buy from this site, they can do so at the last minute—for example, the night before the assignment is due. Again, the site's explicit rhetorical sensitivity to typical student practices—namely, extreme procrastination—sounds a lot more sympathetic than the teacher who says there will be a penalty for late work, even if the extra day or two taken, in the student's mind, would make all the difference in the quality of the writing. Indeed, the voice here is a sympathetic teacher-substitute of sorts, a voice online not found (for good reason, perhaps) in the physical classroom space.

But the most disturbing message sent here that links customer satisfaction with academic notions of authorship is the initial claim for which the Web site is named—that the work is "authentic" and that *refunds* are provided if "even a couple of sentences" in the paper are "word for word" from another source. What does this communicate to students about wholesale plagiarism versus other types of "cheating" that are more easily detectable, and more readily discussed in our student handbooks, our course syllabi, and in our culture's popular presses? What further does it communicate about how to navigate the often delicate weaving of source material into student-authored papers in order to build that fabled "conversation" in the essay? Should students simply not bother—or else risk, taking this statement out of context, the "word-for-word" clause indicating plagiarism?

Clearly, the distinction is made here between whole, "legitimate" authorship—by a paid individual working for AuthenticEssays.com—and "illegitimate" authorship—that which comes from using sources *word for word inside* the purchased paper, an ironic turn on concepts of "intentional" and "unintentional" plagiarism and Howard's research and scholarship on patchwriting, for example. On this site, the company slogans that appear at the top of the page (alongside a happy snowboarder sailing high above the text) are "live life while we work" and "let professionals do your paper." These alluring slogans stem from two common feelings among students—that "life" is different from "work" (and school), and that "professionals" are the preferred source for paper-writing; students aren't even part of the writing equation.

Geniuspapers.com takes this notion of "professional" authorship-for-hire one step further by pointing out on the front page of its Web site just how often its work has appeared in public discourse. This is most likely discourse related to plagiarism, but note how that key detail is omitted here for the student audience. The text reads:

> For over 7 years, Genius Papers has been one of the biggest and most comprehensive research companies on the Web. Not only have we been featured in more publications, conferences, and educational briefings than virtually any other paper assistance service in existence, we have also been included within the top 10 term paper and book report listings of just about every major search engine on the Internet. (www.geniuspapers.com)

Genius Papers additionally claims to have been "featured" in popular news publications such as *The Seattle Times* and *The Washington Post* and on channels such as *CNN*. The sly visual organization of the site lists these publications and corporations on the sidebar, appearing as *sponsors* would on other Web sites backed by "legitimate" companies. Again, the language of commerce justifies the anti-academic product of the site, custom-written papers for sale.

As most students will not know what "publications, conferences, and educational briefings" mean in the context of current research into academic dishonesty, the proud claim here implies that the services of Genius Papers are so valuable that "educational briefings" somehow *emphasize* the quality of the company's service. Genius Papers claims to be cited more than "any other paper assistance service in existence" and is "within the top 10 term paper" listings available on the Internet. The appeal here is to notions of authority—why use other paper mill companies when this one is the "best" (or so it claims)? Why use other companies when this one is part of myriad "conferences" that highlight its services? Genius Papers obviously wants to rise above its own competition—and its competition is vast.[31] But it also wants to appeal to student customers to see its services as *more legitimate* than others, again equating "quality" and legitimacy—a word antithetical to plagiarism. It is a tricky enthymeme that Genius Papers ultimately employs: "Publications, conferences, and educational briefings" are where "legitimate" teachers and scholars work; a degree is for gaining legitimacy; Genius Papers is cited in these legitimate settings; therefore, Genius Papers will make students successful in the "legitimate" work world, because students alone cannot do this in their own writing. At no point, however, does Genius Papers acknowledge that co-opting one of its "original" papers might constitute plagiarism as well.

If our students can be aided in understanding these powerful con games that play on our consumer culture, why are we waiting to have these important conversations? If we start talking with our students about the *value* of writing, and the writing process, and start attending more explicitly in our research to the persuasive power of the paper mills that de-value this process and further alienate, intellectually and socioculturally, the teacher from the student both inside and outside the classroom, we might indeed, in Horner's terms, begin the difficult yet necessary *intellectual* journey of "joining with our students to investigate writing as social and material practice" (526).

CONCLUSION: ASK THE STUDENT-AUTHOR(S)

Revisiting my 2001 survey after a seven-year period has proven to be an eye-opening exercise in the stability of college student perceptions of writing and authorship. With little exception, the UNCG survey responses in 2008 were statistically identical, or nearly so, to those provided by SCSU students in 2001. Given these statistics—which I anticipated, but not to such a degree—I believe it's important to conclude this chapter with a slightly different frame than I did in 2005. The seemingly immovable perceptions of first-year students, even given the likely flaws of the survey instrument itself, indicate to me that we have progressed very little in our attempt to provide students with a greater appreciation of their own abilities and promise as authors, and have perhaps also stalled in our pursuit of the first-year writing course as a site of intellectual and sociopolitical writerly growth, as I posited in Chapter 1.

One element of the survey that *does* demonstrate notable change, however, is in student responses to both their use of the Internet as a research/scholarship tool, a predictable result given the progression of electronic communication between 2001 and 2008, but a notable finding nonetheless. Whereas in 2001, 54% of the SCSU students surveyed found the Internet a "necessary and beneficial" tool in their research, 68% of the UNCG students in the 2008 survey answered in kind. Similarly, whereas in 2001, 45% of SCSU students surveyed noted that "sometimes I use the Internet, sometimes I don't" in research and writing, in 2008, only 26.5% of the UNCG students surveyed agreed. That is a nearly 50% *drop* in the percentage of students who have a passive/nonregular relationship with electronic resources and/or the Internet in their research for academic writing projects. Finally, although a relatively small percentage—7%—of SCSU students surveyed in 2001 stated that the Internet is "not an option for me, either because I don't have Internet access or don't like using the Internet," a nearly invisible percentage of UNCG students in 2008—0.5%—said the same. These findings rather obviously support the hypothesis that the

Internet is a very visible and important part of our students' lives, as well as the hypothesis that most college students at these types of institutions, at least, own or have regular access to the Internet (at other institutional types, these results may differ).

I reinforce these perhaps predictable numbers to emphasize the fact that students *do* consider electronic communication and electronic resources a non-negotiable part of their lives; the fact that although these statistics regarding computer usage have increased, while the other responses in the survey regarding academic dishonesty and plagiarism/cheating have stayed virtually the same, indicates that our methodologies designed to prevent plagiarism and encourage academic authorship are (a) not necessarily working and (b) need to greater account for students' relationship with digital resources and online communities.

Specifically, I think these survey results as a whole indicate a need for a far more aggressive approach to both the teaching of writing as a study in authorship, as Rebecca Moore Howard has experimented with in her undergraduate and graduate courses at Syracuse University, and to more readily and openly regard students *as* authors who must understand and analyze those processes and theories proposed *about them*, as the work of Doug Downs and Elizabeth Wardle and their "Writing about Writing" design for the first-year composition course attempts to do.[32] In the public/nonacademic venue, we now also have the aggregate work of composition studies scholars who sponsor the intellectual work of undergraduates *outside* the classroom (or as stemming from original classroom work) in the undergraduate journal *Young Scholars in Writing*. These scholars have attempted to bridge the connections between student classroom agencies, teacher authority, and the larger enterprise of the first-year course, connections that when flawed or absent lead to potential patronage of these online paper mills.

Ed White, in "Student Plagiarism as an Institutional and Social Issue," warns of the following:

> The response to theft cannot be merely individual. . . . Indeed, we should all expect that much plagiarism will naturally occur unless we help students understand what all the fuss is about; many students simply are clueless about the issue and many faculty think the issue is simpler than it is. Taking moral high ground is important and necessary, but, as with other moral issues, too many of the statements from that ground are hypocritical and not cognizant of the complex motives behind student actions. (207)

White makes it clear that we must combat plagiarism from two sides, "prevention through education as well as punishment for violations" (206). He believes that things will never change unless we help to change them by *educating* the "violators," our students. Like White, I am not against punishment, nor do I believe that it alone will stop plagiarism, or that punishment, for some, teaches any long-term lessons. Those who do not *want* to learn how authorship builds and validates a writer's identity will find ways *not* to listen, and those who are the furthest from the voice of the teacher-figure will find ways to distance themselves even further. Thus, although I agree with Woodmansee's astute observation that "authorship does not exist to innocent eyes; they see only writing and texts" (1), I also recognize that some students—including a few of my own—will remain willfully "innocent" unless, until, and sometimes despite having been proven "guilty."

But there surely is more to this problem than detection and punishment, or even discussion and understanding. At a very fundamental level, first-year student writers are *not seeing* their position as a valued one within the course, or within the university—and perhaps not even within the framework of the teacher and his or her specific course plan. It would seem difficult to convince a student not to plagiarize, not to escape to the seductive online spaces of the welcoming paper mills, if that student sees little value in the enterprise of writing itself, let alone the enterprise of the first-year course as a general education requirement. Certainly, plagiarism happens in other academic courses—and perhaps at an even greater rate; such research, again, is out of my field of expertise—but I am willing to believe that academic dishonesty is certainly not limited to writing courses, or the first-year writing course in particular. The very enterprise of first-year writing, however, suffers the greatest insult when student writers choose to plagiarize the work done within the course, as first-year writing aims to be often politically and socially liberating, per Freirean methods; intellectually comprehensive, per general education guidelines; and institutionally conforming, per public standards of correctness and larger university graduation goals (i.e., senior assessments and alumni surveys).

The latter of these aims has been amply covered by scholars such as Susan Miller and Sharon Crowley, and has been understood to be the main "problem" with the continued viability of first-year writing, via an historical-institutional framework. The second of these aims has been discussed by scholars across composition studies as being problematic as well, as the first-year course is neither a "one-stop fix-it" shop nor an "introduction to all academic discourse" site of instruction. But the first of these aims—to liberate students and allow the course to thus rise above its other two lesser (from an intellectual standpoint) aims—has been far less critically examined, and not at all comprehensively addressed in terms of plagiarism research.

Ultimately, I believe that what we have been doing thus far, particularly where online paper mills and online student discourse about writing are concerned, is *not working*. We *do* have to take note of the now-slippery state of authorship vis-à-vis the expanding Internet, and be diligent about teaching our students that plagiarism is wrong and that academic ethics mean something. But let us not use the exponential—and seemingly unstoppable—growth power of online paper mills as an excuse to give up on the idea of *singular student authorship* altogether; let us instead take this opportunity to revisit theories of authorship with our students and reinforce the value of the writer-author both as an individual and as part of the larger academic community. Although cheating may arise from a complicated notion of self-worth and academic (in)ability, the purchase of essays from online companies strikes an even more basic chord in our students: the power to purchase this worth and ability, and by extension a new academic identity, one that they do not find in their day-to-day interactions with their physical institutions and those institutions' rules and values.

We should continue, in our response to instances of plagiarism, to see the composition classroom as a site for "responsible writing and learning" (White 210) on the part of teachers and students alike. Instead of further sublimating the author ourselves, we should work to solidify our students' ideas of authorship, and their identities as writers, so that if—or when—they visit an online paper mill, they will not be persuaded to erase their writing identity in favor of a good academic bargain. Students and teachers should work to find a way, together, despite their inevitable and growing social and cultural separation, to shape how the ethics of the writing classroom, and the larger university, should operate. In my next chapter, I discuss how the site Rate My Professors seeks to make public the real need for that collective work, where effective teaching and learning are concerned.

APPENDIX

Survey of Student Opinions on Academic Dishonesty in English 101 at SCSU (2001) and UNCG (2008)

1. **When I hear the word "cheating" I think of:**

   a. Copying answers from another student during an exam or in-class work (96%, 98.1%)

   b. Copying lecture notes from another student when I have missed class, then using those notes in a paper or on an exam (11.0%, 11.6%)

   c. Getting help outside of class from another student when writing a paper or take-home exam (30.0%, 24.2%)

   d. Asking another student or a friend to write a paper for me (79%, 87.9%)

e. Buying a paper from an outside source, either a company or an individual (83.0%, 86.5%)

f. Taking source material from the Internet and using it as my own in a paper or take-home exam (71%,74.0%)

g. Taking source material from books, magazine, or journals and using it as my own in a paper or take-home exam (69.0%,67.4%)

h. Using a professor's lecture material as my own in a paper or take-home exam without naming my professor as a source (53.0%,60.0%)

i. Bring notes to a closed-book, in-class examination (73%,79.5%)

j. Other (please specify): _____
   (5.0%,2.8%)

2. **In my experience, students I have known who have cheated in school have:**

a. Always been caught and punished by the teacher or professor (3.0%, 3.3%)

b. Always been caught and punished by someone outside the school (such as a parent) (2.0%, 1.0%)

c. Sometimes been caught and punished by the teacher or professor (39.0%, 51.2%)

d. Sometimes been caught and punished by someone outside the school (13.0%, 19.5%)

e. Seldom been caught or punished by the teacher or professor (51.0%, 46.5%)

f. Seldom been caught or punished by someone outside the school (15.0%, 22.3%)

g. Never been caught or punished by the teacher or professor (22.0%, 17.2%)

h. Never been caught or punished by anyone outside of school (22.0%, 12.6%)

i. I have never known anyone who has cheated in school (4.0%, 2.3%)

3. **The typical punishment for students I have known who have cheated has been:**

a. Failure of the paper or exam for which the cheating was done (83.0%, 92.1%)

b. Failure of the course in which the cheating was done (18.0%, 14.0%)

  c. Higher disciplinary action (such as academic probation) or expulsion from school (14.0%, 20.0%)

  d. No punishment, but the student has dropped the class or has dropped out of school (2.0%, 1.9%)

  e. No punishment at all; no consequences for the student (13.0%, 11.2%)

4. **In my opinion, it is acceptable for me to cheat in school if:**

  a. I am short on time and the assignment is due; if I don't cheat, I won't finish the work (10.0%, 7.0%)

  b. I am under other personal stresses (such as relationship or family problems) that keep me from doing the work on my own (11.0%, 7.4%)

  c. I am confused about the subject and can't do the work well on my own (13.0%, 11.2%)

  d. I am uninterested in the subject and don't care if I do the work well, or if I do it myself (7.0%, 2.8%)

  e. I will be punished by my parents or other authority if I do this work poorly (7.0%, 6.0%)

  f. It is never acceptable for me to cheat (73.0%, 80.5%)

  g. Other (please specify): _____
     (4.0%, 1.4%)

5. **To me, being an "author" means:**

  a. Writing a book or academic article (64.0%, 52.6%)

  b. Writing anything, whether it is "academic" or not, that is then published (61.0%, 56.3%)

  c. Writing anything, whether it is "academic" or not, and whether it is published or not (58.0%, 71.2%)

  d. Writing material for the Internet (either a personal or business Web site) (39.0%, 46.0%)

  e. Writing a paper or a project for a college course (35.0%, 40.0%)

  f. Writing something for which one may become famous or well-known (45.0%, 46.5%)

  g. Co-writing a project of any kind with another person or persons (36.0%, 36.3%)

  h. Gathering different sources and pasting them together as a collection of writing, then putting your name on that collection (6.0%, 6.0%)

i. Other (please specify): _____
    (3.0%, 0.9%)

6. **Most of the papers I have written for college courses could best be defined as:**

    a. Material that has no use outside the particular course or area of study (34.0%, 34.9%)
    b. Material that may be used in other situations, such as a job or professional applications (26.0%, 30.7%)
    c. Material that represents who I am as a writer (45.0%, 52.1%)
    d. Material that in no way represents who I am as a writer (11.0%, 14.9%)
    e. Material that has required extensive research (35.0%, 25.6%)
    f. Material that has required moderate research (59.0%, 60.0%)
    g. Material that has required little to no research (18.0%, 26.0%)

7. **I would define "research" done for college papers as:**

    a. Going to the library and finding books and journal articles to use in my paper (87.0%, 85.6%)
    b. Going to a resource of some kind and learning more about a subject for my paper (69.0%, 83.3%)
    c. Going to the Internet and downloading any and all information that I can use in a paper (63.0%, 64.7%)
    d. Going to friends, family, or other persons and getting ideas or suggestions to use in my paper (52.0%, 55.3%)
    e. Other (please specify): _____
        (4.0%, 3.7%)

8. **My opinion about the overall function or use of the Internet in college research is:**

    a. It is a very necessary and beneficial component of my research for college writing projects (54.0%, 68.4%)
    b. It is a somewhat necessary and beneficial component of my research for college writing projects (26.0%, 21.9%)
    c. It is an option for research in college writing projects; sometimes I use the Internet, sometimes I don't (45.0%, 26.5%)
    d. It is not an option for me, either because I don't have Internet access or don't like using the Internet (7.0%, 0.5%)
    e. Other (please specify): _____
        (4.0%) (0.5%)

4

E-VALUATING LEARNING

Rate My Professor
and Public Rhetorics of Pedagogy

So far in this book, I have argued that the online student discourse about higher education, specifically literacy practices, is a widely undervalued and underrepresented area of study. I also have argued that such discourse reflects students' dissatisfaction with the amount of control they have over their own education, as well as their own acknowledgment that American academic practices and structures are heavily influenced by the current free-market economy, and vice-versa. Liberatory pedagogy, the methodology and ideological position designed to alleviate students of their troubling dissatisfaction over agency and their simultaneous liminal socioeconomic standing in higher education, has its own limitations in the twenty-first-century classroom, as I also have argued.

In this chapter, and for my final in-depth example of "who owns school" in the twenty-first-century Internet age, I return to the core relationship between teachers and students, particularly those in first-year and other lower-level courses, as I discuss the phenomenon of the course evaluation, and how it is changing as both an instrument and a site of student response to higher education as a whole, due to the advent of online evaluative spaces. I examine the most well known of these spaces, Ratemyprofessors.com (RMP), in order to argue that students are now harnessing their online discourse to enact (or attempt to enact) change in the college classroom. Although it is naïve to contend that RMP itself aims to be a great rhetorical machine, I do believe that the ways in which students both contribute to and draw from the discourse on the site—and do so within a cross-national, atemporal framework—illustrates a desire for greater meaningful participation in the evaluative mechanisms of higher education, participation that is typically denied students at the local institutional level.

Universities have used student course evaluations as a means of making pedagogies public for more than sixty years. In the mid-twentieth century, institutions such as the University of California–Berkeley gathered evaluations in the form of "publishing guides rating teachers and courses" that were then considered "irreverent and funny . . . a light-hearted dope sheet" (Gray and Bergmann 44). Similarly, at Harvard, archival collections of course guides from this era exhibit a congenial, "older brother" tone, shepherding new students through the minefield of course selection. For example, the 1939 *Freshman Confidential Guide to Courses* notes that among the "section men" teaching English A (first-semester composition) are "Guerard [who] is brilliant, a hard marker, and conducts good discussions" and "Freeman [who] is able, humorous, and fair, and . . . 'especially swell' in conferences" (27), among other less desirable instructors such as Harrison, who in student surveys "stirred no violent reactions one way or the other" (27). The preface to these brief reports regarding the ability and demeanor of English A instructors is tellingly labeled "Rhetoric and Composition: Not Your Choice," prefiguring many students' view of general education curricula today (26).

But in the data-driven twenty-first century, such collections may be "instrument[s] of unwarranted and unjust termination" for faculty, rather than just advisory guides (Gray and Bergmann 44). Student evaluations now may have greater professional consequences beyond serving as material for anxious, information-hungry students, whom faculty fear to be more interested in their own academic success than in fair instructor assessment. As a result, many faculty caution against the use of student-based evaluative instruments as legitimate measurements of teaching.[33] Such a view certainly stems from the belief that course design and teaching methods are entities inseparable from one's own professional identity, or earned evidence of expertise. This view is backed by a secondary notion that students are in no position to evaluate pedagogy. So, when student-authored measurements of teaching are made public and further, are *publicized*, faculty are frequently quick to take up arms. Students, in contrast, are eager to participate in these publications—and to gain what they perceive to be pertinent information that will augment their complex journey through the system of higher education.

Teaching in the twenty-first century is, in fact, much more than a private expression or representation of one's scholarly and/or professional identity; it is a public, polyvocal enterprise encompassing ideologies that are often internally competing. These ideologies stem from not only the practices of the classroom or the institution, but also from external social groups invested in the dissemination of these ideologies. With the growth of the Internet, public discourse about education is freed from the temporal and spatial boundaries found in historical collections such as the Harvard guide; this boundless online discourse makes possible sites of asynchronous, student-led public evaluation. In keeping with our culture's tendency to use quantitative evaluation as its primary means of assessing not just its products, but also its people and social systems,[34] Web sites such as RMP aim to alter public discourse about higher education via reversals of traditional notions of assessment. This online discourse is led and moderated by students from institutions across the nation, representing myriad social and economic strata, as opposed to the local, institution-specific, homogeneous student groups of the past. RMP as a community is built on shared assumptions about the participatory nature of the college experience; the immediate need to evaluate such experiences in a public setting; and the importance of the "right-to-know" principle where the quality of education is concerned. These assumptions about the public nature of pedagogy and teacher evaluation stand in stark contrast to most assumptions by faculty about teaching and learning, which rely on minimal assurances of privacy and individual choice. Faculty may choose to publicize their pedagogies to colleagues and in scholarship, but rarely will do so in the public domain, in evaluations disseminated outside the physical institution.

On RMP, the previously local, private valuation of pedagogies is subsumed to a greater communal good: the public dissemination of information that enables students to gain some *control* over their education by choosing faculty of "high quality," in RMP terms, based on numerical rankings augmented by commentary. This system, importantly, is regulated by the students themselves, making this inside feedback, once locally community-based in nature, available for public review and uniquely dialogic debate. On RMP, a student can access multiple student testimonies to learn which professors are the easiest (or most challenging), which courses the least stressful (or most rewarding). When disagreements about the quality of a professor occur, a student can witness and engage in that valuation debate online. This online dialogue "unlocks" (in RMP terms) the confidential course evaluation, making it available for public scrutiny and, if warranted, public amendment. RMP participants, for good or ill, seek to engage in a communal support network, one that gives the "real" picture of teaching and learning, in an extracurricular setting free from academic surveillance. RMP thus provides students, arguably the chief agents shaping public rhetorics of pedagogy, a virtual space for engaging in evaluative discourse. This discourse does not always adhere to notions of conversational civility or other institutionally set parameters for evaluating learning, but does allow for a freedom of exchange rarely available in even the most radical pedagogies, and that aims to reify the position of the student in the evaluation and assessment process.

In employing the key term *public rhetorics* here, I first drawing on James Berlin's assertion that "Rhetorics interpellate us, hail us, position us, subject us, put us in our places—and not in others. . . . Rhetorics are made to be broken . . . to be reformed, to recreate who creates, what creations can enter this collusion, what discourse can be voiced and noted" (Enos 6). This definition offers rhetorics as concepts, acts, and mechanisms of resistance, emphasizing the instability of discourse and invoking the ways in which mediums (and certain types of mediation) alter such discourse, specifically that which is selectively "voiced and noted." In this category we may place student rhetorics. Berlin's definition serves as a baseline for Barbara Couture's more specific notion of *public* rhetorics, specifically those that "require the speaker to reconcile a previous conception of a private, closed identity—albeit shared—with the needs of an outside individual or group with whom they will build a relationship, a future, that will change them both in the common pursuit of a public good" (9).

If we consider RMP a display of such public rhetorics, we can recognize its *potential* to mediate between rhetors pursuing a "public good" (i.e., candid, if critical, suggestions for reform). This "public good" in which students perceive they are engaging is, in fact, potentially more powerful than the kind of socially constructed "good" that is typically promoted in the first-year writing class, for example, or within the general aims of liberatory pedagogy. In using RMP, students gain a level of immediacy with their peers, and strive to comment on, and hopefully improve on, what *they* believe most significantly affects their educational experiences: the local act of teaching. Berlin's and Couture's definitions are thus theoretical lenses through which we may study how students invoke faculty evaluation within these public rhetorics of pedagogy. Critical to these public rhetorics, therefore, is RMP's prioritizing of student voices in its discourse of valuation—voices that are often underregarded in such dialogues, or minimized by faculty who see these views as uninformed, or misguided.

Even though I see value in a public hearing of these voices, I do not aim to sanction or promote RMP per se; rather, I view it as a rhetorical phenomenon born of our larger culture's fascination with evaluation, and Internet-based communication, and accompanying student concerns about their relative position(s) and potential lack of power/voice in the teaching and learning processes. I recognize that there are elements of certain RMP postings that do not add to the ongoing conversation about pedagogy, or pedagogical reform; I also recognize, however, that every discourse community has its own "fringe" participants who serve little communal good, the equivalent of those who yell "fire" in a crowded theater. RMP thus represents a realistic range, from the disgruntled to the exuberant, and as such needs to be seen as a democratic space in which some voices are more successful than others in accruing rhetorical agency.

In this chapter, I examine how RMP might enact—even in its less defensible attributes and debates—underlying disagreements between students and faculty over how and where to evaluate and the classroom experience. To illustrate some of these disagreements, I analyze selected student commentary from the site.[35] I then examine in what ways RMP's aggregate public presence suggests a need to address this rhetorical divide in our classrooms. It is my contention that RMP reflects students' desire and ability to engage in institutional assessments, which seem to be otherwise taking place without their full input. I assert that this extra-institutional, evaluative discourse on RMP has the *potential* to effect positive pedagogical outcomes, but only if faculty recognize its presence—and public power—and subsequently engage with its claims in a deliberative, democratic manner in their own classrooms.

VALUING EVALUATION

Faculty know that reading end-of-term evaluations can be a disheartening process, as we sometimes see distortions or misinterpretations of what we believe to be our pedagogical intentions. Because these evaluations are typically distributed at semester's end, faculty is left to ponder the suggestions (or criticisms) made for future use only—making for lingering self-doubt. This doubt is the nature of human response to the intersection of the public/professional and the private/personal. As Andrea Stover notes, faculty and students "tacitly understand that a mix of . . . public and private lives is expected" in the classroom, especially the writing classroom, yet "the tension comes as everyone waits to see exactly how that mix will be concocted" through specific assignments and course interactions that challenge ratios in that concoction (2). Stover thus argues that we as faculty should "make our own understandings of public and private boundaries explicit to our students (even if we suspect they are misperceptions) and . . . invite our students to make their understandings explicit to us" (8–9). This negotiated understanding of the private versus public is especially critical in viewing course evaluation, which risks a public display of personal (i.e., private) impressions of pedagogy and immediately elevates the private student—whose position of linguistic power, for many faculty, is subordinated to a collective in the physical classroom—to the status of public critic.

As Sid Dobrin argues, however, there is no such thing as "private" discourse, which problematizes the notion of a course evaluation suddenly becoming a "public" document, as "discourse does not begin private and then earn a label or stature of public discourse as it is made public. Rather, discourse begins public and is labeled private as needed . . . discourse by its very nature . . . is a public, social, triangulative, interpretive, identity" ("Going Public" 221). Thus, we might argue that any distinction we make between evaluative discourse as "private" when it is limited to our classroom, or to the faculty member's consumption, versus "public" when put online, or opened up to wider consumption, is a false one.

Yet teachers continue to see their classrooms and any evaluations of those classrooms as exceedingly private, and thus exempt from public discourse. Hence, regarding students' role in the evaluative process, faculty seem to be of two minds: On one hand, teachers want students to be critical thinkers, and sometimes active participants, especially in writing courses and/or within classrooms espousing critical/liberatory pedagogies, as discussed in Chapter 1; on the other hand, faculty are still reluctant to allow students too great a voice in pedagogical concerns outside or apart from the course site itself. This tension is over the view of evaluations as truly evaluative mechanisms—those that in isolation from other factors demarcate "quality" and have professional consequences for faculty—versus the view of evaluations as reflective mechanisms, or those that allow students to put a course experience in the context of their overall attitudes toward learning and higher education. Again, in this tension we see manifestations of the private–public divide and its impact on faculty ethos—and conceptions of professional integrity—when translated by students in their course surveys. This may be traced to conflicting views of "participatory democracy" (Weisser, S. 29) evident in assessment tools such as student self-evaluation, often primary in student-centered writing classrooms.

Richard Ohmann addresses this fragile notion of participatory democracy in teaching and learning in "Politics of Teaching." Ohmann defines the "politics" in his title via the interactions in a college classroom. He argues that course participants "enter . . . into a small system of governance, where power is exercised, members have certain rights, laws are made and enforced and broken" (29). This definition of the political in the classroom is pertinent to a discussion of public rhetorics, as democratic principles necessitate that all voices be heard—hence the emergence of the course evaluation in the 1960s, as part of the Progressive Education movement (30). Many faculty, according to Ohmann, believe what students want from an education is a commercial good—a quantifiable product—and thus the idea of progressive education, in its traditional political permutations, is lost. But Ohmann believes that the dream of a progressive education—one that allows students to socially and politically engage with pedagogies—is still potentially alive. Ohmann argues that "strong countermovements to regiment the young" still exist (32), but recognizes the problem is in the translation of this countermovement in the twenty-first-century academy. Specifically, the implications for a democratic politics of learning seem obvious: precisely to the extent that students (and other buyers) base their educational choices on the market advantage they hope to gain—to that extent, they will disregard other educational values they might have, such as the wish to . . . initiate and control their own learning process, or to understand and fight inequality. . . . On this premise, one would predict a continuing place in the agile university and even in corporate culture for democratic relations of pedagogy, so long as they answer to the criteria of efficiency. (34–35)

Such "efficiency" criteria obviously are at work in the course evaluation itself. Herein lies much of the anxiety over evaluation—the format, manner of delivery, the seemingly "corporate" tendencies that it entails, subsequently put into the hands of students who, unlike other public investors, have a stake in the course that is economic and ideological, intellectual *and* personal. Ohmann's call to action assumes that true democracies in learning will "survive in settings where education is not wholly or simply market-driven and in professional fields with a strong ethos of democratic public service—writing instruction [for example]" (35). In short, although he does not sanction the student-driven course evaluation per se, Ohmann does argue for the democracy and advocacy of the classroom, within and against these corporate, externally driven concepts of efficiency. As such, Ohmann's view represents a compromise between fears over the *power* of evaluation and the value of that power in facilitating civic discourse in our pedagogy, something that students seem to want, but could use faculty guidance in accomplishing.

Yet as students want intellectual control over their own discourse of learning and some regard for their ability to improve the discourse of the classroom, faculty want intellectual control over their course structures and their own pedagogical agencies, often without having to consider and/or address disparate student values in constructing that agency. Herein lies a critical disconnect between the methodologies of liberatory pedagogy, which seek to liberate students from the oppressive structures of the educational system, and the evaluative process found at the close of such pedagogies, which operates in isolation from the course setting, is read (or not) after the course is completed, and bears a differential weight almost exclusively depending on the instructor's need for feedback, and willingness to employ it in the classroom. If the primary measure of this disconnect, therefore, is to reconcile classroom experiences and teacher perceptions of the learning process in the *institutional, end-of-term* individual evaluation, a problematic device disregarded by most faculty as ineffective, it is unlikely that faculty and students can agree on any meaningful pedagogical change that will result in—or reflect the values of—a truly democratic classroom.

Part of the problem lies in historical perceptions of what the evaluation stands for—or the ways in which senior faculty instruct junior faculty
(and graduate student instructors) to regard the student viewpoint come
evaluation time. As Stanley Fish argues, institutional evaluations have
been "revised and refined, but . . . have followed political and sociological
trends rather than any advance in our understanding of what is and is not
good teaching" (http://chronicle.com/jobs/2005/02/2005020401c.htm). In
the context of Fish's essay, these "trends" seem to point to the ways in
which knowledge is constructed in the classroom—as a collaborative
enterprise versus a receivership model. Fish's comments also imply that
evaluations do not work as intellectual tools, but instead function as an
unscientific social commentary, which thereby has no real use value in
pedagogical reform. The notion of social versus scientific parameters in
assessment also relates to the varied purposes of teaching itself—including Fish's discouraged classifications of therapy and retail merchandising,
terms that again point to the various cultural roles faculty may fill. To characterize teacher evaluations as somehow victims of politics and sociology
seems problematic, however, if we consider evaluative discourse as an
outgrowth of our larger culture, not just academia. Fish, like many faculty
who doubt student motivations in evaluation responses, questions
whether evaluations do faculty any great service in high-stakes situations
such as tenure and promotion, and supports faculty who loudly protest
putting stock in the student survey as the sole yardstick for measuring
quality of teaching. At my institution, for example—as is likely the case at
many other institutions as well—course evaluations are called Student
Opinion Surveys, putting the emphasis on opinion rather than evaluative
expertise in any way. The data gathered are thus opinions that can be
taken, or ignored, at will.

Fish seems to discount the evaluation process as a whole because of
the apparent lack of intellectual investment students have in their own education. He prefaces his argument about the content and quality of course
evaluation by admitting that after one recent course, he took the "large
enveloped, unopened" student evaluations and "threw [them] into the
trash" unwilling to regard the "ill-informed opinions of transient students
with little or no stake in the enterprise who would be free (because they are
anonymous) to indulge any sense of grievance they happened to harbor"
(http://chronicle.com/jobs/2005/02/2005020401). This action is representative of how many faculty react to their students' course surveys; an alternative approach is not to throw the evaluations away, but to simply file
them in a drawer, among other unused documents. Evaluations often serve
this function—as dusty artifacts that lose meaning the further they become
chronologically separated from the course and students themselves.

Fish's opinions about both the calculated risk of anonymity for faculty
being evaluated and the uselessness of student opinion is borne out in

other similar public rhetorics put forth by faculty, who feel the burden of evaluations and are sometimes openly threatened by the (anonymous) voices and positions they represent. For example, in direct response to RMP, Web sites such as "Rate Your Students" have emerged, which allow faculty to voice their own disgruntlement with the evaluation process, but also take pointed attacks at students, in a manner similar to that which they believe RMP allows. Rate Your Students operates as an open blog, begun by a faculty member in order to create "a public forum where faculty and students can work out the tricky dynamic of the modern classroom" (rateyourstudents.blogspot.com). In general, the blog serves as a site for venting about the ways in which students vex, anger, and annoy faculty across disciplines and course levels. Occasionally, students do post to the site—mostly to note how professors tend to generalize about student behavior unfairly, or to provide insight into how to improve teaching from a student's perspective. Ideally, this would create a productive dialogue online. But more typically, the problem of student attitude and engagement that the site hopes to invoke and critique is global in nature, multifaceted, and framed as already hopeless. Thus, the notion of online commentary resulting in deliberative exchange is absent—perhaps ironic, given that civic discourse is assumedly a goal for many of these faculty's classrooms. As one philosophy professor's response to a student posting on Rate Your Students indicates, critical conversation is not the goal here:

> If your intent is to criticize the content of the course, come chat with me when you have finished your dissertation. . . . Better yet, we can have that discussion once you have taught the course at a few different places over multiple semesters. That will not only give you a point of view on the content of the discipline, but also a perspective on teaching it to undergraduates. By the time you have done all of this, you'll see that your "suggestion" is wrong in a number of ways and you'll be glad you kept it to yourself. (http://rateyourstudents.blogspot.com, posted 03/29/06)

Obviously, this response evidences a few assumptions about student input. First, undergraduate students do not have the experience to comment on or evaluate courses. Second, any "perspective" on teaching can come only from teachers themselves—the student perspective is considered wholly invalid. Finally, such "suggestions" should be private—not public, even as this site allows for just that: the airing of public grievances about the educational system. This publication of evaluative comments is finally, perhaps, the most egregious of all to the poster—as he or she belittles the idea of the student's fairly objective "suggestions" about course structure and reifies them as a public, yet personal, attack.

Also, in contrast to the frequently positive commentary and laudatory postings of RMP, when taken as a segment of the comments posted to the site overall, and that stand in contrast to and serve as balances for negative or hurtful postings, Rate Your Students more typically functions as a general complaint board for professors to post summaries of their negative experiences, or their dissatisfaction with teaching altogether (embedded even in the posting above). For example, one faculty member used the Rate Your Students site to vent his frustrations about choosing teaching as a career:

> Let's get one thing straight. I hate teaching, and I could not care less at [sic] becoming better at it. Yes, I should be doing something else. Yes, I tried. But economic conditions, a poor choice of majors—and no real skills . . . conspired to force me into the position, and now it's a gravy train to retirement. But I don't have to like it. Not even a little. (rateyourstudents.blogspot.com/2006_03_01_rateyourstudents_archive.html)

Certainly, this professor may dislike his career for a number of reasons—none of which we can know given the anonymous format of this and most other blogs and online chat. Motivations for postings and identities of authors—as on RMP—are not measurable in this type of computer-mediated discourse (CMD) on the Internet. But postings such as this one share a common underlying theme: if only students would care more about their education; if only students would want to learn. As long as those conditions are (apparently, assumedly) not met, students do not have the right to evaluate faculty in any meaningful—and especially public—way. This posting is an implied response to the unstated, but assumed-to-be-omnipresent, view of college students: that they do not care about their educations, that they only engage in evaluation to hurt faculty and vent about perceived injustices—in short, that students use the instruments of evaluation to "get" faculty, not to voice legitimate opinions, as they, by definition, have none.

Faculty reaction to public and sometimes "uninformed" scrutiny of one's work—in this case, teaching—certainly stems from the (mis)conceptions just discussed, but also very closely resembles the reaction many scholars have to negative assessments of their professional work outside of teaching—such as unduly critical responses to work under review at academic journals. A September 2007 discussion thread, for example, on the *Chronicle of Higher Education*'s "Forum" section showcases this response to negative assessment in its "What is the Nastiest Peer Comment You Have Ever Received?" thread within its "Research Questions" chat area. As the poster who calls him or herself "Bookish One" writes:

> Yes, it's amazing how much [reviews] sting when you first read them. Sometimes, if I don't look at them again until much later, I can see that

they were right, and not really that harsh. . . . The same thing happens for me with good comments. I'll treasure up some phrase of commendation in a reader's report only to find (when glancing it over a year later) that it's really not that effusive and might just be politeness. Reading negative comments is just really hard. (http://chronicle.com/forums/index.php?topic = 41410.0)

In this posting, and responses to it, myriad anxieties over public review emerge. One category of response invokes the notion that the reviewer doesn't know what he or she is talking about—and thus is not "in a position to judge," similar to the position that students don't "know enough" about teaching to evaluate it. When faculty put their work out for colleagues to judge, and the responses are negative (or in some cases, unduly unkind), the natural reaction is to shun further public opportunities; separating one's self from the work under review, however, is next to impossible. The very existence of this forum thread illustrates the need for faculty to commiserate over such wounded, if justifiable, feelings related to their professional lives.

By the same token, repeated reviews of the commentary—as all scholars know and as the *Chronicle* poster concedes—often unearth elements of truth about the piece of scholarship. The correlation between this type of public review and the type of public evaluation posted on RMP may seem slight, but the emotional response at the core of each is quite similar. People (faculty but also nonfaculty) just don't like to be judged—especially anonymously, which smells of cowardice, even if there is a grain of truth in that judgment. In both anonymous peer review and student evaluations, there is additionally no opportunity to "face one's accuser," in legal parlance. Were these scholarly reviews to be posted online for other scholars to see, surely the anxiety would increase tenfold. On the other hand, such public posting of scholarly reviews also would make the reviewers *accountable* (hence the move, at some journals, to request that reviewers *sign* their work and thus eliminate anonymity in one facet of the process) and would thus potentially provide opportunity to address commentary that is overtly personal, unsubstantiated, and/or wholly derogatory in nature.

The perceptions of these faculty about both students' investment in higher education and the value of public evaluation would seem to contrast sharply with direct statements that students have made about the course evaluation process, both on their own and as part of controlled research studies. In addition to other myriad postings of the "suggestion" genre on Rate Your Students and those frequent postings evidencing positive investments and reflective consideration of pedagogies on RMP, there are perspectives that conflict with the faculty notions above. As one recent graduate asserts in his *Pedagogy* article "Reclaiming Claims: What English Students Want From English Profs," not all students are the "transient" and unaffected people whom Fish describes, or the uninvested, grade-grubbing consumers that Rate Your Students addresses:

> Teaching is not necessarily about giving students what they want—that might amount to little more than free pizza. Still, a student's desires are not entirely insignificant, particularly those desires students didn't know they had. Good teachers have a way of eliciting those deep passions that students are either too embarrassed or too busy or too distracted to realize they possess. (Van Engen 9)

In this view, students are largely potential learners who respond to teachers who will meet them somewhere in the middle of the process—in other words, those who neither discount their abilities nor their potential interests, nor label them as not being invested from the start. This student believes that "the more professors treat students as if they do care—and as if they should—the more they will discover students who actually do" (9). This emphasis on instilling the desire to care in students—and in eliciting responses that regard that care with some sincere dignity—is apparently a baseline issue in the evaluative process. If faculty take the fatalistic view that students are incapable of caring, then certainly evaluation would seem to be a pointless process.

Although this student view comes from within English studies, scholars in other disciplines also have found similar student attitudes toward learning and assessment of learning. James Marlin, an economist, studied 313 first-year students at Western Illinois and Appalachian State universities, and found that "If students have no faith in the system and put little thought and effort into their evaluations, then . . . the results will be useless. [But] if students take the evaluation seriously and view it as a responsibility rather than a chore, evaluation results might improve" (705). Marlin devised a student survey *about* course evaluation, and found, among other results, that "Eighty-three percent . . . felt that instructors changed their teaching as a result of student suggestions only some of the time, while a whopping 25 percent believed that student evaluations accomplish almost nothing" (709). Nonetheless, students believed themselves to be "conscientious" in their assessments (711). Marlin quotes two students who question faculty response to course evaluations. One asks, "How do we know if the teacher changes at all? Give them [the evaluations] out at midterm *and* the end of semester" to ensure some amount of response. Another believes that faculty response "depends on the teacher; I think an older teacher who has been around for a while it won't affect them [*sic*] at all" (709).

Marlin's findings "tend to dispute the sometimes made assertion that students are less than truthful on evaluations for fear of lower grades" (710). He notes, "students would agree with the view that evaluations are a vent to let off student steam. . . . In spite of that, students apparently take the evaluation process seriously" (714). Marlin's study allowed students to collectively assess what qualities of evaluation are the most legitimate for professors to consider, while voicing their own level of investment in this institutional process. However, we do not, as a rule, ask our students to have a community discussion about the effectiveness of their professors or their accompanying pedagogies, as Marlin has done in his research.

Instead, we ask them to do this work individually, in secret (insofar as most traditional evaluations are viewed only by the faculty member). Thus, there is no realistic outlet for students who wish to *share* evaluation, or their views of it, as part of a dialogic community, at least not in the on-the-ground university. As Sharon Crowley points out in *Composition in the University*, it is a myth that in the academy, "fair and adequate socially authorized forms of public discourse are available for interpreting people's needs" (261). Specifically, Crowley contends that

> aside from course evaluations, there is no authorized discourse within the academy that allows students to voice their concerns about curricula. . . . Students do engage in many unauthorized discourses about curricula, of course; they circulate subrosa lists of good and bad courses and instructors. . . . But none of these unauthorized channels give the mass of students regular and equal access to the groups who actually make curricular decisions. (261)

Crowley's argument rests on two assumptions: First, student evaluations are worthy instruments of measurement, and second, said evaluations are not used enough. Aware of this lack of opportunity for students to voice their opinions within the larger institutional setting, RMP advertises itself as a place "where students do the grading," a rhetorical strategy that poaches on traditional faculty valuations of student work. Perhaps a way to bring these two competing notions of evaluation together, therefore, is to look at the typical structure of classroom assessment. As academia is part of an assessment-focused culture, we cannot ignore these markers in our interactions with students, or their responses, especially in extra-institutional settings such as RMP, where the consequences of voicing such assessments are lessened, even erased, and thus comments are more free ranging and potentially useful.

Even with the growth of portfolio assessments, the letter grade remains the singularly most frequent means of assessing student work. Although a complete discussion of the power and function of letter grades is not possible here, it is clear that some students—and some faculty— regard grades as exact, quantitative markers of not just a student's ability, but of his or her motivation and *potential* for success. William E. Knox et al.'s study on long-term effects of the college experience found that "To the extent that one has been rewarded, one forms positive conclusions that go hand in hand with one's identity as a good student. Of course, the causation may be the other way around, with absorption in a positive educational process resulting in good grades" (316). In other words, students who are invested in and rewarded for their work feel better about that work—and may, as a result, continue to *produce* better work in the future. Knox et al. found that college grades correlate positively with a student's assessment of college, which should come as no surprise to faculty. Specifically, "The higher one's college grades, the lower the odds of finding the courses harder than expected and the greater the odds of reporting that courses were interesting, that one performed well, [and] learned a lot" (316).

In other words, students who received high grades had positive perspectives of college; students with low grades tended to express opposite views. We can see this simple yet significant correlative in course evaluations—faculty with overall negative "scores" (and in some institutions, these scores are numerical) are labeled as "ineffective" or "poorly performing." For contingent faculty and those scholars in controversial fields, this can be one rationale for dismissal or nonrenewal. Much as we resist the public posting of student grades outside lecture halls without some coding mechanism for student privacy, faculty similarly resist having these "grades" from course evaluations posted in a public place for others to review, and judge out of context. Subsequently, faculty begin to fear that their "grades" from evaluations will classify them in holistic ways—positively or negatively—to other students, faculty, and the public, building on the already-always present factor discussed previously, namely the human resistance to being judged, in any fashion.

As Kathleen Blake Yancey and Brian Huot argue, teachers as individuals are inextricably and uniquely linked to grades and the grading process beyond the evaluative functions which they perform, perhaps more so than other types of workers or professionals:

> Faculty typically become faculty because they have compiled good grades, lots of good grades. The grades, seemingly, confirm the fact that these people should become teachers, should exercise authority, especially in a classroom. So right from the start, teachers are determined by grades . . . [they] have a right to become part of the institution: to grade others. This right confers power, and its an interesting question as to how many teachers will be, or are, willing to give that power away in some move to negotiate evaluation. (49)

Here, Yancey and Huot interrogate the nexus between the graded and the grader—as well as the linchpin that is the grade, or evaluation point, itself.

They argue, "through the grades we give, we construct a persona that can be used for our advantage in multiple contexts" (49). To return to the analogous relationship between RMP postings and scholarly peer review, faculty begrudge having their authority questioned in either of these arenas, resist giving up the power that is grading agency—even if the faculty member him or herself does not consider such a position "powerful." Ultimately, Yancey and Huot argue, "what we have is an inadequate system for evaluation that is so entrenched that it has real, perceived value on its own" (50). I argue that this "perceived value," as well as its entrenchment, is easily applicable to the system of teacher evaluation, made even more (negatively) valuable vis-à-vis RMP. As long as we allow RMP's public postings to go unaddressed in our classrooms, and fail to recognize the rhetorical import of evaluation as a deeply conflicted mechanism for enabling and also undermining power structures, we are effectively *allowing* our pedagogies to be labeled (and digested) in the same manner as are grades—summative, often incomplete in their recapitulation.

Any assessment that exists as a fixed, summative label is problematic for students and faculty alike; such is the premise to which highly process-based teaching/assessment methodologies such as the writing portfolio respond. As Huot notes, "performative assessment" (i.e., portfolios) is more effective [than individual letter grades] for learning, especially in first-year writing, as it passes "judgments that allow the student to improve" (167). Huot believes that "we have evolved pedagogies that conceive of teaching as a coaching and enabling process, while holding onto conceptions of evaluation as a means for gate keeping and upholding standards" (164). In other words, the grades that we give as "summative" evaluations do little to move our students along in the learning process, and frequently contradict our own desired/targeted teaching methods. Instead, grading "freezes student work and teacher commentary" in space and time (173), disrupting the opportunity for exchange between teacher and student.

We might compare this "freezing" of evaluation to the kind of assessment that faculty receive in regular, institutional end-of-course evaluations. There often is little space for students to annotate their "ratings" when Likert or other numerical scales are the primary means of response. Even when space is provided, students often do not take the time to make written comments, again assuming such comments will potentially not be read. Indeed, faculty often receive "summary" data on their evaluations, quite similar to the "quick-and-dirty" reviews that we give students when assigning grades. As Huot recognizes, "The discourse of assessing student writing is often framed as the worst aspect of the job of teaching student writers . . . 'the dirty thing we have to do in the dark of our own offices'" (qtd in 166). Are we afraid of students doing that "dirty work" to us, in course evaluations?

It also may be important to remember that "returning graded and marked papers to students eliminates the need for response or defines it in very narrow, perfunctory terms. In this kind of assessment, students are accountable rather than responsible, because grades come from a bureaucratic higher authority over which they exert little or no control" (Huot 168–69). Nick Carbone and Margaret Daisley assert that such perfunctory assessments lack a meaningful, shared understanding between teachers and students; simply put, the grade does not "mean" the same to these two large audiences, let alone subgroups within these audiences. Thus, in order to get beyond this hurdle and achieve a kind of stasis, at least, in formulating debates over assessment, "grades-as-texts must represent dialogues between teachers and students who develop a common vocabulary for reading grades as signifying texts" (78). Inasmuch as portfolios attempt to do this work—by exhibiting rubrics that, in some cases, are developed in consultation with students—Carbone and Daisley argue that the final grade itself—the B or the C mark—are not always products of a "common vocabulary of evaluation" (78). Such a vocabulary requires students willing to take part in the process, and teachers willing to share authority.

If indeed we are asking students to be accountable but not responsible for their own learning via our current means of assessment, then perhaps we are inadvertently encouraging them to turn the tables and again absolve themselves of such responsibility (i.e., direct, temporal dialogue with faculty in which identities are disclosed and issues put on the table) when it is time for reflective evaluation of their course experiences.

PUBLIC PEDAGOGY MEETS PUBLIC DISCOURSE ONLINE

As we consider the roles of students in evaluative online discourse, and the way in which this discourse reproduces and complicates public rhetorics of pedagogy that evidence students' desire to have greater control over their educational processes, it is important to recall that RMP's format is *not* new in the context of current institutional assessment mechanisms in place nationwide. Public online sites for faculty evaluation have grown exponentially along with the Internet. Many postsecondary institutions have capitalized on public dissemination of evaluations in recent years, according to the Online Student Evaluation of Teaching in Higher Education (OnSET) organization, which maintains a database of institutions that publicize faculty evaluations on the Internet. OnSET categorizes these institutions by accessibility; institutions receiving a "5" have students complete course evaluations online, and make all evaluations public within the parameters of the institution (via password-protected databases). Institutions receiving a "1" offer some, but not all, evaluations online. Institutions rated 2, 3, or 4 either only report evaluations for distance education courses, or publish a significant percentage of evaluations online.[36] When done as part of the larger assessment movement, such evaluation is nearly identical in scope to what is occurring as a commercial endeavor on RMP.[37]

As academic assessment, this evaluation is controlled and financed by the institution, and is designed to interrogate notions of performance and goal-oriented (or "outcomes-based") instruction in all arenas of higher education, from community colleges to research universities. On RMP, such evaluation is similarly interrogative, yet is underwritten financially by student participants or members and corporate sponsors. Both impulses, when made accessible via these databases, center on electronic publication and dissemination of perceived faculty performance. Both initiatives thereby change the intrinsic value and import of evaluation immeasurably. The chief difference between the OnSET group and RMP is the literal *site* of information—from within the institution versus outside of it, independent of its value system. In either case, these evaluations are reified as public documents rather than private utterances.

Positioning student course evaluations as public documents complicates the notion of what those evaluations *do* as archived, accessible texts versus local, limited artifacts of individual pedagogies. Are we to now see a professor's pedagogy as a larger cultural artifact, open to continued historical scrutiny and comment from individuals who did not participate in the original cultural event (i.e., the classroom in which that pedagogy was formulated and delivered)? To begin to answer that question, we must consider the consequences of pedagogies being not only publicly disseminated and evaluated electronically, but also becoming part of a larger cultural structure in which the sustainability of higher education as a theoretical concept is a burden shared by those who live and work outside academia itself.

As Henry Giroux argues, to protectively limit our definition of pedagogy to those instructional values and activities present within the physical confines of school is a dangerous and ultimately naïve enterprise. Giroux believes that "the work of education takes place in a range of public spheres," including broadcast media and the Internet, and as such we need to consider the role of this "public pedagogy" in our communications with students ("Cultural Studies" 77). Giroux argues that to employ a notion of public pedagogy, faculty must seek to understand "the diverse ways in which culture functions as a contested sphere over the production, distribution, and regulation of power and how and where it operates both symbolically and institutionally as an educational, political, and economic force" (77). In sum, academia should not be regarded as a sheltered community that does not influence and cannot *be* influenced by larger popular culture; education occurs as a social and political act throughout our culture, and is enacted in the context of specific power structures. Giroux thus calls for those in education to recognize pedagogy as an opportunity to "locate oneself in a public discourse" (83). I argue for the value of seeing "public pedagogy" in a highly literal sense—in those locations where public discourse considers varied perceptions of higher education using one of our culture's valued methods of information exchange, the Internet. Seeing students as a critical part of this public discourse, as primary participants in the dual-nature public rhetorics of pedagogy being enacted *outside* the confines of the institution, allows us to revise our notions of teaching and learning as specific to the physical classroom and that specific group of students, with only locally circumscribed boundaries based on the values and needs of that defined community. Such consideration of public versus private spheres, and the role that students play in these spheres, is particularly critical when theorizing higher education as represented via the commercial discourse of the Internet, one of Giroux's already-recognized sites of public pedagogy.

As Theresa Enos and Shane Borrowman argued, the Internet is a "virtual agora in which any rhetor with a small amount of technological know-how and in possession of minimal hardware can make his or her voice heard" (93). Through this apparently egalitarian access, Internet patrons not only must consider who is writing and why, but they also may observe how these individuals create and participate in online communities to formulate and resolve their differences in a public forum. Hence, the often-dialogic postings on RMP, in which one student will modify or augment another's rating with his or her own competing view; this student then may be subsequently challenged him or herself by another. These differences and dialogues are as legitimate as those taking place in on-the-ground conversations of similar ilk, and in some ways mimic the kind of exchanges taking place on Pink Monkey, discussed in Chapter 2. Students on Pink Monkey are reading (and writing) without teacher oversight; on RMP, the students are even further removed from the teacher-figure as they freely discuss the idea of teaching *itself*, as attached to particular teachers and courses, both positively and negatively. In both of these venues, however, the work is highly dialogic, clearly externally motivated in nature, and represents a cross-national, atemporal exchange not available within the traditional institutional setting. The difference in examining RMP in this context, as opposed to Pink Monkey, is that Pink Monkey exists *without specific stakes or consequences* for the subjects (texts) themselves, nor even the curriculum—as posters very infrequently identify where they attend school—whereas RMP has the public power to disseminate person-specific evaluations that may potentially affect the subject(s) of the discourse: the teacher him or herself.

Whether within student-led evaluative sites such as RMP or within other commercially based, demographically diverse sites (e.g., consumer sites such as Amazon, discussion forums/viewer-reader debate venues such as those on MSNBC.com and other news outlets), the Internet's virtual communities do, in fact, operate as "real" communities, as they are "much like most of the ones in . . . real-life communities: intermittent, specialized, and varying in strength" (Fauske and Wade 186). As such, "the provision of information is a larger component of online ties than of real-life ties" and that this produces a "sense of belonging in cyberspace" (186). These groups are formulated on the basis of shared interests and not other social or demographic factors that would otherwise bind individuals (such as gender, class, race) (186). Unlike geographical, on-the-ground communities, there is more "community life" in virtual communities, and this interaction may in fact be better supported, and less socially scrutinized, than in face-to-face settings (187).

This notion of support and belonging is relevant to RMP, as students post ratings there vis-à-vis positions that are not always regarded, or allowed to exist, in the geographical communities in which they live—specifically the classroom that they are evaluating. Their observations are not tied to class or gender, or race—although one may observe higher instances of postings for general education than majors courses. I assert that this has much again to do with "common interests," that is, a community of students new to the university (taking general education courses in their first or second year) and seeking guidance in a global setting because they have not yet become fully integrated into their geographical (academic) communities. Additionally, these first- and second-year students are the ones most directly grappling with new concepts of learning, literacy, and education in their overall course experiences. In RMP as in most online communities, however, belonging and being valued is still key.

The concept of belonging is indeed critical to dissemination of a community's beliefs within the larger public sphere. As Christian Weisser notes, student writing which is designed to go "public" may initially be "most effective if it is aimed at individuals who share common perspectives and goals" rather than immediately broadcast to a variety of interest groups with competing ideologies (107). Weisser's notion of these bounded "counterpublics" as supportive spaces that serve as training grounds for future deliberations for a wider audience is applicable to RMP's shared-interest community setting, as counterpublics allow students to "come away from such interactions with more complex and sophistical views on public topics" (107). Although critics of RMP see this "support" as enabling closed-minded exchanges about professors and pedagogies, I argue that instead we see this online support system through Weisser's lenses—as a proving ground that shows students that "public discourse is worth pursuing in the future" (107) and provides a relatively safe space to exchange ideas outside classroom boundaries.

The Internet's success, in fact, largely depends on the assumption that its patrons will want to use the Web's resources in their capacity as valued and active readers, authors, and citizens of these electronic cultural forums, rather than passive "lurkers" or observers who defer to dominant ideologies represented in the communications of the status quo. The Internet, in many ways, is built on and made powerful by its role as a venue for alternative points of view, even those that threaten implicitly or explicitly our social structure. The rise of the Internet, in fact, provides not just access but also agency for groups who exist on the fringes of public discourse, or who stand in opposition to dominant belief systems, as most media are outside easy public reach, but not so the Internet (Enos and Borrowman 108). As Clawson et al. also argue in their study of student CMD in newsgroups that enable cross-university conversations, online discussions as part of a pedagogy can be beneficial—specifically that these groups, importantly, allow students to "play a proactive role in their own education" (713). But they additionally note that the prevailing evidence is that "high-performing" students are the most likely to participate (713). In using this as a pedagogical tool, their findings suggest that "while news-groups can be a powerful pedagogical tool, not all students participate at the same rates" (716). Thus, such forums—which bear a structural resemblance to RMP—make public deliberation more *possible*, but do not guarantee full participation by all potentially invested individuals. Because dialogue exists does not mean that each exchange is equally operational; in this light, faculty (and students) must weigh the dominance of certain voices or perspectives on RMP, just as they would in face-to-face dialogues.

When CMD occurs in a pedagogical setting, such assessments may "provide interactive learning environments that redefine the roles of instructor and student" (Fauske and Wade 144). Marilyn Cooper and Cynthia Selfe's 1990 study of CMD in their writing classrooms, although pre-Internet, may provide the most extensive and applicable examination of how online discourse communities can enable these interactions and elicit true change. Cooper and Selfe maintain that students have a greater sense of authority and can engage in versions of Brooke's "underlife" through CMD discussions. The conferences in Cooper and Selfe's study are asynchronous and take place outside of class, without teacher mediation—like postings on RMP. Cooper and Selfe argue that such exchanges have the capability to create internally persuasive discourse as well, particularly through the power that anonymity brings. Cooper and Selfe believe that computer conferences "encourage students to resist, dissent, and explore the role that controversy and intellectual divergence play in learning and thinking" (849). Their core contention is as follows:

> Within the traditional forums in our classes, the traditional hegemony of the teacher–student relationship, supported by the evaluative power of grades and the ideology of the educational institution, assures that

most of our students respond as we ask them to. . . . In this way education, even as it empowers students with . . . the ability to operate successfully within academic discourse communities, also oppresses
them, dictating a specific set of values and beliefs along with appropriate forms of behavior. (850)

This oppression of power, which I have argued is possible even in the
most liberatory pedagogy-focused classrooms, is certainly relevant to RMP,
as its format allows student reflection to be asynchronous, thus controlling
the time and space of evaluation; students may post at any time during the
course, or long after it has ended. Herein the idea of evaluation as a reflective mechanism for students is critical, as RMP's format allows students to
comment on a course in the later context of other educational experiences—and potentially even amend a previous rating at a later date.
Traditional evaluations—even Internet-based institutional ones—do not
allow for this reconsideration of views. As such, RMP builds on these
accepted principles of CMD by allowing students greater reflective power
over their course perceptions, freed from the "oppression" of the values
and beliefs present in the classroom, or even the rules and regulations
affecting its in-class discourse. Furthermore, RMP serves as an alternative
to the traditional institutional evaluation, allowing students to control the
means and the dissemination of comments in ways that work outside the
"ideology of the educational institution," in Cooper and Selfe's terms, who
recognize that "although we can encourage students in our classes to resist
. . . we will generally fail to get them to do so as long as we rely only on
traditional forums. . . . Through resistance, individuals identify their needs
and values and, hence, bring about the possibility of change in social systems" (851). Perhaps RMP is one way to provide a forum for this "resistance" that Cooper and Selfe desire.

This idea of resistance may not necessarily be as radical as it sounds—
and as it often appears to faculty when they regard RMP as a wholly negative or even mean-spirited, destructive enterprise. As Jeanette Kindred and
Shaheed Mohammed argue, students "obviously use [RMP] to seek out
information about professors, but they may also simply like the freedom of
expression" allowed by the site. Participants may "post . . . primarily for
interpersonal utility reasons. They want to provide information to others,
and they also feel part of a community of posters. . . . One aspect of the
interpersonal utility motive is to express oneself freely, and venting appears
to [do] this" (http://jcmc.indiana.edu/vol10/issue3/kindred.html). Such
"venting" about teaching is even apparent on Pink Monkey, despite its larger purpose aimed at discussing and interpreting assigned texts. To recall,
such "venting" was apparent in the posting by the student in the *Crime and
Punishment* thread, who claimed that it was not the *text* she disliked, but

perhaps her teacher's way of presenting it. The difference here is that this student neither identified her institution nor her teacher—and as such, the venting is low stakes and, practically speaking, socially "allowed" from the point of view of a faculty member.

Kindred et al.'s study of RMP explains how and why student participation on the site reflects both skewed views of individual teachers and pedagogies, and valid motivations for posting rooted in communal desires, or the need to belong to a community which has a true "voice" in public discourse about higher education. The act of posting on RMP thus becomes a direct response to pedagogical theories already in place in academia, even as specific postings may be discounted as "inaccurate."[38] These postings indeed *resist* the status quo—the traditional institutional evaluation—but not always in ways that seek to harm it. An element of this resistance concerns the singularly defined evaluation, which is recorded but never receives a response. Much like faculty's general views on responding to student work—that such responses must be careful and thoughtful, rather than arbitrary or altogether absent—the evaluative process on RMP allows for extended public consideration of a student's views.

This practice of public deliberation can be beneficial to the larger classroom setting, if translated as a type of public pedagogy. Philip Burns argues that students may be taught, through online discussion, to engage in "deliberative rhetoric that is dialogical (to encourage the give and take among deliberators), inquisitive and informative (to bring about mutual understanding), accommodative (to assure that those understandings are incorporated into public debate) and critical (to promote critical awareness of the deliberative process itself)" (129). Burns' emphasis on reflection again conflicts with our other institutional and traditional notions of assessment, especially that which is quantitative. Encouraging students to see evaluation as a *civic* responsibility, an outgrowth of time spent engaged in the intellectual trajectory of higher education, would allow faculty to better translate RMP's impulses in positive, pedagogically sound ways. Burns argues that "Despite the relative anonymity of the electronic medium and the mitigating effects of a common student status, each student's 'standing' in the deliberative forum will vary according to others' perceptions of her ethos" (135). This comment is again relevant to online power structures—and the ability that RMP participants have to modify and even discount (i.e., "flag") certain postings, all in the space of public view. In these terms, RMP may be seen as a space for public exchange, standing in for those physical sites of discourse where individuals have historically met for debate. Such notions interface with Giroux's criticism of current conceptions of pedagogy as a civic act, in that participants in civic discourse should not only have "the typical right to participate; they should also be educated [in the fullest possible way] in order to be *able* to participate" (qtd. in "Cultural Studies" 83, emphasis in original).

Even though the content of RMP exchanges is certainly far from the intellectual import of classical rhetoricians, one can see the need to "educate" present in the exchanges as they are structured, and a recognition that this is a public dialogue, which means that responses are susceptible to response, modification, even rhetorical negation. The select example responses listed here are in chronological order, with "Poster 1" being the first response in the thread in each case. In four of the five of the exchanges, there is a central negative claim about the professor's pedagogy that subsequent posters seek to challenge or amend, sometimes in direct response to the original poster. In the fifth exchange, there is a supposition about the source of negative ratings, which is carried through later postings. In each thread, there also exists recognition that bias may exist for a variety of reasons within individual ratings/postings, and in at least one case there is explicit consideration of the reasons behind an alternative viewpoint:[39]

Professor A

Poster 1

His was the worst class I've ever taken. This man is a complete jerk. Assigns endless blogs, insults students during presentations. . . . If that's not bad enough, attendance counts big time! He will ruin your life and GPA!!!

Poster 2

He's really not that bad. . . . If you're an English major, you should expect to have to read and write a lot. Once you get used to the way the class goes, it's not impossible. [If] you're a hard worker, you'll do fine.

Poster 3

GREAT professor . . . I say though that by taking his class you do a LOT of writing. There are blogs and worksheets to work on, some books to read, but they are helpful and your writing will improve. Attendance is MANDATORY, so don't slack off. (http://www.ratemyprofessors.com/ShowRatings.jsp?tid = 4614 36)

Professor B

Poster 1

While I found the material that was covered in class interesting, [this professor] had the ability to make me feel like a complete idiot because I did not like to talk in class. I think that some people make him into some sort of godly figure and THIS IS NOT

THE CASE! I worked my butt off and was thankful that I ended up with a C +. Avoid if possible.

Poster 2

[The professor] is beyond brilliant and his class was extremely engaging. Yeah, it is challenging and you have to work your butt off to get an A, it is well worth it. He seems tough at first, but he's really a sweet guy. You just have to actually read and show interest . . . and he'll LOVE ya!

Poster 3

I thought [the professor] was a very helpful professor and he let me edit my paper for a better grade. If you attend his class and actually participate in his discussions then he will take notice of you. If you just sit and stare then you will be bored and eventually get insulted. Don't take this class if you are going to be bored. (http://www.ratemyprofessors.com/ShowRatings.jsp?tid = 208741&page = 2)

Professor C

Poster 1

If you are a woman, expect any grade to have a minus (–) after it!

Poster 2

Best teacher at [University X]. The woman who claimed sexism is a darn fool!

Poster 3

I agree that the woman who claimed sexism is a fool. I am a female and do not see what she means at all. The class I am in is [on the topic of sexuality and humanities] and [the professor] is constantly advocating the equality of women. So that girl is bitter that she didn't do well. (http://www.ratemyprofessors.com/ShowRatings.jsp?tid = 2087 41&page = 5)

Professor D

Poster 1

My god this class was awful. . . . SOOOOOOOOO much reading, and a TON of online reading to boot . . . it's as if he thinks his class is the only one you're taking, and god is he ARROGANT! BOO THIS MAN!

Poster 2

The course work was a bit overwhelming but [this professor] is probably the only [one] that has made me actually think. If you're looking for an easy course . . . don't take [this professor]. If you want a course where you get your money's worth and actually leave a better student . . . [this professor] is the guy.

Poster 3

Take his classes you'll learn. He'll make you work. But, if you can't write papers you shouldn't be here anyways.

Poster 4

This is college, and [this professor] makes it feel like college. A lot of work, but you WILL learn a lot. So shut your mouth, stop whining, get ready to write/read and take this prof at least once. I've taken his classes twice so far. (http://www.ratemyprofessors.com/ShowRatings.jsp?tid = 62240&page = 3)

Professor E

Poster 1

Probably my favorite teacher. I like how the people with all 1s [as numerical ratings] had no comments. Plagiarism? I'd guess so. His classes are fun & interesting. He's extremely intelligent & well rounded. He's a fair grader & wants you to learn.

Poster 2

I thought I would hate this class, yet it turned out to be one of the best classes I've ever taken (I am an Eng. major, so I've taken plenty).

Poster 3

Seems that only those in his lower-level comp classes have problems with him. Too bad they don't know a good teacher when they see one! Most likely they were caught plagiarizing something, he can't be tricked!

Poster 4

He's not very helpful and doesn't answer e-mails. He's an arrogant guy, full of himself and not a very fair grader. I know he also writes all his own ratings on this site, so beware.

Poster 5

I loved him. I can see where some people might say he's arrogant, but it didn't bother me. Very enthusiastic about the mate-

rial, very intelligent. Slow with returning papers . . . plus he
doesn't give many assignments. But overall, fair grader,
extremely nice, fun class, and always returned my e-mails within a day. (http://www.ratemyprofessors.com/ShowRatings.jsp?
tid = 291924)

There is much to note in these postings. First, as a sample set, they visibly discount the notion that *only* lazy or disgruntled students populate
RMP threads—even though one can certainly find professors who have garnered a great number of responses exclusively on the negative end of this
spectrum. These examples illustrate a range of responses—from highly
negative to highly positive—within one set of exchanges, and within one
professor's ratings, across different courses, which highlights another element of traditional evaluation that is limiting—comparing student responses within the context of *one* course/course type only.

These responses fall into several broad categories. First, there are the
enthusiastic student respondents who seek to overturn negative assumptions about a professor, significantly that he is too "hard" on students, or
demands too much work. Sometimes these assumptions are met with consideration for alternative perspectives—for example, the comment that the
student could see "how some people" would see Professor C as "arrogant,"
followed by an explanation of his or her own view. Other times, assumptions are met with the counterargument that it is the *student* him or herself
who has exceedingly low expectations for the course and harbors a misconception of what "college is." This leads to the second thread of
response—that which takes the discussion outside of the professor himself
and into the larger arena of expectations in higher education. A running
argument in these posts, as well as others posted on RMP, is that "this is
college" and that hard work is, in fact, worthwhile. Other respondents
make the popular connection between quality and cost (i.e., that learning
is "worth the money" and that education is an investment worth taking
seriously). Many RMP participants vocalize concerns about course costs,
including textbooks, or the overall cost of college, including transferability
of courses and tuition rates, within their ratings of professors. In many RMP
threads, the students end up judging *one another's* views and attitudes
more than they direct judge the professor him or herself, challenging
unsupported claims and providing counter-examples of positive (or negative) experiences.

A third thread is the recognition of individual student biases that may
affect ratings. Like faculty, RMP student participants are aware of the shortcomings of particular postings, and seem to discount them when appropriate (or even accuse professors of posting their *own* feedback disguised as
students, in the case of the respondent for Professor D). In particular, two
of Professor E's respondents hypothesize that the overly negative postings

are from students who plagiarized or who otherwise skirted the require-ments for the course, and were sanctioned for it. One respondent, follow-ing a positive post by a self-declared English major but a negative post by an assumed general education student of Professor E, hypothesizes that only those in "lower-level comp classes" have problems with Professor E. The implication behind this comment is that such students do not work (or do not want to work) as hard as upper-division majors. Finally, as exempli-fied in the case of Professor C, a thread present in RMP ratings is debate over the conditions of the classroom, including equity for certain groups of students. Although one poster claims that Professor C discriminates against female students, without providing any evidence, subsequent posters dis-count this claim, with the final poster arguing that, in fact, the professor has demonstrated himself to be mindful of both male and female students in her classroom experiences. We cannot know which respondent's view is more "accurate," but participants can *read* both and see that there are mul-tiple narratives to consider.

Although these five sample threads are limited illustrations in the inter-est of space, they exemplify the range of positive–negative dialogic exchanges found overall on the site. I invite readers to use these samples as a starting point for considering the range of rhetorical impulses found on RMP. Importantly, the threads provided assert the *possibility* for such public evaluative forums to be productive sites of student commentary, for students to be valued participants in the discourse regarding teaching and learning. Without some recognition, on the part of faculty, of the potential value of RMP, and lacking any on-the-ground classroom guidance in or con-nections to its aggregate views, the site stands as a lost opportunity to engage students in the art of civic discourse, an art in which they are already exhibiting some interest.

TRANSCENDING VIRTUAL BOUNDARIES: BRIDGING RMP DISCOURSE AND CLASSROOM CONDITIONS

Ultimately, the online format of RMP serves as more than just an opportu-nity for public deliberation among students. RMP has the potential to influ-ence the general public's perception of how higher education is viewed by students; one also might argue RMP reinforces notions of teachers as com-modities within the academic system. Prior to RMP, such discourse about teachers and teaching effectiveness was limited to student communities, and locally conscribed ones at that. Now, as we consider the venue that RMP provides students who wish to take a more vocal role in reflecting on their specific educational experiences, we also must consider the larger consequences of the very *public* nature of evaluative discourse such as that found on RMP. We must further consider how such a community represents our students online to those other potential investors (parents, administrators, governing boards) within higher education.

Patricia Bizzell argues that in a discourse community "what is most significant . . . is not [the members'] personal preferences, prejudices, and so on, but rather the expectations they share by virtue of belonging to that particular community" ("Cognition" 392). Bizzell additionally argues that such communities "can become accustomed to modifying each other's reasoning and language use in certain ways [to] achieve the status of conventions that bind the group in a discourse community, at work together on some project of interaction with the material world" ("Cognition" 388). Bizzell's parameters are critical in analyzing the attributes of the student community on RMP and in bringing that discourse to bear publicly on our classrooms. Their "personal preferences" are indeed less important, I argue, than the "expectations they share" about the subject of their postings, and how these postings seek to "inter[act] with the material world." Seeing RMP students as having shared expectations allows us to account for the often disparate ratings that appear on the site, where one professor might receive a string of wholly positive comments and high numbers, then receive an equal number of negative comments and low numbers, even where the positive and negative comments are in *agreement* about content. When we are able to *interpret* these expectations, which emerge online as contradictions, we can better address this public display of evaluative discourse for other investors[40] and harness the discourse for pedagogical improvements.

Such contradictions relate to the highly individualistic enterprise that college has become in today's economy. Students are making educational choices not always based on traditional notions of prestige, but also (or alternatively) on personal notions of "fit," construed typically as access— socially and structurally defined—and convenience. As Bill Hendricks notes in "Academic Labor and Social Class," "'merit' is still a big player in higher education's social imaginary. But 'merit' is no longer hegemonic, having nowadays to share the stage with two powerful new actors, 'choice' and 'results' . . . 'good' education can today equally well be naturalized in terms of personal preference" (600). Hendricks is arguing that the educational process has been codified such that notions of prestige, selectivity, or even grades, are less important than the overall value of the degree itself. Such important notions of choice and preferences are certainly also in play when students engage in the act of evaluation.

For example, one student in my own aggregate RMP postings from my previous institution viewed the frequent opportunities for class participation as a benefit—giving me an overall positive rating (in RMP terminology, a ☺). Another student, however, saw these opportunities as evidence that I am "always bugging students to participate" in the context of a generally positive, but somewhat irritating, pedagogical style, and thus gave me a neutral assessment, or a ☺. I am assuming, further, that students with an even greater disposition to remain passive in discussions will someday give me a negative rating, or a ☹. To the general public, these evaluations may be a sign of discord in the classroom (what kind of teacher *am* I?). But I can see the equivalent instructional value in these competing perceptions. Each of these responses are *true and valid* assessments, as each is rooted in an individual expectation of respect for the student's needs as a learner, and judges my ability to infer those needs. Our students, after all, are not all the same, and neither are our institutions; if that were so, we would approach pedagogy as a uniform, stable act. If I were to speak with these students about their RMP assessments, I believe that each could adequately defend his or her position in the context of parameters of need, but would not be invested in contextualizing these responses within the larger goals of the course, or the often hierarchical parameters of academia at large.

Thus, faculty must serve as intermediaries between these highly personalized, public evaluations of courses and faculty and the competing messages they send. The true worth of RMP is not its most obviously intended one—its transmission of the inside "scoop"—but rather its collective evidence of how students *view* such courses and discourse opportunities, and how this very public, self-moderated discourse makes higher education and its faculty the topic of national conversation, transcending institutional boundaries. Student participants in the dialogue seek to not only air grievances and share compliments, but also seek to hold each other *accountable* for those opinions, creating a site of civic exchange that stands to alter the phenomenon of the course evaluation in the Internet age.[41] Students who choose to join the RMP discourse community are invested in voicing their *expectations* of quality and effectiveness, and desire to do so in a community setting, rather than in a traditional evaluation. If we let these evaluations stand as is, without any response, we dismiss students' agency in the evaluation process, and the opportunity to shape that agency to elicit positive change.

I propose that faculty—especially those leading reading and writing-centered classrooms—begin to ponder the pedagogical ramifications of public evaluation via online discourse communities as presented by RMP. It does not do faculty any service to spend time wondering whether what students are saying online is accurate without interrogating *why* students say such things at all. These students are interested in being exceedingly public with their evaluative comments, hoping to reach others who otherwise would not have access to these opinions and observations. A posting on RMP communicates a willingness to dialogue about varying expectations of pedagogy. Students and professors might thus have profitable con-

versations in the classroom about, for example, the three categories of evaluation on RMP—easiness, clarity, and helpfulness—that easy may not be
good, or that the definition of "easy" could be negative *or* positive. Students
and professors might also dialogue about the way in which higher education *encourages* such labels in its assessments. These are discussions worth
having—and important to undertake within the construct of "public" pedagogy enacted at all instructional levels, but rarely made available in the
institutional setting, or in singularly voiced evaluative instruments.

I ask that faculty consider RMP's own rationale for existence, worth
reviewing in the context of our own insular stance on students as part of
the evaluative process:

> The purpose of the site is to be a resource for students. Where else can
> you find out what others think of an instructor? When you have the
> option of choosing a teacher, wouldn't you really like some informa-
> tion? It also gives you, the user, a place to voice your opinion. It gives
> you a place to make a difference in your education. (www.ratemypro-
> fessor.com/FAQ.html)

Compare this to Gregory Clark's contention regarding discourse communities:

> The political assumptions that underlie the rhetoric of the discourse
> community as it has been articulated in composition studies during the
> last decade seem to support democracy in principle, yet tend to under-
> mine it in practice. The theory . . . assumes that those people are more
> or less equal politically, that they have equal access to and equal influ-
> ence upon the discourse that determines the beliefs and purposes they
> will share. But . . . once enacted these processes tend to minimize or
> exclude the participation of some people as they establish the domi-
> nance of others. (61)

Are we shutting out students in our theories over how to improve higher education? Are we, as Giroux argues, part of a society for which school
is "no longer considered a public good but a private good" such that "the
only form of citizenship increasingly being offered to young people is con-
sumerism" ("Public Pedagogy" 7)? Faculty must consider how sites such as
RMP seek to validate students' desire to negotiate and even control public
discussion of higher education outside the institutional setting. Too often
academic culture divides itself from public discourse as a protective mechanism; RMP is a reaction to this divide, and while there are certainly
aspects of RMP that academics and students alike find untrustworthy, there
also exists evidence of legitimate and thought-worthy perceptions of teach-

ing. Until we begin to see the connections between such online student rhetorics and the physical and intellectual factors shaping teaching and learning, we cannot begin to see how RMP may someday play a positive role in our literally "public" pedagogies. In the next and final chapter, I discuss these connections more holistically, in the context of the first-year course in particular, and the implicit and explicit roles it seeks to play in modeling higher education's views of literacy acquisition for our students.

5

THE WORK OF TEACHING
IN THE AGE OF ONLINE LITERACY
REPRODUCTION

*Literacy has always and everywhere been the center of the educational
enterprise. No matter what else it expects of its schools, a culture insists
that students learn to read, write, and speak in the officially sanctioned
manner.* (1)

—James Berlin, *Rhetoric and Reality*

*We have a concept of audience as construct, not as lived. Which allows us
to develop all these step-by-step heuristic templates to turn the rhetorical
situation into a parlor game. . . . When there's really only one heuristic
that matters: the person who reads this—and it is one specific person, sat-
urated in lived desire—will that person be changed?* (11)

—Geoffrey Sirc,
English Composition as a Happening

So far in this book, I have argued that students are readily engaging in discussions and allied practices of literacy online, via textual and meta-textu-
al analysis (Pink Monkey), redefinitions of authorship/textual ownership
(the online paper mills), and teacher evaluation (Rate My Professors). In
each of these instances, students are attempting to reify the process by
which they become "literate"—whether that is as readers, writers, or critical evaluators—without the physical or figurative/intellectual oversight of
the teacher-figure. Not only are these students engaging with these online
resources within an extra-institutional *setting*, but they also are doing so
outside of the parameters of institutional teacher *authority*, circumventing

the teacher-centered configuration that is necessarily present in even the most liberally minded college classrooms. I submit that these students participate in this literacy-based/literacy-centered work within student online communities in response to the lack of agency, ergo authority, they feel within higher education's processes of schooling. These online communities serve to challenge, if not contradict, the validity of our institutional notion that the teacher *is*, in fact, the education, delivering the message of the institution, and that students are essentially vessels without significant or lasting input as to their content(s). Contradicting this accepted notion of schooling, the structures of these Web sites and the students who frequent them collectively declare that the teacher is ceasing to *matter* in the practices of postsecondary literacy acquisition. Furthermore, this online student discourse allows for—indeed, is predicated on—the teacher-figure's reconstruction as not primary subject, but as shifting *object* in the larger discourse of higher education.

Given the impending obsolescence of the teacher-figure and the rise of individual student agencies of power and authority in their perceptions of schooling, this chapter thus questions how we come (or bring ourselves) to this place of increasing obsolescence. How do we go forward with literacy instruction in this new role we are asked to occupy *as* teachers, particularly in the first-year writing and reading classroom, wherein literacy principles are inculcated, and teacher-figures have historically taken a personalized, primary importance—arguably more so than in other college subjects/classroom sites—in the student learning process? What happens when the notion of teacher as subject of the classroom discourse is, indeed, vanishing from our students' collective educational lexicon? Short of taking early retirement and abandoning our classroom roles and academic positions in order to duck this problem altogether, how can teachers respond to the hypothesis that our students no longer *want* or, in some cases, even *need* our oversight, expertise, and points of view in order to be "schooled"? What kind of responses—pedagogical or otherwise—can we provide to this impending obsolescence? Finally, and critical to the subject of literacy acquisition, in what ways might these responses be a logical outgrowth of our field's continual reconceptualization of the first-year writing course itself?

CASTING ASIDE THE REBELS: PEDAGOGICAL CONFORMITY AND INTERCHANGEABLE TEACHER-FIGURES

Reconceptualizing the teacher as object is perhaps painful, but theoretically possible, via Walter Benjamin's seminal work "The Work of Art in the

Age of Mechanical Reproduction," wherein, for our purposes, "teacher-fig-ure" may stand in as analogous to "work of art." Although I realize that Benjamin was ultimately arguing for the function (both collective/social and aesthetic/intellectual) of the motion picture as a new technology of "mechanical reproduction," and for understanding our culture's relation-ship with the art object (and the artist), his theorems are also surprisingly applicable to my argument regarding the shifting position of the teacher-as-object in higher education, particularly as a consequence of technolo-gy—in this case, online student-led technologies. The title of this chapter, therefore, deliberately plays upon Benjamin's famous work, so as to argue that teachers must be willing to accept, or at least understand, a similar personal/aesthetic/political re-understanding of themselves as educational objects in the face of increasingly omnipresent reification via emerging Internet-based technologies.

In his 1936 essay, Benjamin states:

> Even the most perfect reproduction of a work of art is lacking in one element: its presence in time and space, its unique existence at the place where it happens to be. This unique existence of the work of art determined the history to which it was subject throughout the time of its existence. This includes the changes which it may have suffered in physical condition over the years as well as the various changes in its ownership . . . changes in ownership are subject to a tradition which must be traced from the situation of the original. (220)

Imagining teachers as "works of art" subject to time and space—their own physicality as well as larger material conditions—and, importantly, history and tradition, and as constructed by the mythologies and realities of our culture—as Benjamin does with the artistic product above, allows us to re-imagine the teacher as a theoretically mutable object. But this comparison is not meant to reify teachers as aesthetic objects alone (although one might argue that, in fact, the aesthetics *of* teaching are quite important). Instead, I invoke in this comparison a larger argument about the specific role of technology in the shaping of the teacher-object. To do so, I turn to the next principle in Benjamin's argument:

> (T)hat which withers in the age of mechanical reproduction is the aura of the work of art. This is a symptomatic process whose significance points beyond the realm of art. One might generalize by saying: the technique of reproduction detaches the reproduced object from the domain of tradition. By making many reproductions it substitutes a plurality of copies for an unique existence. And in permitting the repro-duction to meet the beholder or listener in his own particular situation, it reactivates the object reproduced. This leads to a tremendous shat-

tering of tradition which is the obverse of the contemporary crisis and renewal of mankind. (221)

If we allow that teachers are, like works of art, "reproducible" within a system (education), and if that system "substitutes a plurality of copies for an unique existence," *and* that the system in question *aims* to make available mass reproductions of an original image (the teacher as ideal) that we hold sacred—but now can "meet the beholder or listener in his [*sic*] own particular situation"—we can see more readily the analogy under consideration as one that focuses on mutability of staid objects within our culture, or our subcultures, here higher education. What was once an unique ideal—with unique authority, and lasting physical and intellectual permanence—is now a reproducible object that can take many forms: It can be a genuine "replica" (a new teacher, trained and molded by a postsecondary school of education); it can be a simulacra (to borrow from Baudrillard, i.e,. a copy more "real than the real" in which the ideals, values, and methodologies also take a heightened importance, i.e., the teaching intern, the graduate student training to be a professor); or it can be a mechanical, rote reproduction, exactly as Benjamin argues—in which case, it need not, theoretically, be a teacher at all, but instead a technological apparatus, or system, that does the "teaching" for us. Enter the multiplicity of teacher "stand-ins" that proliferate our electronic settings, including but not limited to machinery created by publishers and other educational software companies or organizations for grading, automated essay "feedback," and of course the deeply flawed authority-granting substitute for instruction in authorship, turnitin.com. In more subtle ways, and with more complex results, the Web sites that I have profiled in this book also function as versions of these technological apparatuses, but are rarely recognized as such.

Thus, I present in this chapter three possible discipline-sponsored permutations of this "reproducible" teacher concept that lead not only to the undermining of our own pedagogical intentions, but also to the polarization between teacher-figures and students, a polarization that not only creates an artificial (and sometimes, but not always, unproductive) divide between these two groups, but that also severely limits the possibility that education, specifically literacy education, will become the democratized, rhetorically driven site of public discourse that best benefits true student learning. If students and teachers continue to work at cross-purposes, and continue to disregard one another's real and tangible agencies in higher education, then the dialogic debates that should and can be at the heart of literacy acquisition cannot be realized. Instead, each group will limit its discourse to its own internalized constituencies, particularly in the case of teacher-figures, who neither benefit from, nor gain agency through, forced entry into student-led online learning communities such as those currently dominating Internet discourse.

THE MECHANIZED TEACHER:
THE TEACHING MACHINE MOVEMENT

I begin with an overview of one of composition studies' earliest encounters with technology: the teaching machine. This encounter reveals that early attempts to experiment with electronic, alternate deliveries so as to streamline the process of writing instruction, and teacher workload, logically led to the re-energized wave of "student-centered" emphasis in literacy acquisition found in today's writing classroom. A review of the principles of the teaching machine, and college composition faculty's response to those principles in practice, also reveals some eerily familiar conflicts that are now represented our current struggle with replicated teaching/teachers as found in online/electronic discourse.

Our resistance as faculty to the machinery of instruction and our near-romance with student-centered "human" classrooms is, in fact, born of the threat of technology reaching back to when the educational possibilities of the machine itself was at its infancy. In order to separate our instinctively human-centered teaching desires from the possible invasion of technology into those protected spaces, we like to console ourselves with the myth that all media is revolution rather than evolution, and that "technology" is a term meaning cutting-edge, complex innovation of either purpose or form. The truth, however, is that technology in writing instruction may be defined in very simple or singular-dimension terms (as many have noted, first it was the pencil, and later the typewriter—neither of which even the most technophobe would now call threatening) and reaches back more than fifty years, to the teaching machine movement of the late 1950s.

In "Drill Pads, Teaching Machines, and Programmed Texts," Neal Lerner details how teaching machines and other devices provided early alterations to the shape of instruction in university writing centers. Lerner argues that "drill-and-practice" work lingers as a popular pedagogy in many writing centers because of the following:

> it performs two powerful functions: (1) By "individualizing" work in the laboratory, the burden of success and failure is clearly shifted onto students and away from the practices and institutions themselves. (2) With drill-and-practice exercises . . . classroom teachers can clearly wipe their hands of the "dirty work" of teaching some things that are very difficult to teach and earn. It is much cleaner to turn such matters over to a laboratory (and later a computer) and this practice acts as a powerful sign that we've done something about the "problem." (123)

In historicizing this mechanized approach to writing instruction that writing centers frequently inherited and were forced to embrace, for various socioeconomic reasons related to student populations, Lerner outlines the main problem with the concept of the teaching machine as promoted by B.F. Skinner in 1958. As Lerner articulates, the teaching machine's approach to student learning "attempts to 'individualize' instruction, [and thus] is firmly at odds with the ideas of writing as a social activity. Not only do students proceed 'at their own pace,' but they learn, essentially, alone" (126).

The idea of learning in isolation is especially critical to my argument here about teachers versus teacher-functioning replacements, whether they be machines or larger systems of technology. Inasmuch as faculty often have relied on the writing center, for example, as an initial site of displacement of authority—as in, "go to the writing center to get *help* with that paper," where "help" is the primary function of the teacher him or herself—that displacement still results in a teacher-figure guidance relationship, in which the student sees the pedagogy of literacy as a personalized, individualized one. In the *further* displacement of the teacher in the figure of the teaching machine or technological system, however, the "personal" attributes are completely absent, as the relationship is human with (not versus, importantly) machine. When such further displacement happens in the writing center, Lerner notes, faculty have limited worries—as they are nonetheless "freed" from the more difficult task of teaching writing, particularly grammar, usage, and mechanics. But when the student moves directly from the teacher in the writing-based classroom to a machine or machinery/system itself, and does so by *choice*, I argue, the concerns are greatly magnified on the part of faculty, in ways apparent in faculty reaction to Web sites profiled in this book.

Skinner's original article is worth brief examination here because it seemingly intended to argue for technology as an *aide*, not a hindrance or competitor, to the teacher. Further still, Skinner explicitly sought a technological means to make students take more *control* and have more *authority* over their own education, through self-guided instruction vis-à-vis the teaching machine. Skinner argued that randomized instruction in basic concepts—such as mathematical computation, but also grammar and usage—should be employed via machines positioned within introductory-level classrooms, in order to promote active and reinforced learning among students, and to supplement classroom/teacher instruction in efficient, quantifiable ways that make individuated learning possible. Skinner's article proposed that the increasing demand for an education nationwide went far beyond "building more schools and training more teachers"; in fact, Skinner argued, "Education must become more efficient," but not at the expense of providing machinery that encourages the growth of "the student . . . as a mere passive receiver of instruction," one of his core fears about the direction that efficiency-based instruction was heading at the time (969).

Instead, Skinner proposed that schools begin to employ "a capital equipment which will encourage the student to take an active role in the instructional process" (969). This equipment, Skinner claimed, had already been invented, in the 1920s, and was predicated on the "automatic testing of intelligence and information" wherein student responses to questions led to differentiated learning or response challenges presented via subsequent randomized material; students who offered a correct answer received reinforcement and a new question, whereas students who offered an incorrect answer were directed toward material that would double-back to highlight their error(s) (969). Skinner believed that the prototype teaching machine developed by Sidney L. Pressey in 1992 was, importantly, not a machine designed to stand in for the teacher him or herself, but a device "to be used after some amount of learning had already taken place elsewhere" (969).

Skinner's first and primary condition of the ideal teaching machine built on two core principles of learning: first, that the student have a significant responsibility in creating the correct answer, and second, that the student's long-term ability *to* select the right answer is reinforced by the lack of incorrect alternatives that confuse this process:

> The student must *compose* his response rather than select it from a set of alternatives, as in a multiple-choice self-rater. One reason for this is that we want him to recall rather that recognize—to make a response as well as see that it is right. Another reason is that effective multiple-choice material must contain plausible wrong responses, which are out of place in the delicate process of "shaping" behavior because they strengthen unwanted forms. (970)

Such a proposal immediately undercuts the traditional notion of "testing" in a mechanized (i.e., formulaic, form-based) situation, in that multiple choice is seen as easier for the test-taker him or herself, but less desirable for actual *learning* (i.e., long-term retention).

Skinner asserted in this article that despite how the machine might sound, it "does not teach. It simply brings the student into contact with the person who has composed the material it presents. . . . This may suggest mass production, but the effect upon each student is surprisingly like that of a private tutor" (971). Skinner maintained that, like the tutorial relationship, students working with the machine would experience "sustained activity"; would be "always alert and busy"; would be required to demonstrate that a point had been "completely understood"; would only work with the material for which he or she "was ready"; and finally, would help the student "come up with the right answer" (971). Finally, the machine would help to reinforce "correct behavior" in student learning, an attribute obviously of great interest to Skinner, as a behavioral scientist (971).

Although the bulk of the remainder of Skinner's article goes on to out-
line the specifications of the machine, the testing situation, including a
description of the machine itself and the optimal seating arrangements for
implementation, and the charting of appropriate levels of material that the
machine should or could handle, in the closing of his piece, Skinner
answers "some questions" related to the teaching machine, chief among
them "Will machines replace teachers?" Skinner responds that "On the
contrary, they are capital equipment to be used by teachers to save time
and labor. In assigning certain mechanizable functions to machines, the
teacher emerges in his proper role as an indispensible human being" (976).
In marrying education and economics in this statement, Skinner lays bare
the value of the teaching machine: its capacity to economize the classroom
space (and growing student body, a significant concern mid-century) and
work as a kind of infinitely replicable aide to the teacher him or herself.
Skinner also assuages the fears of readers (some of whom are surely teachers) who anticipate the "machine" taking over their jobs.

   I find Skinner's two central concerns to be prescient in imagining
today's concerns over mechanized instruction, or any third-party machinery, including online spaces controlled by students, which aims to do some
of the work of teaching in a particular classroom or context. These concerns are, in fact, continuing ones for teachers considering technology in
the twenty-first century; whether they are technologies officially sanctioned by the institution (such as Blackboard or other platforms); technologies created by companies and testing corporations for use in the classroom, but is not created by the institution itself (from innocuous-seeming
programs such as spell check to textbook companies' tutoring/writing programs, to larger money-generating systems such as SmartThink or the
afore-mentioned turnitin.com); or technologies that stem neither from the
corporate world per se, nor the institutional world, but from the organic
spaces of student learners (i.e., the sites profiled in this book).

   Skinner's initial theories led to some college-level experimentation
with the teaching machine in English composition classrooms during the
1960s; reports on these experiments can be found in the 1961 and 1966
convention reports published in *College Composition and Communication*
(*CCC*), as well as in the textbook generated on the basis of the teaching
machine theory, *English 2600*, by Joseph C. Blumenthal. A brief look at
these reports and the opening rhetoric of this textbook's pages give us
some insight into the evolution of machine-centered pedagogical theorems
to the longer-standing human-centered pedagogical approaches that would
soon pervade writing instruction in the 1970s and beyond. Although I do
not believe that making these two approaches oppositional—human versus
machine—is accurate or productive, I *do* think that in terms of this early
era in mechanized instruction, and in applications of technology in the
writing classroom, the opposition is an apt contextual one. One cannot

help but see, in the suspicion raised by these reports and the subsequent rise of expressivist, student-centered writing classrooms, a clear continuum of pedagogical strategy that leads away from the machine-as-subject (or any representation thereof) and toward the rigorous reinforcement of the teacher-as-subject in the writing classroom. Even though the classrooms of iconic expressivist figures such as Murray and Elbow would never claim to have been "teacher-centered," the agency given to the teacher-figure to serve as a very *human* role model for students is about as anti-machinery as one can get, and neatly coincides with the failed experiments and eventual demise of the teaching machine movement in composition studies.

In the 1961 *CCC* report on the twelfth annual convention, report No. 15, "Teaching Machines and Programmed Instruction," the advantages of programmed instruction are described as:

> The opportunity for individualized instruction—The self-evaluating materials free the student to go at his own pace; (2) The operation of reinforcement—the answer is accepted or corrected immediately, thus strengthening the correct response; (3) The removal of anxiety caused by competition and grades—all the questions must be answered correctly by all the students; (4) The freeing of the teacher from the drudgery of marking drill papers—the teacher is afforded the opportunity to improve her own preparation; (5) The motivation of a fresh approach—time-worn material may be taught more effectively by a new model; (6) The counter-acting of the effects of poor teaching; and (7) The removal of social stigma for incorrect English usage. (182)

One conclusion drawn was that true to Skinner's original admonition, the machine should be used as a teacher aide rather than a teacher substitute: "The value of the machine lies in the learning of material which may be transferred to the solution of problems or to the acquisition of more complicated skills. This transfer lies in the province of the teacher" (182). The above suggested benefits, however, evidence a view of the teaching machine as potential savior for exhausted, frustrated teachers who can no longer see new ways to approach old problems (such as teaching mechanics) and for anxious students who falter under the pressure of the imposing and demanding teacher-figure who seeks the right answers, right now. Finally, the idea that the teaching machine could remove "social stigma" by improving students' writing in a private, mechanized setting (rather than, implicitly, in basic writing courses or other tutoring situations in view of fellow students) also reinforces the conflict during the late 1950s and early 1960s over how and where to educate at-risk, underprepared, or otherwise intellectually marginalized student writers.

By 1966, the focus of the *CCC* report had changed significantly, from one designed to explore the possible benefits and drawbacks of the teaching machine, to a gentle but pointed critique of the methodologies behind the teaching machine and the need for more data that proved its effectiveness. Even though the workshop title focused on teaching machines, the very first sentence of the report reads as follows: "Teaching machines were virtually ignored in the lively discussion which developed on programmed learning and the programmed texts currently available in the teaching of English" (192). By 1966, workshop participants were questioning whether such mechanized learning could even be *possible* in any setting, especially in more nuanced curricula such as English literature—implicitly a heavy-reading and critical-thinking curriculum not suited to drill–practice learning. As the report noted, "There was a discernible impression from the statements of several consultants and participants in the workshop that there are no current programmed texts which can be wholeheartedly endorsed for English. Yet, several at the workshop believed that the present criticisms of programmed texts could also apply to more conventional textbooks in English" (193). Such comments exhibit a worry among participants that other teacher stand-ins—such as grammar or writing texts—were ill-equipped to assume the teacher's role in meaningful pedagogy. Moreover, the report emphasized the limited physical capacities of the teaching machine versus a human evaluator in highlighting the issue of sensory learning: "Programming in the future might involve other factors in the learning environment: its current focus on written materials has ignored important senses in the process of learning, for example, hearing" (193).

Such anxiety over the eventual erasure of human facilitators of the learning process (i.e., classroom teachers) also is present in other contemporary literature on this subject, such as Bloom and Bloom's 1967 *College English* article, "The Teaching and Learning of Argumentative Writing." The authors begin with a somewhat revolutionary premise—that the teacher also is a student (in his or her continuing learning regarding essay evaluation) and the student also is a teacher (in his or her interpretation of available materials, posing of solutions to problems, and developing strategies) (128–29). Echoing some of Skinner's own concerns, they argue that "teaching depends on selective rewarding of appropriate behaviors. Traditional methods of teaching are relatively ineffective; they encourage over-dependence on the instructor rather than promoting independence in the student" (134–35). But a few pages into the essay, Bloom and Bloom begin to argue not for teacher-free or teacher-less learning, but instead for what they call the "symbolic presence" of the teacher, as that which extends beyond the classroom and/or the specific lesson to conferences, representative and applicable written commentaries, and other lasting measures of the teacher's advice and authority beyond fleeting verbal instructions (130). Such symbolic presence is necessary, according to Bloom and Bloom, because of the following:

> A reinforcement learning theory of theme writing would suggest that a teacher be present to sort out and reinforce the more adequate solutions to problems which the student has created for himself. It is impractical to have a teacher physically present-and disconcerting, according to the student who was observed, even when no grades were involved. And so we must fall back on the symbolic presence of the instructor. (130)

When the concept of symbolic presence is extended to non-human teacher stand-ins, however, Bloom and Bloom find that the concept fails in its execution. They note that "The books of rhetoric typically used fail to provide true symbolic presence because they do not and cannot tell the student how he is to apply a given rule at a given time and place . . . appropriate usage depends on the instructor's continual (symbolic) presence" (130–31). Additionally, Bloom and Bloom argue that despite the benefits of self-pacing that teaching machines allow, "A programmed learning device cannot tell the student what content to apply . . . and hence teaching machines are seldom used when the content is as complex a thing as the writing of a paper" (132).

These are not surprising conclusions, as one can see how Skinner's proposed teaching machine would have its limitations to only certain types of subject matter. Obviously, teaching machines—at this historical moment—were limited in their purview. Bloom and Bloom's argument is notable in this context, however, for its simultaneous championing of independent student learning and the blurred roles of teacher and student and its continued assertion that books and machines will *always* fall short of the human teacher. They note that "The reinforcement proposed [here] concerns ideas, not discrete responses typical of the usual Skinnerian teaching machine. The judge of the correctness of the complex response is not a machine (which has had its omniscience programmed). Rather, the judge (or teacher, if you will, the person who is active during the process when knowledge and skill are being imparted) is the student himself" (131). However, they also concede that the ultimate indicator of student success (at least in our system of higher education today), letter grades, are in fact symbolic representations of the *teacher* rather than the learning process, as grades are "at best learning about the teacher, not about the writing" (133).

The actual *English 2600* text, built on Skinner's principles of the teaching machine and designed to be used with such a device, actually promotes a strange combination of student independence and "forward-thinking" learning. As the first page, titled "What Is English 2600?" proclaims, "What a strange-looking book!" "This is what you are thinking as you glance through its pages and notice how different it looks from the many other textbooks you have studied" (iii). This second-person "student-friendly" rhetorical approach not only catches the attention of the skeptical reader, but also later becomes a familiar trope in rhetoric and composition hand-books from the 1970s forward, speaking directly to the student instead of to the teacher (who would have his or her own "teacher's guide," perhaps). Of course, such rhetoric resembles that found on the student-led Web sites profiled in this book: direct address, bypassing the authority figure other-wise at the center of the learning experience, the teacher. But *English 2600*'s introduction then goes on to explain why its streamlined approach is valuable, invoking cultural anxieties over falling behind (or getting ahead) in the arenas of science and technology:

> One of the great things about our country is that we don't stand still. We are constantly trying to create better products and discover better ways of doing things. Millions of man-hours and billions of dollars are spent on research each year to build better homes, cars, refrigerators, TV sets, and countless other things. Why can't we, through scientific research, make similar progress in matters that pertain to the mind and education? The fact is that we can and we do! (iii)

Unlike today's prototypical writing textbook, this pitch from *English 2600* quite casually and effortlessly brings economic values and cultural con-sumerism into the argument over teaching methodologies. Rather than espousing the value of the personal connection between teacher and stu-dent, the social aspects of the learning process, or even the working habits of the developing writer, as composition studies texts would later privilege almost exclusively, *English 2600* gets right to the efficiency point: The world is moving fast, and so can your school work. Get on board!

Such rhetoric sounds much more like the economically based argu-ments of sites such as the online paper mills inhabit, as discussed in Chapter 3. But *English 2600*, while selling itself as a product, also is selling a larger *philosophy* of learning that was undoubtedly uncomfortable to many faculty who read its claims. The book notes that "the advantages of 'reasoning your way' instead of 'being told' have been known to good teachers ever since the days of Socrates. There is no separation between explanation and exercise, as in other textbooks; the two are woven tightly together [in this book]" (iii). Such weaving—although on one level com-pletely logical—seems to elide the teacher's role in being the explicator, the guide that bridges listening to the lesson (back to Bloom and Bloom's "hear-ing" complaint) and executing mastery of its concepts in written form.

But the real nail in the coffin for those faculty opposed to the method-ology of *English 2600* on "thinking" grounds comes two pages further into the introduction, wherein the guide to "getting the most" out of the book includes the following admonition:

> Don't cheat yourself out of the valuable experience of thinking! Don't
> look at the answer in the next frame until after figured it out for your-
> self. You are not working for grades on these lessons because the les-
> sons will not be scored. In fact, you will always end with a perfect score
> because you are expected to correct each error immediately. . . . Since
> your teacher will score the tests and you will not be able to look ahead
> for the answers, you will have to think for yourself. (v)

Thus, the book assures students that its methodology will provide the two
key functions that teachers have served up until this point in time: (a) a
platform for making students *think* about their answers, rather than simply
an exercise in guessing (provided the students use the book "correctly"); (b)
an error-free and virtually grade-free environment for learning that does
not *correct* errors, as teachers have historically done by supplying the right
answers in turn, and does not *punish* mistakes, as teachers must do when
this supply method fails. Instead, *English 2600* will allow students an open
space to select responses and then give those responses to the teacher off-
stage—a teacher who has now been reduced, through the role-reversal
rhetoric of the book's overview, to little more than a *grading* machine, fulfilling the prophecy that indeed, a machine *can* replace a teacher in some
respects, and can do so in the name of progress.

   If such a move is possible—and certainly the fact that English 2600 is
still in print today indicates that its philosophies were not rejected in total—
then it is not surprising that composition studies as a field would want to
provide a counter-solution to the problem of overworked writing teachers,
underchallenged students, and eclipsing values regarding the personal
interaction necessary to teach reading and writing in a meaningful, lasting
context. But how could this happen? One potential answer lies in self-repli-
cation, or the creation of a pedagogical system, or systematic theory, that
itself is hearty enough, and appealing enough, to withstand threats by the
machinery waiting to erase the human teacher-figure and his or her ethos.

THE SIMULATED TEACHER: REPRODUCIBLE
PEDAGOGIES AND SYSTEMATIC EMULATION

If the essence of the teacher-figure him or herself were not so susceptible
to, and predicated on, such possible replication and reproduction by
machinery or external systems, it is likely that my earlier analogy to
Benjamin's work of art would be less apt, even indefensible. But at least in
the American system, we continue to treat teachers as if they were able to
adhere to a magic formula for "getting it (teaching) right," after which

many are less-than-inclined to change or grow with the changing times, as it were, especially in relation to new strains of technology. We are collectively guilty of this formulaic approach to teaching in our schools of education, our secondary school structures, and our postsecondary school professorial culture, which claims to champion pedagogical innovation but rarely allows for real *change* in light of existing material and social conditions found within the classroom.

Once we *do* find the "magic"—in a particular pedagogical practice, assignment, or entire course plan that makes our teaching lives easier, and so we believe more effective—we freely encourage its replication across eager masses of newer, knowledge-seeking teachers. It is admirable to share our pedagogies, especially with those new to the profession, and such impulses often result in productive educational collaboration. But such oddly stalwart practices and traditions—especially when sanctioned at the administrative/institutional level—also ironically demonstrate to students that if teaching is a formula, it's a formula that need not reside in the authoritative (or senior/elder) individual in the room. Thus, the problematic equation results in a teacher who, in crass economic terms, outlives his or her use-value, such that his or her pedagogy may be separated from his or her *self*, and his or her identity thus elided by virtue of the pedagogical replication taking place outside of the teacher's physical presence. We already see this in the spread of online education, for example, wherein some institutions jointly own the rights to the teaching materials produced and posited on the course Web site. But we also see it in smaller ways, in English departments that employ a standard syllabus for the first- or second-semester composition course, often to account for, and easily assist, the tremendous turnover in contingent faculty teaching in the program, many of whom are hired last-minute and armed with little teaching experience or course-specific preparation.

Although I would be the first to stand up and declare that some degree of agreement or consistency is a good thing—that fifty teachers creating fifty goal-divergent and potentially methodologically and/or ideologically opposed courses within one course number (e.g., first-year writing) usually leads to some degree of chaos, and that replication can at some level make for a significantly positive cultural change within a department or area of study—one of the tenets of this difficult formula is that conformity, ergo *uniformity*, is always already good, whereas rebellion, and thus rejection of such uniformity, on even a micro-level, is always already bad. There can be no room for grey areas of value within this formula. Teachers who adhere to the system—even if it is a flawed one—are valued for their ability to be shuffled, reproduced, and realigned where needed. Teachers who diverge from currently accepted practices are outliers, nonassessable objects within the larger assessment system. Moments of rebellion, such as the process pedagogy movement in the 1970s in composition studies, thus often *become* systems onto themselves and therefore gain slavish follow-ings (as post-process theorists such as Sid Dobrin and Gary Olson have compellingly argued).[42] Such distaste for rebellion and difference ultimate-ly more often is translated in the act of teaching itself, and the message sent to students, for example, about acceptable literacy practices. This is especially true when the machinery of the public school/secondary school system overwhelms the individual and continues to linger—even if it is less visible and/or visibly problematic—in the mindset of students, and some teachers, into the first year of college.

Considering this problematic construct of teacher as unwilling staid authoritative figure in the context of a classroom that *itself* does not change is Geoffrey Sirc, in his book *English Composition as a Happening.* As is clear from the quote provided in the epigraph to this chapter, Sirc resists the "cor-porate seminar" approach to composition studies that pervaded its instruc-tion the 1980s and 1990s, and to his mind, continues into the twenty-first century (9). Instead, Sirc maintains that the artistic and aesthetic experi-mentation of the 1960s had a momentary influence on the act of compos-ing in first-year writing as well—as a "happening" rather than a formulaic act replicated from classroom to classroom. Sirc, echoing Benjamin's argu-ments about art and the spectator, argues that in the first-year required course (with the emphasis on "required," as Sirc points to scholars such as Bartholomae and Lindemann who advocate for a utilitarian approach to the course, designed to serve upper-division majors and fields):

> Our pedagogical, then, is the curatorial: we teach connoisseurship. . . .
> As instructors, our classroom activities combine the docent's tour (explaining how the great master-Pieces are put together) with the hands on workshop of family day (now that the Gallery-goers under-stand how the masterpieces work, they get to try to make one). The scene of classroom writing is peculiarly over determined, then, as Gallery—as physical space in a larger institution (Museum/University), lying on the cusp between the curatorial and the commercial. (4)

In Sirc's argument, then, our susceptibility to the uniformity of the system of teaching readily bleeds into our approach to teaching itself in the specter of the first-year writing course. Rather than teach students that writing is an artistic act, a mode of expression, certainly a site of experimentation—indeed, a vehicle by which one might know *self* in a tangible way—we teach writing as a replicable act that is heavily reliant on the success of acts that came prior to it, published in textbooks, readers, and course manuals (formerly our enemies, and now our rhetorical teacher-power re-enforcers) to become simply the purview of the writing classroom (i.e., dead artifacts for emulation). One might argue that even in our attempts to teach more "progressive" forms of writing—such as those found in alternative delivery systems (i.e., online spaces) we often are victim to relying on modeling and emulation, in electronic communication that modeling often resulting in echoes of form and design, especially that which seems "groundbreaking" in its effusive youthfulness.

Other critics of the system that Sirc theorizes to be true in writing instruction similarly argue that the writing course *itself* keeps any notion of writing-as-self (or as active rebellion against systems) institutionally in check. Although such a stance also may be heard in the historical studies of Robert Connors, Stephen North, and Sharon Crowley, in his 2001 *CCC* essay, "School Sucks," T.R. Johnson engages his readers in this stance from a slightly different, localized angle, with a hypothesis aimed at what he believes to be the core of literacy-based pedagogies: Namely, that teachers do more to regulate and suppress student individualities and the "rhetoric of rebellion" than to encourage in these pedagogies the free-thinking that composition studies otherwise aims to promote as a field. Johnson argues that "dominant traditions in our thinking have insistently constructed the renegade . . . as antagonistic, combative, even apocalyptic. In this tradition, the body in general and pleasure in particular are the Medusa-like villains that pedagogy must vanquish" (631). Johnson, echoing the work of Nancy Sommers, exemplifies this impulse in the search for error that pervades the pedagogy of writing teachers:

> Although we rarely detect the errors that dot the texts of professionals, we actively seek them out in student texts, and when we find them, we figuratively slash them, often with "bloody" red ink: that is, we expose the texts as unclean, impure, and thus unfit for full membership in the academic community. By embarrassing them in this way, we slowly but surely initiate them into a certain set of affiliations . . . [one of which is that] pain is an essential ingredient in writing pedagogy. . . . This pain may be a primary instrument by which the academy perpetuates itself. (632)

In Johnson's view, the student associates writing (and by extension, reading) with this act of "pain" and is not encouraged otherwise, at least not explicitly by teachers or other authority figures within the institution. Johnson's characterization of the teacher as one who wields intellectual as well as social power in the classroom setting is reflected in the absence of teachers on sites such as Pink Monkey—a site providing socialization through education, as it were—as well as the often vilification of teachers, rather than *courses,* or *curricula,* on sites such as Rate My Professors. The teacher-figure as interchangeable demon of the system bears the weight of the flaws of the system itself, at least in the mind of many students who have suffered from the system's judgments, assessments, and valuations.

Such opposition to the teacher-figure as the symbol of institutional oppression results in the "us-or-them" mentality that composition studies implicitly claims is the guiding principle of nearly all disciplines other than its own. Such opposition also leads to an unproductive stand-off in arenas where powerful stands and unmovable positions are the easiest to uphold: online spaces. The outcome of these virtual standoffs, as represented through polarized views of the validity of student-led learning online, rarely results in true educational collaboration between teachers and students, and more rarely still results in faculty gaining a greater understanding of how to harness and challenge students' online agencies for classroom discussion and rhetorical growth.

IT'S THEM OR US: THE SEPARATIST TEACHER AND THE MYTH OF STUDENT COLLABORATION

The method by which the teacher is sometimes characterized as the non-feeling, antistudent entity that, again using Benjamin's theory of reproduction, can be negatively reproduced regardless of the classroom setting, is a great leveler of students within socially or spatially defined communities. Yet in contrast to the professors who seem to be constantly manufactured to work interchangeably within higher education generally and first-year education specifically, students are often romanticized in our cultural lore (including our writing textbooks) to be only able to work *with* rather than against one another, and to share a common understanding of how to write *for* one another. Given that such impulse is evident in the sites of electronic discourse profiled in this book, I argue that certainly students are more than agreeable to help one another learn without teacher or institutional-authority figure oversight. But what is striking about this desire for student–student collaboration is how it has become an either–or principle in higher education: with the depersonalization of the teacher-figure, the student remains humanized and the "true" center of educational discourse. The student also remains a constant that is positively reproduced, but now as *subject* rather than object, particularly in Internet spaces wherein teachers are disallowed or themselves the object of student scrutiny. Although such "us-versus-them" mentality may seem organically grown, the result of the "me" generation now simply doing its sociocultural work online, I posit that composition studies has, for many years now, been fueling this opposition through its interchangeable systems and resistance to more open, and even oppositional, definitions of student agency in the classroom.

As I argued in Chapter 1, attempts to "liberate" students through theories such as liberatory pedagogy did little, in the long run, to change the view of the teacher as authority; in many cases, the authority was simply shifted to a *moral* one, in which the institution itself was viewed as the oppressor, and the student and teacher thereby automatically realigned as agents against oppression. When the pursuit of higher education became significantly *economic* in the late twentieth-century, however, the notion of teachers as "liberators" became less viable as the moral and ethical construct of higher education itself shifted. Now, in the first two decades of the twenty-first century, teachers of writing seek to reposition themselves as knowledgeable of student economic systems that pervade online technology by bringing said technology into the writing course itself. But quite often, this co-opting of student agencies for classroom instructional purposes when accompanied by the negation of this technology's powers *outside* the classroom space, particularly in social network settings, rings hollow to many students. These students wonder, whose side (of the digital divide) is my teacher *on*?

As Jeff Rice compellingly argues in *the Rhetoric of Cool*, composition faculty's use of technology in the teaching of writing has been limited thus far to three approaches, specifically "through anecdotal or empirical foundations, or hermeneutical readings of media texts ('this is what the media artifact means'), or continued laments regarding the technology gap ('we must first address access')" (9). Rice articulates these positions as ones that resist performativity, or do not engage with the media under discussion in any theoretical, tangible way. Rice further posits that accepting in 1963 as the "birth" of composition studies—a chronology of our disciplinary history heralded by Stephen North and others—we fail to re-examine that inception and its resulting practices, including, for Rice, the "digital relevance of cool" (15). As a result, Rice argues, "we do not problematize or attempt to reify technological innovations circa 1963; instead, the repetition of the composition grand narrative has done little to startle us, to provoke us, to cause us to wonder what else could have shaped our writing pedagogies, theories, and practices . . . why hasn't composition studies refocused its narrative for the postmodern, the multiple narratives, the differing stories, the unrecognized moments, the idea of, of all things, cool?" (16).

As someone who finds herself newly yet completely engaged with the value of recovering the history of composition studies—in my case, as a history of its (undervoiced) people—I agree with Rice that as a discipline, we tend to ride a party line that immediately invokes agreement over teaching philosophies, for examine process and then liberatory pedagogy, that apparently set us apart from other disciplines and fields of study. Yet in doing so, there are certain lines we will not cross in order to usurp the powerful ideological traditions voiced in our scholarship. I posit that our love–hate relationship with technology, as not only a mediator between students and faculty but also as a potential faculty doppelganger, has been similarly undertheorized, resulting in the three limited perspectives on technology and writing instruction that we often find in the pages of our journals and more often witness in the classrooms we inhabit.

In order to keep the status quo of composition as a "personal" field that embraces its humanistic principles, for example, and to keep alive the dwindling myth that our students need teachers more than they need each other as peers in learning (and, sometimes, in teaching), many faculty employ new media in their writing classes in distinctly unchallenging ways. They do so not to illustrate how the technology may, in fact, serve a teacher-function in itself within certain contexts, but instead to say that they have "used" the same technology that students use—with little understanding of or interest in the larger socioeducational import of the technology itself (as an example from this book, the entry of the teacher "Mrs. Houston" into the discussion forum on Pink Monkey falls into this category). To "use" the technology is to appropriate it, like one would any text, for augmenting one's teaching; such appropriation keeps the teacher at the focus of the pedagogy, as the controller of the technology and its resulting discourse(s). In other cases, faculty bring student-centered technologies into view in the writing classroom as seemingly "fun" alternatives to "real" pedagogical strategies; this approach assumes that students will like writing instruction, and composition courses, "better" if they incorporate technologies with which students are familiar (blogs, wikis, and other sites for public Internet discourse), rather than critically examining the base pedagogical principles already present and asking whether "fun" is really the core goal—and whether "fun" technologies will, in fact, improve the ethos of the teacher him or herself.

Much less frequently do we see faculty engaging with these student-led technologies due to a theoretical understanding of how or why the technologies *mean*; even more rarely do we see faculty refusing to engage with said technologies on *similar* theoretical grounds, rooted in an understanding of the sanctity of these spaces for *student*, rather than teacher–student, discourse. Instead, faculty often see technology as an apparatus for "improving" teaching, or elevating the approval position of the teacher, as opposed to either a legitimate site of public rhetorics/public discourse, or a theoretical platform with which students might engage in rhetorical analysis in order to introduce and sustain meaningful debates. This use of technology in writing instruction aims to solidify the teacher-as-subject, even in a room full of computers (connected to a world full of other students, in rooms of their own).

This mixed message about students, teachers, and classroom agencies didn't begin with the advent of the Internet and the ensuing scramble to adopt new technologies for classroom appropriation, however. For many years, composition studies itself has been validating this view—that teachers are mostly concerned with the effectiveness of their own methods as extensions of their teacherly ethos, rather than as a means for understanding how and why students learn both inside and outside the classroom. Despite the myriad research on student learning, student writing practices, and student engagement with literacy practices, composition has still perpetuated the myth of the unengaged teacher—or, more accurately, the myth of the collaborative student network that above all else, seeks to help itself against the implicit power of the teacher. More specifically, composition has aimed itself as the *field* that harnesses student energies in order to overturn the "typical" teacher that fails to advance student knowledge or student self-growth. In doing so, composition studies ironically promotes a "student-led" discipline (and, by extension, first-year course), but oddly fails to recognize how and when that student-led focus can be most powerful: in learning outside the classroom, without the field's supremely "sympathetic" teachers, unique among university faculty.

We see an early invocation of this unsympathetic teacher-figure who is unaware of the deeply seated values of her students positioned in opposition to the myth of the understanding and meaningful peer group in Peter Elbow's reasoning for "why the teacherless class helps make writing better," in *Writing Without Teachers* (1977), which pointedly and progressively uses the second person to speak directly past the teacher-reader and to the students who will take charge of the "teacherless" class in Elbow's pedagogical paradigm:

> A teacher is usually too good a reader in the following ways. He usually reads and writes better than you do and knows more about the subject you are writing about. you are probably writing the thing because he asked you to, and, if it's an essay, he may well have picked a topic that he knows a lot about. If writing is an exercise in getting things into readers and not just onto paper, then usually it is too easy to get everything in a teacher's head. *Yet at the same time too hard to get anything in.* What I mean is that though he can usually understand everything you are trying to say (perhaps even better than you understand it); nevertheless he really isn't listening to you. He usually isn't in a position where he can be genuinely affected by your words. He doesn't expect your words to actually make a dent on him. He doesn't treat your words like real reading. (127, emphasis in original)

In Elbow's view, teachers are able to operate in these nonlistening, depersonalized ways when reading student writing because their pedagogy is an example of the "doubting" rather than "believing" game, as doubting "seeks truth by indirection—by seeking error" whereas the believing game takes as its motto, "I believe in order to understand" (148–49). Elbow's theories, posited at the height of the Expressivist movement in composition studies and now appearing as slightly dated, still compare favorably to the standard assessment of the teacher-figure function in the classroom.

Composition studies as a field has duly promoted this notion in order to better rationalize and argue for the validity of efforts such as liberatory pedagogy, which assumes the teacher will take a role completely antithetical to Elbow's teacher, above: to care deeply about the students' writing, and to be immediately affected by the students' words, within a framework of writing-as-liberation, and therefore writers as subjects/agents rather than blank slates to be written on. In liberatory pedagogy, the students are, per Elbow's call to action, the unique subjects of the writing process and the teacher is the minimized (yet still present) co-agent in helping said students to achieve literacy consciousness.

There is nothing wrong, in theory, with either Elbow's narrative or with the general response to it that comprises the student-centered pedagogies of today's composition studies classrooms. But the fact that we use terms such as "student-centered" at *all* belie the notion that faculty still do not see some significant divide between their own subject-positions as teachers and their students' subject-positions as those who consume, ingest, absorb—pick your pejorative verb—pedagogies—rather than truly enact their core principles in their own rhetorical spaces.

RECONCILING THE REPLICATION: COMING TO TERMS WITH EXTRA-INSTITUTIONAL TECHNOLOGIES AS SITES OF PRODUCTIVE PUBLIC LITERACIES

If the reader of this book is to believe my assertions as outlined in this final chapter, then he or she can break down the "problem" as follows: First, teachers resist wholesale uses of technology because they fear the computer/technological device will replace them in person and, importantly, in spirit, as classroom leaders; this we know to have been historically true in the case of Skinner's teaching machines. Second, teachers do themselves somewhat of a disservice in accruing unique teacherly identities when they rely on pedagogical systems of their own—or rely on interchangeable teaching philosophies, approaches, and the like—to keep the teacher-centered pedagogy of writing instruction as a stable one. Third, building on the reproducibility of teachers and the systems on which they rely, students are asked to work with technology in writing classes typically insofar as it will reinforce the teacher as innovator, as understanding of student technological trends, or as one who mediates his or her unfavored teaching methods with seemingly favorable technology tools, which appeal to students *as* students, rather than as potential rhetors or theorists of rhetoric.

If the reader accepts these premises, he or she sees the future of literacy education as one guided by large groups of students who meet online to circumvent traditional teachers and teaching methods in favor of collective learning within atemporal/cross-geographic (and cross-demographic) settings, and one tolerated by faculty who acknowledge the existence of said technologies, but either ignore their rhetorical potential in students' reading and writing lives, or pander to their popularity vis-à-vis pithy classroom engagement with these technologies under the guise of widening writing pedagogies and teacherly agencies. Because these premises may now be providing my readers with a grim outlook on the impasse facing us in literacy educational spaces, I stubbornly close this chapter, and this book, with a prompt for those left feeling hopeless and confused, especially those readers who are writing faculty.

Now is the time, I believe, to overcome our powerful and sometimes irrational fears of students learning *en masse* and instead gather our intellectual resources to consider the core purpose of literacy education: to give students the tools to engage in public discourse, widely construed, so as to become productive actors in civic community exchange. Let us respect and appropriately employ online student-led technologies focusing on literacy discourse to challenge and improve our own staid views of writing instruction, even if we consider ourselves technologically "literate" within our own spheres of influence—and even if we personally consider those spheres to be wide and enlightened ones. If you, the reader, opened this book and found yourself doubting what I might reasonably theorize about literacy education and Pink Monkey, Rate My Professors, and other Web sites with silly, faddish names that you had never heard of, nor cared to visit, then I'm directing a prompt personally to *you*—because your spheres, I'm sorry to say, are not as wide as you may have previously thought.

To make this leap, you, the reader, first must acknowledge that literacy instruction encompasses many other subgoals along its way: to appreciate great texts (as we decide how we define "great" and "texts," that is); to communicate effectively in workplace situations, and in vocational positions (as much as we hate to admit it, eventually we all read and write in *jobs*); and to understand the power of language as both the great leveler and the great divider in modern societies (i.e., to train students to be effective *rhetoricians*). But are we really effective rhetoricians *ourselves*—and are we serving as effective rhetorical models—when we observe the increasing technological and philosophical divides between ourselves and students and do nothing to bring those debates into full pedagogical view? When we haltingly co-opt the discourse of youth technology by inserting ourselves into online spaces wherein we are not only sociologically out of step with the values and motivations of the other agents present, but also are fundamentally *unwelcome* as late-comer guests who crashed the party? When we furiously assert that we are willing to give students a certain amount of limited agency in the classroom, but only so long this agency does not accrue and subsequently travel into online spaces *outside* the classroom, and become a viable extra-institutional agency of literacy discourse that threatens our own complex teacher-ethos?

As faculty, we need to be at least as reasonably critical as our students clearly are about the imbalances of power, authority, and personal agency in literacy acquisition for today's college students. Harnessing the technological spaces that students have created and inhabited shows us for the posers that we are: the replicants of a system that we believe might now be *moved* online, even though this move makes us virtual squatters in rather than true proprietors of technology-based learning communities. Our desire to reproduce "what works" over and over in our teaching strategies easily leads us to the fallacy that if we do what "works" for student groups online—if we set up shop on Pink Monkey, or direct our students to say nice things about us (or our colleagues) on Rate My Professor—we will be speaking their "language" and thus realizing a bridge in the technological divide. To respond to this fallacy in the teen-speak from my own college years: *As if*.

My proposal suggests that instead of colonizing student spaces and student-led technologies for our own tired uses—instead of putting our old pedagogies in new shiny twenty-first century packaging (a packaging that, incidentally, appeals strongly to tech-desiring administrators at many universities)—we force ourselves to leave these spaces *alone*, and instead bring the spirit of the discourse and debate found in those online spaces more strongly to bear on our own systematic pedagogies that currently encourage students to be pupils of rhetoric, but not *public* rhetoricians in a highly democratic and potentially charged classroom. This may sound an awful lot like liberatory pedagogy, which I have somewhat mercilessly critiqued as limited in its ability to counteract the pull of students' extra-institutional agencies and their own newly minted views of readerly and writerly ethos. The difference between what I am proposing and the pedagogy enacted by dedicated followers of Freire is that my proposal seeks a high level of comfort with students as, in some online venues, wholly *independent* learners who are capable of enacting the principles of civic discourse in Internet spaces, for socioeducational ends. Thus, my proposal also requires that writing teachers embrace—or at least acknowledge—the *social* element of education that pervades, for good or ill, the sites profiled in this book. Teachers must also subsequently accept twenty-first-century literacy education as a highly social endeavor, informed certainly by the art of technology but made most meaningful by the interactions that said technology enables students to have *outside* the space of the classroom, and within diverse and ever-shifting online communities, led by the principle of the "moving wall"—wherein the boundaries and timeframes of the communities may shift and be redefined depending on the issue at hand and/or the question posed.

How can we accomplish what this proposal sets out to do? First, we can be cognizant of new technologies—and we should, if we are serious about keeping up with the ways in which students learn in this age of new media—but we need not, in my view, seek to bring all or even most of those technologies into our classrooms. I believe that computerized classrooms are highly beneficial for those faculty who use them well, and in no way should this book be seen as an argument against technology in general, or as an argument against the use of computers in the classroom. On the contrary, such technologies can be great learning tools. What faculty *do* with those technologies is what concerns me here. If we simply ask students to, for example, replicate their otherwise extra-institutional discourses within the more "supervised" settings of the writing classroom, we do not replicate the discourse at all—we simply mimic it, and in somewhat pandering ways. Rather, faculty should ask students to engage in critical discussions *of* these technological spaces, and in doing so, respect that all responses may not be voiced in the space of the classroom, but instead within the very public spaces where the technologies originated and continue to proliferate, in spite of the institution's loftier goals against such proliferation.

Second, we as teachers of writing and literacy should begin to reconceptualize our classroom roles *as* teachers, and require that our students make a concerted effort to see themselves as rhetors outside the classroom, and outside our spaces of oversight. We cannot complain about irresponsible uses of agency and authority in online spaces if we do not invite students to see the connections between their in-class and out-of-class rhetorical utterances, or their home and school community literacy roles. Rather than see ourselves as authoritative directors of students' rhetorical (and sometimes moral/ethical) choices within their larger community spaces, we should invite students to take a larger responsibility for showing *us* how those choices operate in extra-institutional spaces, and among rhetors who are not their classmates.

Finally, as teachers, we should try to reconcile our new—and likely unchanging—positions as objects within higher education, and not necessarily see this as a wholly negative shift. In particular, our collective fears of evaluation and evaluative discourse, whether it be on a personal, student-review level, or on an institutional level, within assessment paradigms, are creating a wide chasm between ourselves and our students, who have been raised on a culture of evaluation, assessment, and "feedback" (both in educational and commercial terms). Many students do not see evaluation of their products, services, and fellow humans as a negative thing (note CNN's constant request, for example, to "tell us what you think," as part of its regular news programs and delivery format. Walter Cronkite would *never* have asked us that!). In 2009, our typical/traditional first-year college writer will have been born in 1991, and will have never known a life without some sort of evaluative technology and personal media devices. What is shockingly invasive to us, is not so to them; what we see as an uncomfortable amendment to the accepted and highly successful structure of educational hierarchies and classroom instruction, many students see as necessary augmentation of an otherwise-stagnant system that fails to address their particular and individual agencies in the process of literacy acquisition.

It's an old philosophy, but it bears repeating, at least in paraphrase: There is a generation gap that must be acknowledged here, and realized as extant, but not, in my view, rendered seemingly invisible by teachers who seek approval through misuses of technology that in no way will ever "mean" the same as they do to students in their original forms, and within their original student-led communities. In profiling the Web sites in this book, and by framing these Web sites with the larger (perhaps provocative) question of "who owns school?" in this technological context, I hope to raise awareness of how and why students may learn "without" teachers, yet in the process learn to truly appreciate and be changed by their individual paths toward the acquisition of literacy.

NOTES

INTRODUCTION

1. One recent example of this in-person to online shift would be the December 2008 student protests at the New School in New York City, in which participants demanded the resignation of the institution's chancellor, Bob Kerrey, due to both his political beliefs and his perceived mismanagement of the institution. The on-the-ground, physical protests were widely reported as being "not representative" of the student body as a whole, and amounted to fewer than 100 students participating in the protests at any given time. On the other hand, the Web site organized by the protesters, titled "New School in Exile," allowed for a much wider dissemination of the group's views, and generated 550 online petition signatures as well as an allied Facebook site (www.newschoolinexile.com). This Web site also remained a viable, interactive URL into 2009; long after the physical protests had come to a close, with the semester's end.

2. See for example Robillard's essay "Young Scholars Affecting Composition: A Challenge to Disciplinary Citation Practices." *College English* 68.3 (2006): 253–70.

CHAPTER 1

3. I have chosen not to discuss Paulo Freire's work here as a primary source, first because I assume that my readers are at least conversationally familiar with his theories, and second, because I do not take issue with Freire *per se*, but rather with the enactment of his theories in English studies, specifically in composition studies/first-year writing. Thus, I find more benefit in discussing Freire in the context of secondary sources that discuss his work, such as those examined in this chapter.

4. Here I would draw readers' attention to studies of basic writing students within privileged/higher status populations, including my look at Yale and Harvard basic writers in the mid-twentieth century (*Before Shaughnessy: Basic Writing at Yale and Harvard, 1920–1960*. Carbondale: Southern Illinois University Press, 2009).

5. Bizzell makes another critical assumption about the structure of the basic writing classroom in this 1991 essay: the content of the course readings. She states that in contrast to the literature-based composition courses of old, "Now the students' own papers are likely to form the only set of texts for the course; or if we use a reader, we use one that is pluralistic as to the race, gender, ethnicity, and sexual preference, and social class of its contributors, and we assign or let students select essays whose subject matter is likely to be of interest to them" (66). Certainly there are basic writing classrooms that follow this model, however, I believe it is a gross overstatement to characterize this approach as the norm—definitely in 2009, and even to a degree in 1991. By making this assumption, however, Bizzell's argument regarding the importance of critical pedagogy in basic writing classes is far better served, as students already (in this model) have a great deal of control over the course curriculum, and thus should logically be an integral part of the theoretical approach to the teaching of the course itself.

6. I discuss grading in more depth in the context of Rate My Professors, in Chapter 4.

7. I add my own anecdote in relation to this issue, and to a hallmark of Nelson's current agenda, namely contingent labor. At the 2008 Modern Language Association (MLA) convention, I was participating in my second Delegate Assembly meeting as a special-interest delegate. On the issue of MLA taking a public position on working conditions for adjunct/contingent faculty, several delegates, myself included, stepped up to the microphone to offer comments for the assembly on this initiative. Although many supported the idea, and offered specific parameters that the MLA might consider in regard to contingent faculty, I instead suggested that we (a) consider as a tenure-track/tenured faculty how our consistent teaching of upper-division and graduate courses leaves a professional gap for contingent faculty (e.g., they only are able to teach first- and second-year courses repeatedly, thus limiting their professional development), and (b) that a better resolution for the MLA to take regarding contingent labor would be to take a stand against it altogether, and ask its members to stop accepting contingent employment. Interestingly, in contrast to the often vociferous, affirming back-and-forth between delegates following a voiced suggestion, and/or an uproar of appreciation (verbal, clapping, etc.) regarding advocacy for adjuncts, there was no follow-up discussion at all to my suggestions from the 150 delegates present, and only the weakest of polite applause when I finished.

8. At this point I would say that a glossing of the literature on the teaching of writing to secondary (or primary, or middle school) students evinces this truth for readers. Although teachers are encouraged to engage in expressivist-leaning models of instruction (journals, reading logs, visual interpretations of arguments, stories, and other written work), I do not see a significant push to raise the critical consciousness of these students through writing. My take on second-

ary writing instruction, given my recent experience teaching a methods course on this subject, is that students are encouraged to *enjoy* writing, to *appreciate* it, and to *readily engage* in it as a means of expression and analysis. But I would not argue that a primary goal alongside these is to become self-empowered through the act of writing, at least not in the public schools in the United States.

9. One could also ask, what happens to the liberal consciousness-raising of students who do not *take* first-year writing at all (either via exemption, advanced placement, or some other set of institutional circumstances)?

10. Here I am referring to Nancy Hass' essay "In Your Facebook.com," which I think is actually an interesting and insightful piece. My comment means to highlight how textbook publishers in particular have been quick to incorporate works on, or invent educational technology that resembles, these popular sites in order to reach students. This strikes me, in such cases, as pandering to students' perceived extra-institutional social networking preferences for the sake of profit.

11. Here I ask readers to recall the BBC broadcast news program—available on many National Public Radio outlets in the United States—of the same title. I believe this title nicely invokes the push–pull in our American popular culture between our desire for viewer/listener/consumer feedback and our educational culture's lacking desire to hear what *students* think about equally pressing—if not more critical—aspects of their own education. Even CNN wants to know "what you think" as part of its regular daily news programming, and encourages viewers to participate in hourly polls, blogs, e-mail remarks to the anchors, and so on. Rarely in public schooling do we hear such calls for feedback directed at student populations. To ask students to live in a culture of constant evaluation and re-valuation while being schooled in a setting that ignores and even aims to counteract such a culture is perplexing, at best.

CHAPTER 2

12. Here I think specifically of tenure cases in which faculty who co-author articles, monographs, or textbooks are ranked lower than their peers who do single-authored work. Composition studies prides itself on being more invested in collaboration and co-authorship than is English studies as a discipline, but in the larger lexicon of the humanities, collaborative work is generally still seen as easier, less demanding, less intellectual—pick your adjective—than single-authored work. In addition, the continued question of where the limits of tutoring in writing centers lies, in terms of "help" with improving a piece of writing, complicates even the best efforts at collaborative views of authorship. Student processes which thus mimic these collaborative efforts in their design lead to similar anxieties, not to mention the more obvious fears of "cheating" via reliance on, and use of, peers' greater knowledge of the subject matter/text in completing a given reading.

13. Bauerlein also writes a blog for the *Chronicle of Higher Education*; as such, his ideas reach a fairly wide readership, not limited to journal subscribers such as those reading *College English*.

14. A variety of communities use the "pink monkey" label as a controlling metaphor for difference and communal rejection of that difference among

their constituents. For example, see http://www.hoagies gifted.org/pink_monkey.htm, a site for "gifted education," which contextualizes this definition for parents of nonconforming, gifted kids.

15. Indeed, parents and children within the American home-schooling community also have taken a significant interest in the benefits of Pink Monkey, as the site allows these students to come together online both within and without home-schooling groups, and also provides many online study guides, study aides, and teacher-directed learning supplements that are of interest to home-schooling parents who frequently lack the institutional resources available to classroom teachers.

16. As ethnographer Margaret Finders observed, in her study *Just Girls*, "underlife" is a logical response to the ironic structure of schooling itself: Although these students need to be social beings as part of their human development, the academic setting is one that discourages such socialization, and sets it in opposition to learning. Students who seek to make social practices a part of learning also struggle with power balances in their roles as students, friends, members of a community, and emerging readers and writers. This struggle is reinforced outside the classroom as well; as Finders notes, even the parents in her study desired for their daughters to be "academic, not social," contributing to complex underlife-influenced literacy practices that subvert the school system, even as they originate in the sites of schooling.

17. Harrington is building on the seminal work of Martha Woodmansee, renowned expert on copyright and authorship in textual studies in pre-twentieth-century Europe. Woodmansee's article "The Genius and the Copyright" outlines the origins of the "genius" label that Harrington describes, arguing that the concept of "author" is a distinctly modern (and recent) one. Woodmansee asserts that the modern concept of authorship originated in eighteenth-century Germany, wherein writers "sought to earn their livelihood from the sale of their writings to the new and rapidly expanding reading public" but had "[none] of the safeguards for its labors that today are codified in copyright laws" (426).

18. I have left the original spelling errors and informal usage—for example "u" instead of "you"—to keep the responses intact and to provide their original presentation, particularly since computer-based discourse (text-messaging, forums, etc.) allows for a looser or even alternate rules-system for grammar and spelling, especially among young adults and college-aged students.

19. I have pulled out selected responses here, presented in chronological order. The few responses that I have chosen not to spotlight/include were typically off-topic postings that had only a tangential connection to the theme/issue at hand.

20. Given that this is the student's original work, posted in its entirety, I feel it unethical to reproduce it here without being able to access her permission.

21. Hea notes that "edentity" is "not equitable to an online persona," but instead is "created through technological experiences including interactions with technology as well as negotiations of cultural constructions of technology" (343). As such, Hea's definition allies nicely with Fleckenstein's argument about mutually constructed ethical identities online, which emphasizes action as well as reaction, text as well as context.

CHAPTER 3

22. See Robillard, Amy and Ron Fortune. "Toward a New Content for Writing Courses: Literary Forgery, Plagiarism, and the Production of Belief." JAC 27.1/2 (2007): 185–210.

23. See Ritter, Kelly. "The Economics of Authorship: Online Paper Mills, Student Authors, and First-Year Composition." *College Composition and Communication* 56.4 (June 2005): 601–31, as well as Ritter, Kelly. "Buying In, Selling Short: A Pedagogy Against the Rhetoric of Online Paper Mills." *Pedagogy* 6.1 (January 2006): 25–51.

24. Since I first began my research into plagiarism and paper mill Web sites, I have corresponded frequently with Rebecca Moore Howard, who freely acknowledges the validity of the "whole-text" argument. As such, whereas in my original version of this research I cited Howard as a scholarly source, and perhaps one in conflict with my own theoretical position, I now regard her as a friend and trusted colleague whose interest in complicating and dissecting the criminalized notion of plagiarism among faculty and the general public I certainly share.

25. Some online paper mill companies actually are predicated on the notion that students are comfortable with erasing their identity, even in the specific writing occasion for which "identity" and its trappings counts the most. As Kelly McCollum reports in the *Chronicle of Higher Education*, "IvyEssays" sells pre-existing, successful admissions essays from Ivy League students to paying Internet clients. Although the company stresses that it is "not interested in helping students plagiarize" and also sells tailored essays that fit the students' interests or goals ("One Way to Get Into College" A25), the temptation to instead select an already proven successful admission essay, particularly for those students wishing to gain entry to a top school, is obvious. This is an instance of complete identity erasure perpetrated by those who advertise authorship for sale to students who have already devalued their ability to "own" their own texts through authorship.

26. To assist in readers' parsing of the comparative data, given the common course title, I have referred to the students as "SCSU students" or "UNCG students" throughout the discussion of their respective, collective responses.

27. As of 2005, English 101 at SCSU has been changed to English 112, to account for a renumbering of the entire first-year composition sequence, including basic writing, which changed from a pre-100/non-credit course to a 100-level (English 110) credit-bearing course.

28. It is important to recall that students were allowed throughout both of the survey versions to circle/select one or more responses to each question; for the question that focused on being an author, multiple responses were the norm, with each student circling/selecting on average four of the options listed.

29. In her May 2002 *Chronicle* piece, Andrea Foster argues that services such as turnitin.com, which keep submitted papers in a large database for future faculty reference, may infringe on students' own copyrights, particularly when done without the students' knowledge or consent ("Plagiarism-Detection" A37). She also cites Howard as an "outspoken critic" of the detection serv-

ice, and indicates that Howard believes that the service may also violate students' Federal Educational Rights and Privacy Act rights (A38). As of May 2004, at least one student in Canada has initiated a lawsuit against the turnitin.com, contesting the inclusion of his academic paper in the company's database.

30. At some colleges and universities, a variety of institutional measurements are in place that are designed to combat plagiarism vis-à-vis specifically internal, tougher punishments based on peer reporting and/or institutional honor codes. Studies have shown, however, that these more progressive peer-based measures involving self-policing may not curb cheating, even if they raise awareness of individual acts of academic dishonesty. These measures are of the most relevance to a study of paper mill usage and related acts of plagiarism, since this sort of cheating may take place without peer complicity (i.e., allowing a friend to see answers in an exam) but with peer awareness (those who know a friend had purchased or downloaded his or her paper). Donald McCabe, Linda Klebe Trevino, and Kenneth D. Butterfield studied the influence of academic honor codes and peer reporting among college students, and determined that while students who attend institutions that have some sort of honor code in place along with peer reporting are afforded a great deal of trust and freedom, these same students react negatively to the notion that they must report on their fellow students, and "find reasons why it is not appropriate to report peer cheating" (42). Reasons range from the student feeling it is "none of (his/her) business"; to a feeling that the penalties for cheating are "too severe"; or the risk of being ostracized by one's friends if a report is filed (42).

31. See the often referenced, helpful Georgetown University plagiarism/academic dishonesty Web site, www.Georgetown.edu/honor/paperframe.html, for a comprehensive list on which I built my research and the list of Web sites that my students analyzed in their English 101 papers. Also see William McHenry's concise 1998 piece listing comparative details of price and conditions of purchase on several paper mill Web sites, available on the Georgetown Web site (www.Georgetown.edu/honor/papermill.htm). See Peggy Bates and Margaret Finn's page at Coastal Carolina University, www.coastal.edu/library/mills2.htm, for a more recent and extremely comprehensive listing of the paper mill sites operating online, including many that now offer papers for trade as well as sale/resale, for example Swaptermpapers.com. This system is particularly interesting in that the financial aspect of the paper mill is waived in favor of a kind of barter system that gives paper for paper, author for author, again without a sense of "stealing" work of any kind, although surely the overall commerce of the site is funded by company sponsorship, "membership" fees, and the continual purchase of papers by students without papers to trade. As the company Swaptermpapers.com puts it, theirs is a site "by students, for students, and with students" (www.swaptermpapers.com).

32. See Downs, Doug and Elizabeth Wardle. "Teaching about Writing, Righting Misconceptions: (Re)Envisioning 'First-Year Composition' as 'Introduction to English Studies.'" *College Composition and Communication* 58.4 (2007): 552–84.

CHAPTER 4

33. See for example the overwhelmingly positive/assenting response to Gray and Bergmann's *Academe* article, at http://www.aaup.org/AAUP/pubsres/academe/2004/JF/LTE/birg.htm.

34. See Doug Hesse's insightful take on the similarities between academic publishing and the rating/review system on Amazon.com. Hesse argues that Amazon's format of rating *reviews* (i.e., "was this review helpful to you?") "creates a corporate ethos of being helpful and adding value, supplementing the words themselves with one measure of the authors' reputations. The system of blurbs and ratings mimics, after a fashion, the academic publishing system" (141). When we consider this rating system in comparison to RMP's similar format—with qualitative commentary serving as "blurbs"—it is striking to consider the similarities of not just format, but ethical intention, that is, for a student's ethos to be represented, even anonymously, in his or her "helpful" review that "add(s) value" to the overall assessment of the faculty member. If we further link this to academia—as Hesse does—it becomes an interesting triangulation of the academic, public (nonacademic), and corporate—on which RMP also thrives.

35. Although RMP is a public site, accessible to all (in limited fashion; those who wish to see all of a faculty member's ratings must become a member), I feel it is important to choose my samples from institutions where I know the curriculum, faculty, and students, all the while keeping the identity of the faculty under discussion from being explicitly identified. In order to reference/document the sources for these comments, however, I do provide links to the postings as they are cited.

36. According to OnSET, of the one-hundred eighteen institutions that currently use this type of evaluation, sixteen, or 13.5%, are category 5 in their methods. This group includes several prominent, top-twenty research universities, such as Yale, Northwestern, and Carnegie Mellon. The majority of the institutions tracked by OnSet—seventy-three—are category 3 or 4. These two categories tend to consist of smaller state and private institutions. These data suggest a rapidly growing trend among colleges and universities to publicize their faculty's course evaluations outside the local context in which they were constructed, even if that "public" is for other students and faculty within the college. For a complete listing of all colleges and universities participating in online course evaluations, see http://onset.byu.edu. This site includes a more detailed explanation of how such evaluations are classified and how the overall project is conceptualized, including relevant scholarship on the topic.

37. In discussion threads on the WPA-L during September 2007, several composition and rhetoric faculty commented on the relative successes and failures of online course evaluation as part of a posted query on WAC/WID course evaluation. See https://lists.asu.edu/cgi-bin/wa?A2=ind0709&L=WPA-L&D=1&T=0&P=63250 for the thread.

38. I freely admit that some postings on RMP are not defensible. The infamous "chili pepper" designation, as well as other offensive (sexist) postings, are certainly not dialogic, nor valuable. However, even as we can discount these types of postings, we cannot discount the desire to post, nor can we say that such

surface assessments do not occur outside the electronic confines of RMP. For a fuller discussion of how such ratings may be interpreted, see James Felton, John Mitchell, and Michael Stinson, "Web-Based Student Evaluations of Professors: The Relations Between Perceived Quality, Easiness, and Sexiness." *Assessment and Evaluation in Higher Education* 29.1 (2004): 91–108.

39. Because the exchanges themselves and not the professor whom these students are "rating" is the important element here, I have chosen not to identify the professors. In all but one case (Professor D, a history professor) these are professors of English who teach first- and second-year students, a significant population on RMP. I also have chosen faculty with a significant number of ratings (twenty or more), in addition to varied opinions within those ratings, to allow analysis of emerging patterns within exchanges, rather than just two or three limited postings/views lacking a significant sample set.

40. I am deliberately using "investor" here instead of Deborah Brandt's established notion of "sponsor" because I wish to invoke a more aggressive notion of the economies of higher education that often are behind large-scale assessments, and the resulting working conditions of faculty, particularly those in the positions of nonguaranteed renewal or contingent funding. I recognize, however, the value in Brandt's seminal term and its larger implications for the social machinery behind the literacies in our students' home communities, as well as how those communal perceptions of higher education greatly influence not just where or whether students attend college, but how it is they approach the very act of learning itself.

41. See also the "forum" section of RMP, wherein students—and sometimes faculty—engage in longer, threaded discussions of particular courses and other larger issues at work in the college classroom. For example, recent forum threads on RMP concerned the use (and value) of professors' office hours; the qualities of a typical Honors program; and the question of whether faculty read their RMP ratings. Other threads are unrelated entirely to the RMP site, including political debates or other such seemingly extra-institutional issues (http://www.ratemyprofessors.com/jive/vodka/viewForum.jsp?forum = 2).

CHAPTER 5

42. See for example Dobrin, Sid. "Paralogic Hermeneutic Theories, Power, and the Possibility for Liberating Pedagogies" and Olson, Gary. "Toward a Post-Process Composition: Abandoning the Rhetoric of Assertion," both in Thomas Kent, Ed. *Post-Process Theory: Beyond the Writing Process Paradigm.* Carbondale: Southern Illinois University P, 1999.

WORKS CITED

Anonymous. "Authentic Essays." http://www.AuthenticEssays.com. Accessed 16 November 2003.

Anonymous. "Genius Papers." http://www.GeniusPapers.com. Accessed 16 November 2003.

Bates, Peggy and Margaret Finn. "Cheating 101: Paper Mills and You." 12 August 2002. http://www.coastal.edu/library/mills2.htm.

Bauerlein, Mark. "The Dumbest Generation." www.dumbestgeneration.com. Accessed 30 January 2009.

Benjamin, Walter. "The Work of Art in the Age of Mechanical Reproduction." *Illuminations: Essays and Reflections*. Trans. Hannah Arendt. New York: Schocken Books, 1969: 217–51.

Berlin, James. *Rhetoric and Reality: Writing Instruction in American Colleges, 1900–1985*. Carbondale: Southern Illinois UP, 1987.

_____. "Freirean Pedagogy in the U.S.: A Response." *JAC* 12.2 (1992): 414–21.

Berthoff, Ann E. "Paulo Freire's Liberation Pedagogy." *Language Arts* 67.4 (April 1990): 362–69.

Bizzell, Patricia. "Power, Authority, and Critical Pedagogy." *Journal of Basic Writing* 10.2 (1991): 54–69.

_____. "Cognition, Convention, and Certainty: What We Need to Know About Writing." *Cross-Talk in Comp Theory*. Ed. Victor Villanueva. Urbana, IL: NCTE, 2003: 387–411.

Bialostosky, Don. "Should College English Be Close Reading?" *College English* 69.2 (November 2006): 111–16.

Bloom, Lynn Z. and Martin Bloom. "The Teaching and Learning of Argumentative Writing. *College English* 29.2 (November 1967): 128–35.

Blumenthal, Joseph C. *English 2600: A Scientific Program in Grammar and Usage*. New York: Harcourt Brace, 1962.

Brandt, Deborah. "Remembering Writing, Remembering Reading." *College Composition and Communication* 45.4 (December 1994): 459–79.

_____. "Sponsors of Literacy." *College Composition and Communication* 49.2 (May 1998): 165–85.

Brereton, John. Rev. of *As If Learning Mattered: Reforming Higher Education* by Richard Miller. *College Composition and Communication* 51.3 (February 2000): 494–98.

Brooke, Robert. "Underlife and Writing Instruction" *College Composition and Communication* 38.2 (May 1987): 141–53.

Burns, Philip. "Supporting Deliberative Democracy: Pedagogical Arts of the Contact Zone of The Electronic Public Sphere." *Rhetoric Review* 18.1 (Autumn 1999): 128–46.

Carbone, Nick and Margaret Daisley. "Grading as a Rhetorical Construct." *The Theory and Practice of Grading Writing: Problems and Possibilities.* Eds. Frances Zak and Christopher C. Weaver. Albany: SUNY P, 1998: 77–94.

Clark, Gregory. "Rescuing the Discourse of Community." *College Composition and Communication* 45.1 (December 1994): 61–74.

Clawson, Rosalee A., Rebecca E. Deen, and Zoe M. Oxley. "Online Discussions Across Three Universities: Student Participation and Pedagogy." *Political Science and Politics* 35.4 (2002): 713-18.

Cooper, Marilyn. "Really Useful Knowledge: A Cultural Studies Agenda for Writing Centers." *Writing Center Journal* 14.2 (1994): 97–111.

Cooper, Marilyn and Cynthia Selfe. "Computer Conferences and Learning: Authority, Resistance, and Internally Persuasive Discourse." *College English* 52.8 (1990): 847–69.

Couture, Barbara. "Reconciling Private Lives and Public Rhetoric: What's at Stake?" *The Private, The Public, and the Published: Reconciling Private Lives and Public Rhetorics.* Eds. Barbara Couture and Thomas Kent. Logan: Utah State UP, 2004: 1–13.

Crowley, Sharon. *Composition in the University: Historical and Polemical Essays.* Pittsburgh: U of Pitt P, 1998.

Dobrin, Sidney. "Going Public: Locating Public/Private Discourse." Couture and Kent, 216–29.

_____. "Paralogic Hermeneutic Theories, Power, and the Possibility for Liberating Pedagogies." Ed. Thomas Kent. *Post-Process Theory: Beyond the Writing Process Paradigm.* Carbondale: Southern Illinois UP, 1999: 132–48.

Downs, Doug and Elizabeth Wardle. "Teaching About Writing, Righting Misconceptions: (Re)Envisioning 'First-Year Composition' as 'Introduction to English Studies.'" *College Composition and Communication* 58.4 (2007): 552–84.

Edmundson, Mark. "How Teachers Can Stop Cheaters." *New York Times* 152 (September 9, 2003): A29.

Elbow, Peter. *Writing Without Teachers.* New York: Oxford UP, 1973.

Ellsworth, Elizabeth. "Why Doesn't This Feel Empowering? Working Through the Repressive Myths of Critical Pedagogy." *Harvard Review* 59.3 (August 1989): 297–324.

Enos, Theresa. "Professing the New Rhetorics: 1990 CCCC Roundtable." *Rhetoric Review* 9.1 (1990): 5–35.

Enos, Theresa and Shane Borrowman. "Authority and Credibility: Classical Rhetoric, the Internet, and the Teaching of Techno-Ethos." *Alternative Rhetorics: Challenges to the Rhetorical Tradition.* Eds. Laura Gray-Rosendale and Sibylle Gruber. Albany: SUNY P, 2001: 93–110.

Faculty Center at Brigham Young University. "Institutions Using Online Student Evaluation of Teaching." *ONSET: Online Student Evaluation of Teaching in Higher Education.* http://onset.byu.edu/OnSETinstitutions.htm. Accessed 20 June 2005.

Fassbinder, Polly. "Professors and Students' Perceptions of Why Students Participate in Class." *Teaching Sociology* 24 (January 1995): 25–33.

Fauske, Janice and Suzanne E. Wade. "Research to Practice Online: Conditions that Foster Democracy, Community, and Critical Thinking in Computer-Mediated Discussions." *Journal of Research on Technology in Education* 36.2 (Winter 2003–2004): 137–53.

Felton, James, John Mitchell, and Michael Stinson. "Web-Based Student Evaluations of Professors: The Relations Between Perceived Quality, Easiness, and Sexiness." *Assessment and Evaluation in Higher Education* 29.1 (February 2004): 91–108.

Finders, Margaret. *Just Girls: Hidden Literacies and Life in Junior High.* Urbana, IL: NCTE, 1997.

Fish, Stanley. "Who's in Charge Here?" *The Chronicle of Higher Education* (February 4, 2005). http://chronicle.com/jobs/2005/02/2005020401c.htm. Accessed 6 February 2005.

Fleckenstein, Kristie. "Cybernetics, Ethos, and Ethics: The Plight of the Bread-and-Butter-Fly." *Plugged In: Technology, Rhetoric, and Culture in a Posthuman Age.* Eds. Lynn Worsham and Gary Olson. Cresskill, NJ: Hampton Press, 2008: 3–23.

Foster, Andrea. "Plagiarism Detection Tool Creates Legal Quandary." *Chronicle of Higher Education* 48.36 (May 17, 2002): A37 + .

Freshman Confidential Guide to Courses. 1939. Harvard University Archives. Cambridge: Boston, MA.

Gee, Paul James. "Discourse and Sociocultural Studies in Reading." Reading Online.org. www.readingonline.org/articles/handbook/gee/. Accessed 18 January 2009.

_____. "Teenagers in New Times: A New Literacy Studies Perspective." *Journal of Adolescent and Adult Literacy* 43.5 (February 2000): 412–23.

Giroux, Henry. "Public Pedagogy and the Politics of Resistance: Notes on a Critical Theory of Educational Struggle." *Educational Philosophy and Theory* 35.1 (2003): 5–16.

_____. "Cultural Studies and the Politics of Public Pedagogy: Making the Political More Pedagogical." *Parallax* 10.2 (2004): 73–89.

Gray, Mary and Barbara Bergmann. "Student Teaching Evaluations: Inaccurate, Demeaning, Misused." *Academe Online* (September–October 2003). http://www.aaup.org/AAUP/pubsres/academe/2003/SO/Feat/gray.htm.

Halpern, Faye. "In Defense of Reading Badly: The Politics of Identification in 'Benito Cereno,' *Uncle Tom's Cabin*, and Our Classrooms." *College English* 70.6 (July 2008): 551–77.

Hardin, Joe. Rev. of Miler, Richard. *As If Learning Mattered: Reforming Higher Education. Rhetoric Review* 18.1 (Autumn 1999): 206–10.

Harrington, Dana. "Composition, Literature, and the Emergence of Modern Reading Practices." *Rhetoric Review* 15.2 (Spring 1997): 249–63.

Hass, Nancy. "In Your Facebook.com." *Composing Knowledge*. Ed . Rolf Norgaard. New York: Bedford/St. Martin's, 2006: 590–94.

Hea, Amy Kimme. "Rearticulating E-dentities in the Web-based Classroom: One Technoresearcher's Exploration of Power and the World Wide Web." *Computers and Composition* 19 (2002): 331–46.

Hendricks, Bill. "Teaching Work: Academic Labor and Social Class." *JAC* 25.1 (2005): 587–622.

Herring, Susan C. "Questioning the Generational Divide: Technological Exoticism and Adult Constructions of Online Youth Identity." *Youth, Identity, and Digital Media*. Ed . David Buckingham. The John D. and Catherine T. MacArthur Foundation Series on Digital Media and Learning. Cambridge, MA: MIT P, 2008: 71–92.

Hesse, Doug. "Identity and the Internet: The Telling Case of Amazon's Top 50 Reviewers." Couture and Kent, 139–52.

Horner, Bruce. "Students, Authorship, and the Work of Composition." *College English* 59.5 (1997): 505–29.

Howard, Rebecca Moore. "Plagiarisms, Authorships, and the Academic Death Penalty." *College English* 57.7 (1995): 788–805.

_____. "The Ethics of Plagiarism." *The Ethics of Writing Instruction: Issues in Theory and Practice*. Ed. Michael A. Pemberton. Norwood, NJ: Ablex, 2000: 79–90.

_____. *Standing in the Shadow of Giants: Plagiarists, Authors, Collaborators*. Stamford, CT: Ablex, 1999.

Hull, Glynda and Katherine Schultz. "Literacy and Learning Out of School: A Review of Theory and Research." *Review of Educational Research* 71.4 (Winter 2001): 575–611.

Huot, Brian. "Toward a New Discourse of Assessment for the College Writing Classroom." *College English* 65.2 (November 2002): 163–80.

Johnson, T.R. "School Sucks." *College Composition and Communication* 52.4 (2001): 620–50.

Johnston, Bill. "Putting Critical Pedagogy in Its Place: A Personal Account." *TESOL Quarterly* 33.3 (1999): 557–65.

Jolliffe, David. "Learning to Read as Continuing Education." *College Composition and Communication* 58.3 (February 2007): 470–94.

Jolliffe, David and Allison Hurl. "Studying the 'Reading Transition' from High School to College: What are Our Students Reading and Why?" *College English* 70.6 (July 2008): 599–617.

Kindred, Jeanette and Shaheed Mohammed. "He Will Crush You Like an Academic Ninja!: Exploring Teacher Ratings on Ratemyprofessors.com." *Journal of Computer-Mediated Communication* 10.3, article 9 (2005). http://jcmc.indiana.edu/vol10/issue3/kindred.html. Accessed 16 June 2005.

Knox, William E., Paul Lindsay, and Mary N. Kolb. "Higher Education, College Characteristics, and Student Experiences: Long-Term Effects on Educational Satisfaction and Perception." *The Journal of Higher Education* 63.3 (May-June 1992): 303–28.

Kopelson, Karen. "Rhetoric on the Edge of Cunning; Or, The Performance of Neutrality (Re)considered As a Composition Pedagogy for Student Resistance." *CCC* 55.1 (September 2003): 115–46.

Lerner, Neal. "Drill Pads, Teaching Machines, and Programmed Texts: Origins of Instructional Technology in Writing Centers." *Wiring the Writing Center.* Ed. Eric Hobson. Logan: U of Utah P, 1998: 119–36.

Lunsford, Andrea and Susan West. "Intellectual Property and Composition Studies." *CCC* 47.3 (1996): 383–411.

Marlin, James W. Jr. "Student Perceptions of End-Of-Course Evaluations." *The Journal of Higher Education* 58.6 (November–December 1987): 704–16.

McCabe, Donald, Linda Klebe Trevino, and Kenneth D. Butterfield. "Dishonesty in Academic Environments." *Journal of Higher Education* 72.1 (2001): 29–46.

McCollum, Kelly. "One Way to Get Into College: Buy an Essay that Worked for Someone Else." *Chronicle of Higher Education* 43.25 (February 28, 1997): A25–26.

McFarland, Daniel. "Student Resistance: How the Formal and Informal Organization of Classrooms Facilitate Everyday Forms of Student Defiance." *American Journal of Sociology* 107.3 (November 2001): 612–78.

McHenry, William. "Reflections on the Internet Paper Mills." 15 January 2002. http://www.Georgetown.edu/honor/Papermill.html.

Miller, Richard. "The Arts of Complicity: Pragmatism and the Culture of Schooling." *College English* 61.1 (1998): 10–28.

_____. "Fault Lines in the Contact Zone." *College English* 56.4 (1994): 389–408.

_____. *As If Learning Mattered: Reforming Higher Education.* Albany: SUNY Press, 1998.

_____. *Writing at the End of the World.* Pittsburgh: U of Pittsburgh P, 2005.

Mohr-Corrigan, Lori. "Role of Women: Renaissance and Today." The Paper Store, Inc., 2000: 1.

"New School in Exile." www.newschoolinexile.com. Accessed 2 January 2009.

Ohmann, Richard. "Politics of Teaching." *Radical Teacher* 69 (Spring 2004): 29–35.

Olson, Gary. "Toward a Post-Process Composition: Abandoning the Rhetoric of Assertion." *Post-Process Theory: Beyond the Writing Process Paradigm.* Ed. Thomas Kent. Carbondale: Southern Illinois UP, 1999: 1–15.

Pemberton, Michael. "Threshold of Desperation: Winning the Fight Against Term Paper Mills." *The Writing Instructor* 11.3 (Spring/Summer 1992): 143–52.

Pink Monkey. www.pinkmonkey.com/index2.asp. Accessed 15 August 2008.

Price, Margaret. "Beyond Gotcha!: Situating Plagiarism in Policy and Pedagogy." *College Composition and Communication* 54.1 (2002): 88–115.

Rate My Professor. www.ratemyprofessors.com. Accessed 30 March 2006 and 18 September 2007.

Rate Your Students. www.rateyourstudents.blogspot.com. Accessed 31 March 2006.

"Research Questions" Discussion Forum. *Chronicle of Higher Education.* (http://chronicle.com/forums/index.php?topic=41410.0). Accessed 17 September 2007.

Rice, Jeff. *The Rhetoric of Cool: Composition Studies and New Media.* Carbondale: Southern Illinois UP, 2007.

Ringer, Jeffrey M. "Liberating 'Liberatory' Education, or What Do We Mean by 'Liberty' Anyway?" *JAC* 25.4 (2005): 761–82.

Ritter, Kelly. *Before Shaughnessy: Basic Writing at Yale and Harvard, 1920–1960.* CCCC Studies in Writing and Rhetoric Series. Carbondale: Southern Illinois UP, 2009.

_____. "The Economics of Authorship: Online Paper Mills, Student Writers, and First-Year Composition." *College Composition and Communication* 56.4 (2005): 601-31.

_____. "Buying In, Selling Short: A Pedagogy Against the Rhetoric of Online Paper Mills." *Pedagogy* 6.1 (2006): 25-51.

Robillard, Amy. "Young Scholars Affecting Composition: A Challenge to Disciplinary Citation Practices." *College English* 68.3 (2006): 253-70.

_____. "We Won't Be Fooled Again: The Absence of Angry Responses to Plagiarism in Composition Studies." *College English* 70.1 (2007): 10-31.

Robillard, Amy and Ron Fortune. "Toward a New Content for Writing Courses: Literary Forgery, Plagiarism, and the Production of Belief." *JAC* 27.1/2 (2007): 185-210.

Roy, Alice. "Whose Words These Are I Think I Know: Plagiarism, the Postmodern, and Faculty Attitudes." *Perspectives on Plagiarism and Intellectual Property in a Postmodern World.* Eds. Lise Buranen and Alice Roy. Albany: SUNY P, 1999: 55-61.

Sanjek, David. "'Don't Have to DJ No More': Sampling and the 'Autonomous' Creator." *The Construction of Authorship: Textual Appropriation in Law and Literature.* Eds. Martha Woodmansee and Peter Jaszi. Durham, NC: Duke UP, 1994: 343-60.

Skinner, B.F. "Teaching Machines." *Science* 128.1330 (October 24, 1958): 969-77.

Sirc, Geoffrey. *English Composition as a Happening.* Logan: Utah State UP, 2002.

Sosnoski, James and Ken McAllister. "Circuitous Subjects in Their Time Maps." *Plugged In: Technology, Rhetoric and Culture in a Posthuman Age.* Eds. Gary Olson and Lynn Worsham. Cresskill, NJ: Hampton P, 2008: 125-44.

Spigelman, Candace. *Across Property Lines: Textual Ownership in Writing Groups.* Studies in Writing and Rhetoric. Carbondale: Southern Illinois UP, 2000.

_____. *Personally Speaking: Experience as Evidence in Academic Discourse.* Carbondale, IL: Southern Illinois UP, 2004.

Stander, Aaron C. "The Reading/Writing Connection." *FFORUM: A Newsletter of the English Composition Board, University of Michigan* 3.2 (Winter 1982): 83-83.

Stover, Andrea. "Redefining Public/Private Boundaries in the Composition Classroom." *Public Works: Student Writing as Public Text.* Eds. Emily J. Issacs and Phoebe Jackson. Portsmouth, NH: Boynton/Cook, 2001: 1-9.

Sullivan, Patrick. "An Open Letter to Ninth Graders." *Academe* (January/February 2009): 6-10.

"Teaching Machines and Programmed Instruction (Workshop Report 19)." *College Composition and Communication* 17.3 (October 1969): 192-93.

Tingle, Nick. *Self-Development and College Writing.* Carbondale: Southern Illinois UP, 2004.

Weisser, Christian. *Moving Beyond Academic Discourse: Composition Studies and the Public Sphere.* Carbondale: Southern Illinois UP, 2005.

Weisser, Susan Ostrov. "Believing in Yourself as Classroom Culture." *Academe: Bulletin Of the American Association of University Professors* 91.1 (January/February 2005): 27-31.

White, Ed. "Student Plagiarism as an Institutional and Social Issue." *Perspectives on Plagiarism and Intellectual Property in a Postmodern World.* Eds. Lise Buranen and Alice Roy. Albany: SUNY P, 1999: 205–10.

Woodmansee, Martha. "The Genius and the Copyright: Economic and Legal Conditions of the Emergence of the 'Author'." *Eighteenth-Century Studies* 17.4 (Summer 1984): 425–48.

_____. "Introduction." *The Construction of Authorship: Textual Appropriation in Law and Literature.* Eds. Martha Woodmansee and Peter Jaszi. Durham, NC: Duke UP, 1994: 1–14.

Yancey, Kathleen Blake and Brian Huot. "Construction, Deconstruction, and (Over)Determination: A Foucaultian Analysis of Grades." *The Theory and Practice of Grading Writing.* Eds. Frances Zak and Christopher C. Weaver, Albany: SUNY P, 1998: 39–51.

AUTHOR INDEX

SUBJECT INDEX

Agency
  Participation in online communities
    and student, 148
  Teacher-figure as role model, 155
AuthenticEssays.com, 104–105
Authority
  Ethos and online environment, 60
  Graduate students in introductory
    courses and, 29–30
  Investment in students as, 60
  Sources and, 92
  Student discursive, 59
  Student-led spaces and, 76
  Student movement away from
    teacher as, 77
  Student rebellion against, 35–36
  Teacher-figure as villain, 162–163
Authorship
  Borrowing ideas, 94–95
  Capitalism and property vs. academic
    reading, writing, and text produc-
    tion, 102
  Consumers and, 81
  Co-writing as, 90–91, 175(n12)
  Definition in 21st century, 82
  Higher education and student, 80
  Legitimate vs. illegitimate, 105
  Ownership of text, 83–84
  Plagiarist/author role, 82
  Professional, 106
  State of in relation to Internet,
    109–110
  Student definitions of, 89

Student perception of, 78
Student self-conceptions vs. assign-
  ment, 92
Student view as published and com-
  plete, 93
Student view of own, 90
Teaching of writing as study in, 108
Valuation of student, 94
Author/student binary, 78, 85–86

Banking concept, 18, 19
Blame of students, 45–46
Borrowing, 95, 97
Business transactions, stealing and, 96,
  178(n31)

Canon
  Exclusivity of, 28
  Great Books and, 28
  Writers as distant entities, 92
Cheating
  Consumer culture and, 101
  Enforcement of academic policies
    and, 99
  Faculty fear of, 99
  Internal conflict about, 101
  Peer policing and deterrence, 100,
    178(n30)
  Prevalence of, 100
  Rise in enforcement levels vs. prob-
    lem of plagiarism, 99–100
  statistics, 99
Chicago Great Books, 28
Collegepaperexchange.com, 101

Composition, first-year
  Assimilation into academic community, 102
  Assumed knowledge of students, 29
  Author/student binary, 85–86
  Avoidance of writing, 78
  Classroom as political space, 22
  Course content, 174(5)
  Critical reading and, 52
  Critical thinking and, 21–22
  Definition of reading, 48
  Elimination of teacher figure in, 34–35
  Evaluation processes, 77–78
  Failure to recognize power of student-led focus and, 166
  Less privileged population of, 21
  Liberatory pedagogy in, 18
  As location of liberation, 32–33
  As marginalized field, 32
  Peer review and, 74
  As preparatory for real world application, 93
  Print-based ideological assumptions, 57
  Public good and, 118
  Remedial coursework, 21
  Scholarship and, 32
  As site of liberation, 32
  Student definitions of authorship, 89
  Student inability to achieve perfection required, 86
  Student needs and paper mills, 80–81
  Student underlife and, 56
  Teacher *vs.* student role, 18–19
  Use of graduate students and, 29–30
  Value-free classroom and, 25
  Worth of writing outside course, 91
  Writing about Writing design for, 108
  Writing as product which is produced, 86
  Writing as replicable act, 161–162
Composition studies
  Classroom interaction, 36
  Classroom power and, 21
  Compliance with assigned reading, 47–48
  Definition of plagiarism, 79

Emotional relationship to students and writing, 98
  Oppositional reader stance, 52
  Overworked writing teachers and, 159
  Paulo Freire and, 173(n3)
  Peer review, 74
  Process pedagogy movement, 160–161
  Self-aware student writer, 32
  Student-centered pedagogues, 167
  Student-led focus, 166
  Success of paper mills, 79, 81–82
  Teaching machine and, 151–157
  Traditions of, 164–165, 166
  Us-or-them mentality, 163
  Value of reading and writing about humanist texts, 18–19
Computer-mediated discourse
  Benefits of, 134
  Motivations for postings, 124
  Redefining instructor and student roles, 134
  Student authority, 134
Course evaluations
  Anonymous peer reviews and, 125
  Assumptions about student input, 123
  As civic responsibility, 136
  Consequence for faculty, 116
  Criteria of efficiency and, 121
  Cultural and generational views of, 170–171
  Cultural tendency toward quantitative evaluation and, 117, 179(34)
  Early versions of, 116
  Faculty disregard for, 122
  Faculty resistance to publicizing, 128
  Faculty self-doubt and, 119
  From within institution *vs.* outside, 130–131
  Knowledge construction in classroom and, 122
  OnSET (Online Student Evaluation of Teaching in Higher Education), 130–131, 179(n36)
  Participatory democracy and, 120, 175(n11)

Internet
  Agency for fringe groups, 134
  Community and, 133–134
  Student participation and, 134

Liberatory pedagogy
  Aims of, 15, 18
  Classroom as democratic space, 20
  Core goals of, 15–16
  Definition of liberty, 37
  English studies and, 18–19
  Evaluative process and, 121
  False consciousness and, 32
  First-year writing and, 18
  History of, 18
  Linguistic roots of, 37–38
  As moral conscience, 27–28, 175(n9)
  Oppression of power, 135
  Position of teachers in, 31
  Reward for student of, 23–24
  Role of teacher, 18, 36–37
  Socially constructed "good," 118
  As spiritualism, 20
  Student disenfranchisement and, 15
  Student resistance to difference,
    24
  Students as informed reader, writer,
    and reader, 34
  Students as part of community and,
    36
  Students as subjects of writing
    process, 167
  Student writing as fixed, 93
  Teacher as authority, 163–164
  Teacher-figure and student freedom,
    36–37
  Terms of, 22
  Vs. ethos represented on Pink
    Monkey.com, 60–61
  Vs. traditional classroom, 23
Literacy
  External forces contributing to, 55
  Home life and, 55
  Minimizing teacher-figure and online
    discourse, 57–58
  New capitalism and, 54
  Sponsors of, 55

Literary acquisition
  External forces contributing to, 55
  New capitalism and, 53
  Online circumvention of authority-
    led, 75
  Presentations and venues for text,
    48
  Sponsors of literacy and, 55

Machine-centered pedagogy
  Advantages of programmed instruc-
    tion, 155
  Effectiveness of, 156
  Reinforcement of teacher-as-subject,
    155

New capitalism
  Definitions of literacy, 54
  New Literacy Studies model and, 53
  Pink Monkey.com and, 54
  Types of workers, 53–54
New Literacy Studies, 53

Online discourse
  As alternative to "real" pedagogical
    strategies, 165
  Circumvention of authority-led liter-
    ary acquisition, 75
  College and high school participation,
    66
  Commercialization effects on, 39
  Conflict with liberatory pedagogues,
    16
  Control of course, 39–40
  Co-opting to classroom space, 38
  Criticism as dumb, 46
  Decoding process and, 26
  Defiance of teacher or institutional
    authority and, 35–36
  Dependence on teacher as guide and
    controller of information, 39
  Discussion and, 45
  Edentities, 76, 176(n21)
  Elimination of student motivations
    affecting performance, 61
  Elimination of teacher figure, 34–35
  Ethos of performance, 63
  Fulfilling institutional needs and,
    74–75

Breinigsville, PA USA
03 March 2010
233547BV00002B/2/P

9 781572 739536